Demand management, supply constraints and inflation

edited by
M. J. Artis, C. J. Green,
Derek Leslie and Graham W. Smith

Manchester University Press

Published by
Manchester University Press
Oxford Road, Manchester M13 9PL

British Library cataloguing in publication data

Demand management, supply constraints and inflation.
  1. Economic policy
  2. Supply and demand
  I. Artis, M.J.
  339.4'7   HD82

ISBN 0-7190-0846-8

Printed in Great Britain by
Biddles Ltd, Guildford, Surrey

Demand management, supply constraints and inflation

Contents

List of tables   *page* vii
Preface   ix

Demand management

1 Recent developments in the theory of demand
   management   *M. J. Artis*   2
2 Using the Treasury model to measure the impact of
   fiscal policy   *M. J. Artis* and *C. J. Green*   29
3 Crowding-out in UK macro models
   R. C. Bladen-Hovell   48

Labour supply

4 Labour supply in the UK: a review   *Derek Leslie*   72
5 Absenteeism in the UK labour market   *Derek Leslie*   97
6 The production of an adjusted employment series
   R. J. Apps and *J. S. Ashworth*   111

Wage determination and incomes policies

7 Wage inflation: a survey   *M. J. Artis, Derek Leslie*
   and *Graham W. Smith*   134
8 Incomes policies   *J. L. Fallick*   153
9 The real wage hypothesis: some results for the UK
   R. J. Apps   170

Prices and inflation

10 Pricing behaviour: a survey   *Simon Domberger* and
Graham W. Smith   192
11 The normal cost hypothesis: a reappraisal
Graham W. Smith   213
12 Industrial structure and the inflationary process
Simon Domberger   238
13 Inflation expectations: direct observations and their
determinants   *Graham W. Smith*   255

References   275
Name index   287
Subject index   290

List of tables

2.1 Fiscal policy effects, 1974.II–1979.I *page* 38–9

2.2 The fiscal mix: the output effects of changes in taxation and expenditure considered separately 40

2.3 Stabilisation impact of fiscal policy 43

2.4 Comparison of GDP effect of different fiscal measures 44

3.1 Crowding-out in three UK macro-econometric models 60

3.2 Response of GDP and expenditure components to a one percentage point rise in $2\frac{1}{2}\%$ Consol rate; earnings and exchange rate exogenous 65

5.1 Sickness and voluntary absence, by range of overtime hours: full-time manual workers in all industries and services 103

5.2 Regressions explaining absenteeism 107

5.3 Elasticities at mean values from regression coefficients in equation 2, table 5.2 108

8.1 Increases in gross earnings, prices and net real income from employment: periods with and without incomes policies compared 156

9.1 Incomes policy dummies 177

9.2 'Real wage' equations utilising adaptively formed price expectations; best-fit results for the six DHSS real net earnings variables, estimation period 1950.I–1975.IV 178–9

9.3 'Real wage' equations utilising adaptively formed desired real net earnings and adaptively formed price expectations; best-fit results for the six DHSS real net earnings variables, estimation period 1950.I–1971.IV 182–3

9.4 'Real wage' equations utilising adaptively formed
desired real net earnings and adaptively formed
price expectations; best-fit results for the six
DHSS real net earnings variables, estimation
period 1950.I–1966.IV   184–5

9.5 Forecast rates of change of money wages, using
RNE4 equation, 1976–77   188

10.1 Pricing behaviour and concentration: some previous
results   199

11.1 Preferred estimates of the structural parameters
for male and female operatives and female
administrative, technical and clerical staff   228

12.1 Industrial concentration in the UK   239

12.2 Price adjustment and industrial structure   246

12.3 The impact of concentration on the inflationary
process: the oil price rise simulation under different
adjustment regimes   248

12.4 The rate of inflation under different adjustment regimes 249

13.1 Generalised second-order error-learning model for
each sub-period   267

Preface

The contributions to this volume represent (with the partial exception of one joint-authored paper) the work of members of the Manchester University Economics Department on various aspects of macroeconomics. The agenda for macroeconomic analysis today is a wide one and we were conscious, in preparing the volume, of the need for papers which would survey the field as a complement to original research papers; accordingly, each of the sections into which the volume is divided contains a chapter which sets out to review, in the brief compass afforded by space constraints, the state of the art in the area concerned.

The reader may be impressed or, alternatively, distressed by what might seem to be the disparate range of topics. But our concern would rather be that the volume may not be sufficiently eclectic. For the observer of British economic policy cannot fail to be struck by the extent to which the single-minded concentration on demand management policy and analysis has given way to wider fields of analysis and policy initiatives; indeed, the vaunting of 'supply side' economics reached an apogee with the assumption of power by the Conservative administration in 1979. Perversely, events since then seem only to have demonstrated the proverbial dangers of throwing out the baby with the bath-water. A more balanced view suggests that successful economic policy requires a subtle blend of demand and supply-side policies, and for this a great deal of knowledge is required.

The chapters that follow concentrate successively on demand management, labour supply, wage behaviour and pricing behaviour. The list of topics could have been larger, but there is a strong case for saying that all these are key areas of analysis for policy formulation.

For an analytical innovation of recent years, which is at the same time of great simplicity and of considerable cutting power, is the distinction between flex- and fix-price markets, or between 'auction' and 'administered' prices. This distinction is vital to the powerful analytical insights afforded into the behaviour of economies in respect of inflation and unemployment by such distinguished economists as Hicks, Kaldor and Malinvaud and provides a means of reconciling the traditional insights of 'Keynesian' economics and the arresting contradiction of those insights afforded by proponents of the rational expectations school. Analytical reconciliation of theories based on alternative 'stylised facts', however vital, is of course no substitute for empirical work which aims to refine and describe more precisely, if not finally to explain, those stylised facts. The fix-price markets which analysts draw attention to most importantly include the labour market and the market for industrially processed goods, and it is in this light that the concentration in this volume on those markets seems justified.

But whilst, on this view, there is an underlying unifying thread to the volume, we do not pretend to more than that. The authors do not subscribe to a monolithic view, and despite the interactions of views which took place as a result of discussion of the individual papers each contributor is singly responsible for the views expressed in his own chapters.

We should like to acknowledge the assistance of Helen Grindrod, Julie Owen and Jean Ashton in typing the manuscript and that of Ronnie McDonald in preparing the indexes.

M.J.A.
C.G.
G.S.
D.G.L.

Demand management

1   M. J. Artis

Recent developments in the theory of demand management

1. Introduction

Around the end of the second world war many governments pledged themselves to economic policies which would guarantee full employment. The intellectual basis of these commitments lay in the work of J. M. Keynes and his followers. Keynes's *General Theory* (1936) had elaborated the theory of effective demand and gave an intellectual foundation to the use of fiscal policy as a response to slump conditions, whilst his *How to Pay for the War* (1940) provided a brilliant translation of this concept to the quite different conditions of modern war.

Commitment to the demand management policies based on this contribution were not, of course, adopted simultaneously or pursued with the same vigour throughout the world; important differences in national historical experience, the attraction of rival traditions of thought, political obstacles in the form of sentiments in favour of balanced budgets and simple inertia in the spread of ideas ensured this. Notwithstanding, Keynesian theories of demand management became the intellectually dominant mode of thought about economic policy formation, and the subsequent development of analytical macroeconomics and the problems and successes of economic policy were correspondingly closely connected.

The central idea of demand management required and received a great deal of refinement in line with the constraints perceived by the policy-makers and the problems experienced by them. A significant attraction of the *General Theory* was tractability to quantitative estimation of its behavioural postulates; accordingly, and especially after the advent of electronic computers, further sophistication of the empirical basis of demand management policy proved possible. By perhaps the mid- to late 1960s the inheritance of the *General Theory* had assumed impressive proportions. At the operational level, the problems of producing regular estimates of the national accounts had long since been resolved; and, in response to the call for more frequent observations, quarterly accounts were becoming generally available. In response to the need for more flexible policy, a wider range of more flexible policy instruments have been provided. In recognition of the time delay in economic responses, economic forecasting had become a major routine activity, calling on the assistance of econometric models. At the analytical level, the problem of optimising policy subject to constraints had been addressed and resolved in different ways by economists like Meade (1951), Swan (1955) and Mundell (1962). The theory of economic policy developed by the Netherlands school (e.g. Tinbergen, 1956, and Theil, 1958) clarified the distinction between instruments and objectives of policy and provided a setting in which econometric estimation and optimal policy design could be considered simultaneously, promising, it seemed, a scientific reduction of policy problems to matters of technical detail.

However impressive this progress seems, the reader will need little reminding that since the late 1960s 'Keynesian' policy-making and Keynesian theory have lost their former dominance. It is perhaps as well, at this juncture, to mention that not all Keynesian economists would subscribe to the catalogue of progress described above. In particular, it would be wrong to omit mention of the fact that many of the earliest contributors to the Keynesian revolution saw the limits of demand management techniques in the problem of control of money wages (e.g. Kalecki, 1944; Worswick, 1944; Robinson, 1937).

What is important about this, of course, is that many would date the beginning of disillusionment with demand management policy with the onset of rapid inflation, at the end of the 1960s and during the 1970s. This period marks the recrudescence of 'classical economics', monetarism in its modern guise. There were other significant developments in this period, too, which disciplined the progress of macroeconomic theory and policy: the much increased integration of national economies through international trade and finance, and the breakdown of the international monetary system established at Bretton Woods. These developments have helped focus attention on the small open economy as the object of analysis, and on factors affecting the determination of the exchange rate. The accumulation of large masses of mobile funds in a world of comparative freedom from controls has given markets the power to undermine policies which do not strike them as convincing: and this in turn has implied that attention must be given to the way in which foreign exchange markets use information about national government policies. In particular, since these markets stand to make or lose money on the long-run outcomes of current policies, the long-run solution of policies cannot be ignored, even if, on other grounds, they could be.

This, and the connected problem of inflation control, has plunged macroeconomic analysis into what seems — compared with the confidence of the mid-1960s — a morass of doubt and confusion. At the analytical level, the most challenging and exciting developments in macroeconomics — the rational expectations revolution on the one hand and disequilibrium macroeconomics on the other — seem to point in divergent directions. The subject matter of the one is a world of clearing markets functioning up to an informational error at equilibrium; of the other, of market failures leading to 'short run' (but nevertheless significant in calendar time) deviations from the long-run equilibrium. Yet both lines of investigation appeal to important facts of life. The policy-makers meanwhile, presiding over the greatest recession since the inter-war slump and still rampant inflation, are confronted with the task of devising policies which make sense both in the short and in the long run.

Epitaphs have been written and unwritten for the macroeconomics underlying demand management policy. In what follows we attempt to cover the uncomfortably broad canvas implied by the title of this chapter by, first, recounting the principal elements of the conventional wisdom on demand management in a world of trading economies. We go on to review a recent extension which deals with wealth adjustments. The following section deals with the question of supply constraints, and reviews the pure flex-price model with 'rational' expectations. This is then contrasted with the rationed equilibrium approach. In the final section we turn to a discussion of rules versus discretion in economic policy. This highlights the tension between the 'optimal policy' tradition of demand management policy and the modern version of classical economics. We end with a paragraph of conclusions.

2. The conventional wisdom

The purpose of this section is to establish some of the key elements in the conventional macroeconomics underpinning demand management policies; the versatility of the IS–LM apparatus enables us to do this in comparatively short order. It is worth while first of all recalling the key abstractions underlying what is to follow, the more so in that the developments reviewed in subsequent sections derive from relaxing these simplifying assumptions. First, then, the analysis is taken to be sufficiently short-run that supply constraints on output responses to demand stimuli can be neglected; second, although current saving and investment are occurring, the time interval under consideration is short enough that the effects on asset accumulation can be ignored; finally, domestic 'value added' prices (wages and profits) are assumed constant.[1]

The key propositions for economic policy developed on the basis of these abstractions concern the relative effectiveness of fiscal and monetary policy in raising output; the associated proposition that crowding-out of fiscal policy is a consequence of inappropriate financing policies; the requirement that the number of independent policy instruments should at least equal the number of policy objectives if a multiple-objective policy is to be successful; the requirement that policy design be tested for robustness in the face of stochastic errors; and the proposition that the short and long-run effects of policy actions may differ.

Figure 1.1 is designed to illustrate the first two of these propositions. From an initial position of equilibrium at A, with associated income y_0 and interest rate r_0, we consider a fiscal stimulus which shifts the IS schedule from IS_0 to IS_1. A new point of equilibrium is established at the income level and interest rate associated with point B in the figure. (Dealing with a closed economy for the moment, the BB schedule may be neglected.) Evidently the income expansion associated with the move from point A to point B is less than that which would have occurred had the interest rate remained constant at r_0, in which case the system would have moved from point A to point D. By the standard of this

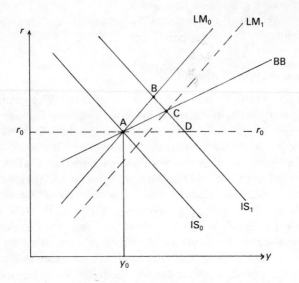

Fig. 1.1   Aspects of 'crowding out' under fixed exchange rates

constant interest rate 'base line', some expenditure and output has
been crowded out. The following propositions are evident: the
crowding-out would have been greater, for the same fiscal stimulus
(horizontal shift in IS) the flatter the IS schedule (complete in the
limiting case of a horizontal IS curve); it would also have been
greater the steeper the LM schedule (and complete in the limiting
case of a vertical LM schedule); in any event, crowding-out could
be avoided altogether if the fiscal expansion were accompanied by a
monetary expansion sufficient to maintain a constant interest rate.
More precisely, the first two propositions taken together indicate
that fiscal policy (not accompanied by monetary expansion) is the
more potent the less the interest elasticity of expenditures (which
defines the slope of the IS schedule) and the greater the ratio of the
interest elasticity of money demand to its income elasticity (which
defines the slope of the LM schedule). Moreover there is a
symmetry here; where the conditions imply that fiscal policy is
potent, monetary policy will be impotent, and vice-versa.[2] The
third proposition restates the obvious; since the model contains no
supply constraints which would compel crowding-out, its existence,
far from being inevitable, is simply the result of inappropriate

financing policies.

We now review these conclusions in an open economy context but assuming for the moment a fixed exchange rate; the BB schedule must now be brought into play. This schedule describes overall balance in the external account, with some upward slope indicating imperfect capital mobility: this slope is conventionally assumed to be less than that.of the LM schedule, foreign demand for domestic bonds being assumed more elastic than the domestic demand for money. For the moment we adopt the convention that sterilisation policy is infeasible: this means that any potential equilibrium implied by an intersection of LM and IS above (below) the BB schedule implies a potential surplus (deficit) on the overall balance of payments and consequentially an increase (decrease) in the supply of money. Such intersections must, on these assumptions, give way to a shift in the LM curve such as will provide for an IS–LM intersection *on* the BB schedule. To illustrate, assume the same fiscal stimulus as before, producing the potential equilibrium point B. The 'no sterilisation' assumption implies that the money supply must increase, shifting the LM schedule to LM_1, providing for equilibrium at the point C. Compared to point B, there is less crowding-out because our 'no sterilisation' assumption guarantees an accommodating financial policy. Had perfect capital mobility prevailed, the BB schedule would have been horizontal, and the fiscal stimulus would have generated the no-crowding-out equilibrium point, D. Whilst this is the usually quoted 'paradigm' result for a small open economy (defined to have perfect capital mobility),[3] it is possibly more illuminating to say that if external factors require a completely accommodating financial policy there will be no crowding-out, but if they prevent it, as in the case of imperfect capital mobility, then (at least as judged against the hypothetical and, in this case, infeasible baseline of a constant interest rate policy) there must be some. The imperfect capital mobility possibility may be judged as a real constraint on the opportunity to finance the fiscal stimulus without provoking a rise in interest rates.

An early refinement of demand management theory was the result of responding to the problem posed by multiple objectives of policy. The solution was to require at least as many independent instruments of policy as objectives of policy. An illustration may be provided, using a fresh version of fig. 1.1 and with similar

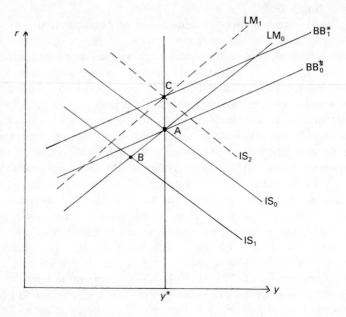

Fig. 1.2   The sterilisation case

assumptions, except that for simplicity of exposition we now
suppose that sterilisation is in general quite feasible and that the BB
schedule may now be defined for any desired surplus or deficit,
rather than for exact balance, as in the previous no-sterilisation
example. (Stressing this, we denote the schedule BB^*.) The
economy (fig. 1.2) is depicted as in initial equilibrium at the point
A. A collapse in world demand for the country's exports is
hypothesised, driving the IS curve to IS_1, equilibrium to B and the
BB_0^* schedule to BB_1^*. At B the economy fails to attain its target for
either income, y^*, or the balance of payments, as embodied in BB_1^*.
A fiscal stimulus sufficient to shift the IS schedule back to its
original position would suffice to restore output to its target level
y^*, but at A there would now be a deficit relative to the desired
balance of payments position. To achieve *both* targets, a tight
monetary policy must be used in conjunction with a more
expansionary fiscal policy, restoring full equilibrium at point C,
where both targets are met.[4]

   In the previous example we motivated the required matching of

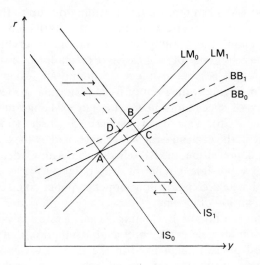

Fig. 1.3 Aspects of 'crowding out' under flexible exchange rates

the number of policy instruments to the number of policy objectives by suspending the no-sterilisation assumption; in doing so, we created both the possibility of a balance of payments policy target and an independent monetary policy which, along with the fiscal policy, fits the bill of requirements.

We move on to reconsider the previous crowding-out proposition in a world of floating exchange rates; no question of sterilisation now arises, since the floating exchange rate assures zero net reserve flows. Figure 1.3 illustrates the case where capital flows are imperfectly responsive to domestic interest rates (relative to world rates) net of any expected exchange rate depreciation; but initially we assume that exchange rate expectations are stationary, so that expected depreciation is always zero. Trade flows are assumed responsive to the spot exchange rate, domestic value-added prices being fixed. Consider again a fiscal expansion from the initial equilibrium at A, which promises a new potential equilibrium at point B: this is infeasible, for the implied surplus here indicates a pressure on the exchange rate to appreciate, reducing net exports and driving the IS schedule back to its original position. Crowding-out appears to be complete. But, once again, an accommodating increase in the money supply (taking the LM schedule to LM_1) can remove this crowding-out up to the amount dictated by the imperfect mobility of international capital. Replacing now the assumption of stationary exchange rate expectations by one of regressive expectations, a somewhat different result is obtained; even without an accommodating monetary policy, crowding-out of fiscal policy may be lessened by the activity of speculators in the foreign exchange market (see Dornbusch, 1976). Thus if, in response to a fiscal stimulus, the current rise in the exchange rate is accompanied by the expectation of a future depreciation, the BB schedule shifts upward (as to BB_1), permitting a possible equilibrium at point D. It is still true, however, that an accommodating monetary policy could underpin a greater expansion of income.

One of the features of the floating exchange rate analysis which is clearly uncomfortable is the continued assumption that domestic value-added prices remain fixed in the face of variations in the domestic price equivalent of foreign prices as the exchange rate changes. The speed and degree of response of domestic wages and prices to such variation are obviously of the greatest significance for the scope of the analysis: we return to the subject in section 4.

Up to this point the analysis has been conducted on a deterministic basis, but some of the more important issues in policy choice arise only in the context of a stochastic setting. Figure 1.4 can be referred to for some illustrations. We first of all consider the propositions that barriers to interest rate variations provide a premium on flexibility in fiscal policy response and that fiscal policies oriented towards targets for the actual budget surplus are destabilising. Thus suppose, for the sake of argument, that for given settings of the policy instruments (government expenditure and tax rates for fiscal policy, the money supply for monetary policy) stochastic variations or unforeseen shocks imply that the IS schedule may 'wander' from its 'best guess' position (IS) up to the barriers shown by the schedules IS' and IS". Clearly, in order to preserve output at y^*, a flexible monetary policy would result in substantial variations of the interest rate (as at equilibrium points D and E). This implication would have no further consequences if there were no barriers to such variations, but in practice economic policy-makers seem to be very sensitive to such variations; clearly, one 'moral', then, is to design a more flexible fiscal policy (tax 'regulators', mini-budgets and the like), so that policy-induced

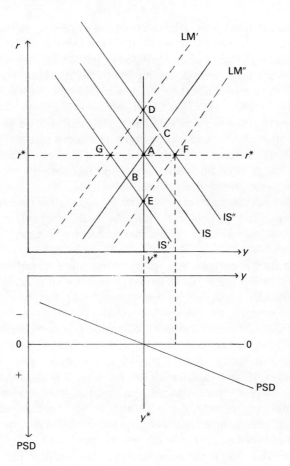

Fig. 1.4 A stochastic model

shifts in IS can offset shifts induced by unforeseen shocks. It is also easily seen, referring to the bottom part of the diagram, that a policy targeting the actual budget deficit would be destabilising: the budget deficit schedule shown here slopes downward against output as tax revenues rise with income. Shocks which raise output against target (y^*) reduce the deficit (raise the surplus) and call for fiscal contraction, whereas targeting the actual budget deficit would call for expansion, exacerbating the effects of the output-raising shock.[5]

Consideration of the robustness of policy rules is enjoined by a stochastic setting of the analysis. If, in the face of shocks to the IS schedule, monetary policy consisted in pursuit of a money supply rule, output target misses are implied by the resultant equilibria B and C. A rate of interest (r^*) policy would be even less optimal, implying equilibria at G and F. If, on the other hand, the shocks exclusively concern money demand, shifting the 'best guess' LM curve between LM′ and LM″, a constant interest rate policy would be optimal.[6] Results of this kind give a degree of comfort to advocates of discretion, fine tuning and flexible policies, up to a qualification provided by irreducible policy time lags and the fallibility of economic forecasts, and by recognition that pursuit of pre-announced policy rules may in itself alter private-sector behaviour in ways which are favourable to obtaining superior outcomes.

As a final illustration of aspects of the conventional wisdom in demand management, we illustrate recognition of the effect of lags in behaviour. Specifically, we assume that the 'true' income variable entering the money demand and consumption function is permanent rather than current income and that permanent income is a weighted average of current and past actual income. These assumptions imply that in the IS–LM diagram (fig. 1.5) the long-run LM and IS schedules, drawn on the assumption that permanent and current income are equal, have corresponding short-run counterparts, drawn on the assumption that permanent and current income are not equivalent. Specifically, at the equilibrium point A, a rise in current income from y^A would imply a smaller rise in permanent income, a smaller increase in consumption, a larger increase in savings and hence a steeper slope in the IS schedule in the short run than in the long run. *Mutatis mutandis*, similar arguments imply that the short-run LM schedule (LM′) will be flatter than its long-run counterpart. A fiscal stimulus shifting the long-run IS schedule to IS_1 promises long-run equilibrium at C, and short-run equilibrium at the intersection (at point D) of the short-run IS and LM schedules (IS_1' and LM′). Point D may lie to the right or left of C.[7] Predictions and diagnosis of the economy are accordingly more complicated when these effects are taken into account; the demand management 'bias' is to draw from this a conclusion favouring the construction of more refined econometric models capable of incorporating these effects.

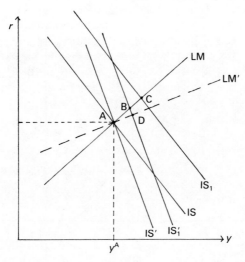

Fig. 1.5 The effect of lags on behaviour

3. Wealth adjustment

A theme of the previous section was that, in the short-run setting of traditional demand management analysis, crowding-out is an artefact of financial policies. This conclusion is not disturbed by a comparatively recent extension[8] of traditional analysis which, in recognising the effects of asset accumulation on behaviour, implicitly pushes the conventional analysis towards a longer-term setting.[9]

The extension to take account of these effects consists in respecifying the money demand and expenditure functions underlying the LM and IS schedules to incorporate terms in financial wealth (positive in both cases), explicitly accounting at the same time for the government budget constraint (the financing identity for government expenditures) and, in an open economy, the current account of the balance of payments, since a deficit in the one and a surplus in the other imply additions to the net financial wealth of the private sector.[10] In a closed economy setting, or a fixed exchange rate open economy, these modifications of traditional analysis result, if the processes can be counted on to produce a stable equilibrium, in more powerful fiscal policies. The reason is not far to seek. In the new equilibrium, net wealth must be

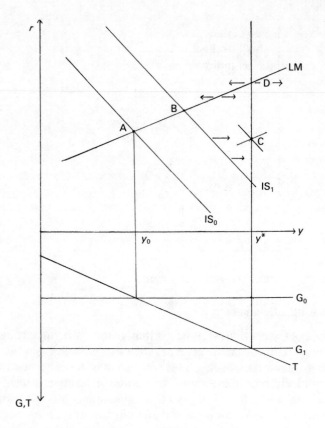

Fig. 1.6   Wealth effects: the closed economy case

constant, so that the budget deficit (in a closed economy) or the sum of the budget deficit and current account surplus (in an open economy) must be zero. In the absence of supply constraints, income and output move so as to ensure this, increases in output and income helping to produce a new equilibrium following fiscal expansion through the mechanism of rising tax revenues (closed economy) or a combination of rising tax revenues and increasing imports (open economy). Figure 1.6 illustrates the case of the closed economy; the lower part of this figure shows the generation of the budget balance. From initial equilibrium at A we suppose an expansionary increase in government spending shifting the IS schedule to IS_1, and G to G_1 in the lower part of the figure. The new equilibrium will not be at B, however, since this would imply a continuing budget deficit, and hence increases in private-sector wealth driving the IS schedule further to the right, and the LM curve to the left (as indicated by the arrows). The latter may be offset if the increase in the money supply associated with the financing of the deficit is at least sufficient to satisfy the added demand for it. The new equilibrium must be along the y^* line, where the budget is again balanced. If money financing is more than sufficient to offset the increase in money demand, full equilibrium might be reached at a point like C. If money financing is just enough to meet added money demand, equilibrium is at D, whilst if money supply increases fall short of the added demand for money due to wealth increases, equilibrium will be determined at some point on the vertical line through y^*, but above D. The process at work need not be stable, however: if the expansion of the money supply is sufficiently small, the wealth-induced contractionary effect on the LM schedule may outweigh the expansionary effects on the IS schedule, and income may decline as the budget deficit increases and net wealth rises. This 'crowding-out' result, however, can always be avoided simply by ensuring that the monetary expansion is sufficient to prevent it: very strong wealth effects on the demand for money relative to those on expenditure call for a correspondingly large proportion of the deficit to be money-financed. This 'sensible' conclusion, though less exciting than the implication that crowding-out, if it occurs, implies an unstable economy and so cannot be a feature of a monetarist world, is much more robust, since monetarists will argue both that instabilities can be induced precisely by foolish monetary policy and also that the fix-price assumptions of the analysis betray a short-run orientation which is in no fundamental way altered merely by accounting for wealth effects. *Mutatis mutandis*, similar conclusions carry over to the floating exchange rate open economy.

To reiterate, it is, of course, not surprising that, if no constraints are imposed on the ability of output to respond, crowding-out can be reduced to a matter of financing policies. We now turn to the question of supply constraints.

4. Supply constraints

The earliest, and quite explicit, recognition of supply constraints in the demand management prospectus must be dated to the concern voiced by the architects of the Keynesian revolution for the behaviour of money wages at 'full employment'.[11] A characterisation of this concern may be expressed as follows. Demand management policies can in principle so manage 'real' things as to maintain full employment. Given technology and productivity, this will imply a certain real wage, with corresponding real money supply, etc. But the real wage is the quotient of two nominal variables, the money wage and the price level. What is to tie down the level and rate of growth of nominal wages and prices? The suggestion at this time, which has remained the classic Keynesian solution, is a wages or incomes policy. This insight, though not the exact solution advocated, has something in common with the much more recent development of the rational expectations school.

However, the 'discovery' of the Phillips curve (Phillips, 1958) seemed for a time to let demand management policy formation off the 'incomes policy hook'. To the extent that the Phillips curve could be thought of as reasonably steep, control of inflation could be purchased at a comparatively small cost in terms of unemployment and demand management policy chosen so as to locate an optimal trade-off with respect to policy preferences. This is a matter not of optimal policy combination, as in the case of the employment/balance of payments problem, but simply — in the fatal absence of an additional policy instrument — of compromising one target in favour of the other. Figure 1.7 illustrates the Phillips curve 'menu of choice' (Rees, 1970). The Phillips curve, PC, represents the technical trade-off of inflation and unemployment, the curves $I_A I_A$ and $I_B I_B$ the hypothesised preference schedules of an employment-preferring (Labour?) and stable currency-preferring (Conservative?) government, with corresponding optima A and B.

Demand management theory has made ample use of the distinction between product real wages and real wage incomes, i.e. the distinction between the wage in terms of domestic output and the wage in terms of consumables. This distinction is significant for the treatment of devaluation and appreciation, and changes in the real terms of trade. In the analysis reviewed earlier (section 2), exchange rate changes — given the assumption of fixed domestic value-added prices — caused changes in the real wage in terms of

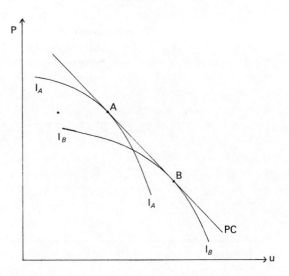

Fig. 1.7   The Phillips curve 'menu of choice'

consumables whilst leaving product wages unchanged. For this reason, exchange depreciation reduces the foreign currency cost of domestic value added and increases demand for domestic production, an appreciation having the opposite effect. In the light of experience this traditional treatment has come to seem particularly arbitrary, for it seems natural to suppose that labour supply decisions are made in terms of the consumables version of real wages, so that a devaluation (for example) will simply tend to raise domestic value-added prices, at a constant level of employment, in line with the rise in price of foreign exchange. This line of argument is expressed with particular severity in the doctrine of 'real wage resistance', but it is also implied in the natural rate-augmented Phillips curve.[12] If real (consumables) wages cannot be changed, except by higher unemployment (permanently in the real wage resistance view, transitorily in the Phillips curve view), economic policy in an open economy is in for a hard time. Fortunately, matters cannot be quite as difficult as this: real wages do change significantly, though incomes policy and spells of unemployment may be a help in securing the alteration. Meanwhile fig. 1.8 (derived from Mackinnon, 1976), illustrates the case in which, with inflexible real wages, domestic demand management is

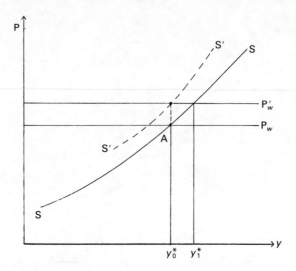

Fig. 1.8   Supply constraints

useless and output and employment are determined by world conditions. Here the supply schedule SS is drawn for a given nominal wage and expresses output supply for an economy producing a composite tradable good under conditions of diminishing returns; prices rise, and real wages fall, along it. The horizontal line P_w represents world demand for the good. Output is initially determined at y_0^*. Demand management has no purchase in this economy, except to the extent that it raises world demand, the effective supply curve of goods being SAP_w: added demand merely raises the import bill. A devaluation which raised the domestic price of the goods to P_w' could raise output to y_1^* provided that the real wage falls. If, however, the devaluation encounters resistance and SS shifts to $S'S'$, real wages will not fall and output will not rise. In this picture of a small open economy neither direct demand management (government purchases) nor the management of demand for domestic production via devaluation is helpful, unless real wages fall simultaneously. The supply side is dominant and — if at the cost of excessive simplification — the lesson is nonetheless salutary.

Its appeal to specialised assumptions dependent on the 'small open economy' definition, however, marks this example off from

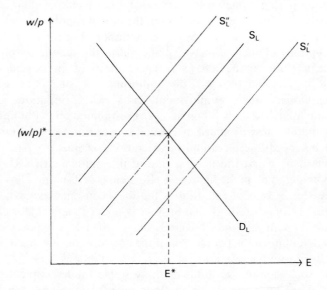

Fig. 1.9 The natural rate hypothesis

the more general and ambitious rational expectations (RE) version of monetarism, the development of which has been interpreted as qualifying the scope for demand management policies to the point of annihilation.

Friedman's classic paper (1968) on the Phillips curve is really the key here, even though Friedman has not espoused rational expectations. The paper introduced the notion of the natural rate of unemployment, and with it foreshadowed the suspension of employment objectives for macroeconomic policy, the key *desideratum* of demand management theory. It also highlights the key assumption of RE monetarism of market clearing and equilibrium subject only to informational disturbances.

Figure 1.9 is a diagram of the labour market, with equilibrium at $(w/p)^*$, and E^*, as shown. Friedman assumes an informational inequality between firms and workers. Firms make no mistakes and the demand for labour schedule stays constant. Workers, on the other hand, have imperfect access to information. Both labour supply and labour demand schedules are to be thought of as holding against perceived or expected values of (w/p). From equilibrium, an inflation raising money wages coaxes out more employment as perceived real wages rise against actual: the labour supply schedule shifts to the right (as to S'_L). As inflation begins to fall, misperceptions about this may equally cause the labour supply schedule to shift to the left (S''_L). The pattern of employment response is related not to disequilibrium as such but to misperceptions. Since employment rises when inflation is underestimated and falls when it is overestimated, the Phillips curve should be drawn against misperceived inflation ($\dot{p} - \hat{\dot{p}}$). On Friedman's specific accelerationist expectations scheme, $\dot{p} - \hat{\dot{p}}$ may be replaced by $\ddot{p}$. At the natural rate of unemployment (NRU) corresponding to E^* in the figure, employment is at its natural level and any steady rate of inflation is feasible, consonant with no perception errors. It follows that for macro-policy to aim at a level of unemployment less than NRU (E bigger than E^*) requires a sustained 'fooling of the people' (or, if the accelerationist version is correct, a constant acceleration in the rate of inflation).

If the real economy *is* fundamentally stable, and this picture applies, then the rational expectations hypothesis suggests that agents will form their expectations in the 'best possible way'. Specifically — and sooner or later — this suggests that they will form expectations using relevant economic theory. But if the economy is always at equilibrium in this sense the relevant economy theory *is* classical theory and this theory incorporates the quantity theory. So (taking a few more steps here) we arrive at the idea that output varies round *its* natural level according only to monetary 'surprises' (see e.g. Sargent and Wallace, 1975).

This theory gives no scope to demand management policy. In truth none is necessary, for equilibrium is a foregone conclusion. However, the theory does provide some important qualifications of demand management policy even if not all its underlying assumptions are granted.[13] For example, the theory suggests that agents will act according to what they expect of, among other things, government policy. This implies that the evidence of agents' responses to one kind of policy cannot be readily used to work out their response to another kind of policy, the 'Lucas critique' (Lucas, 1976). This is a salutary constraint on policy optimisation exercises conducted on econometric models which reflect behaviour conditioned by other types of policy. Another point at issue is the effectiveness of counter-cyclical policy: again, to the extent that (say) tax reduction policies are known to be counter-cyclical, tax reductions today will be expected to be followed by tax increases tomorrow. This limits the scope for the policy to work if there is any sort of income averaging in expenditure behaviour.

Nor is this all. We may not accept that markets clear and establish long-run equilibrium up to an informational error, but most economists would accept that there is a long-run tendency for long-run equilibrium! This being so, it seems unlikely that short-run policy can neglect all the lessons of the rational expectations model. In the next section we turn to the 'market failure' rationale for demand management policy before taking up a current policy issue, that of rules versus discretion, which illustrates the present tension between the traditional lines of demand management theory and the impact of rational expectations monetarism.

5. Rationed equilibrium

A recent analytical development which has significant repercussions for traditional demand management policies and theorising is provided by the so-called disequilibrium macroeconomics or rationed equilibrium approach associated most notably with the work of Barro and Grossman (1971) and Malinvaud (1977 and 1978).[14] This literature clarifies the purchase of Keynesian economics and in doing so provides a counterpoint to the rational expectations alternative; and, whilst its policy applications have to date been limited, Malinvaud has nonetheless provided illuminating accounts of current policy concerns using this framework, accounts which are the more interesting in that they indicate a role for supply-side actions (incomes policies) as an essential complement to demand management, not so much in curbing inflation as in bearing upon real wages.

The argument begins with the observation that in the absence of an 'auctioneer' or *tâtonnement*-cum-recontracting process there is no presumption that the market will hit upon the vector of market clearing prices appropriate to equilibrium. Granted this, the failure of a market to clear has system-wide repercussions, as agents' behaviour in other markets is conditioned by their experience of disappointment in respect of the quantities they can trade in the

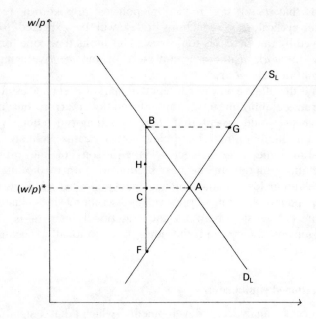

Fig. 1.10   Rationed equilibrium

market which fails to clear. For example, workers unable to trade as much of the quantity of labour as they expected in the labour market will revise downward their demands for goods. This self-reinforcing process implies the possibility of many rationed equilibria and renders it unclear how equilibrating market forces can get to work. It is, however, clear that government action can relieve quantity-constrained equilibrium by demand management; indeed, the analysis clarifies what Keynes left unclear, that demand management has scope for action without (necessarily) bearing on real wages. Figure 1.10 illustrates the argument: it depicts the labour market with equilibrium at A. At a point like B, by contrast, the real wage is too high, there is involuntary unemployment (BG), and the classical remedy is a reduction in the real wage; on this understanding of the matter, demand management would work only by somehow devising a fall in the real wage.[15] If, however, there is a demand constraint in operation, as shown by the vertical line through BCF, employers are to be thought of as minimising the cost of producing the constrained quantity of sales available at the going wage. A point like C is conceivable: here the marginal product of labour is greater than its cost (which by chance is at its equilibrium value) but the sales constraint prevents the realisation of what would otherwise be the corollary — namely to employ additional labour up to the point at which the marginal product and cost are equal. A demand stimulus to relieve the sales constraints has an obvious rationale. It is also clear that unemployment in this model may be overdetermined, in the sense that both demand management to shift the constraint and a policy to bear on the real wage may be called for (say, as at point H in the diagram).

Malinvaud (1977) has argued that the unemployment of the mid-1970s should be thought of as 'Keynesian with classical contamination'; some unemployment can be regarded as overdetermined, in the sense that neither pure demand management nor wage–price (incomes policy) remedies is sufficient in itself. This diagnosis can be conveyed by reference to the sort of diagrammatic representation favoured by its author. Malinvaud assumes the presence of wealth effects in the labour supply function and that wealth (real money balances) is also an argument of consumers' utility and demand functions; hence, for given nominal money balances, the price *level* (p) is relevant to full equilibrium as well as the real wage (w/p). There are also autonomous demands (like government expenditure) in the system. For given values of these autonomous demands and nominal money balances there is a unique real wage and price level which determines a full 'Walrasian equilibrium', with no rationing. A rise in autonomous demands would require some rise in prices to reduce real money balances and private expenditure ('crowding-out'), although this would also increase labour supply somewhat.[16] An autonomous fall in productivity, other things being equal, would require a fall in the real wage to maintain equilibrium. Malinvaud describes the 'oil price shock' as having had both a productivity-reducing and a demand-reducing effect. Thus, in terms of fig. 1.11, if W_0 corresponds to the initial equilibrium, the productivity-reducing effect of the oil price shock pushes the equilibrium w, p vector to the right (real wages must fall), say, to W_1. The terms of trade effect on aggregate demand, however, implies the need for absolutely lower prices (given nominal money balances and autonomous expenditures), pushing the equilibrium w, p vector in towards the original, say, to W_2. Through any one of

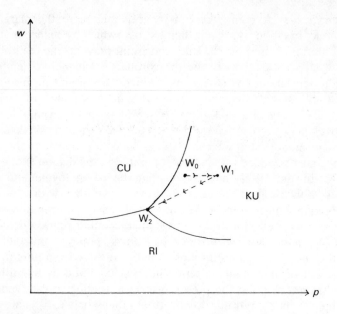

Fig. 1.11   Malinvaud: the three regions

these equilibrium points lines may be drawn which demarcate
Keynesian from classical unemployment and each from repressed
inflation; classical unemployment is defined for too high a real
wage, Keynesian unemployment for too high a price level (hence
too low an aggregate demand), repressed inflation for too low an
absolute price level, leading to excess demand. For simplicity, in
fig. 1.11, these areas have been shown for the point W_2 only. Thus if
the effect of the oil shock is as described, and actual wages and
prices remain at the original equilibrium point W_0, the economy is
plunged into what seems to be Keynesian unemployment (for W_0
appears in the KU zone of W_2). However, simple expansionary
demand management policies will not be enough; they would move
the equilibrium of the system towards W_1, which — if the actual w,
p sector stays at W_0 — simply converts Keynesian into classical
unemployment. Unemployment is overdetermined and the real
wage also needs to fall for full equilibrium to be restored: incomes
policy is required as well as demand management.

    This approach thus seems to be comparatively rich in its policy
implications, though they have yet to be amplified to take full

account of open economy considerations,[17] and clearly require some specification of the dynamics of wage–price movements to be integrated. We note, however, that meantime the traditional concerns and abstractions of demand management theory and policy do receive some support, and a more rigorous foundation, from this development.

6. Rules versus discretion

The debate between the advocates of rules and the advocates of discretion in economic policy is an old one, and one that might have been thought to have been decisively resolved in favour of discretion and fine-tuning demand management many years ago. Today, however, many governments conduct their economic policy on the basis of pre-announced rules (typically for the rate of monetary expansion) in a development which is perhaps some measure of the extent of the decline of demand management in contemporary policy-making. Underlying this is, of course, the unfavourable experience of inflation and the limited success of, and political problems associated with, incomes policies. But there is undeniably a deep irony in a situation in which demand management is eschewed in the face of the deepest recession since the inter-war slump.

Of several arguments for the adoption of publicly announced monetary growth rules the dominant one is that there is a long-run relationship between inflation and monetary expansion, and that policy cannot aim for an employment level different from the 'natural rate' if the goal of steady (perhaps zero) inflation is to be achieved. Discretion would still be superior to publicly announcing a rule for monetary growth, however, were it not for a presumption that the announcement itself conditions private-sector expectations.[18] The public announcement of a rule must then undergo a cost–benefit analysis: does the beneficial effect of announcement in conditioning expectations offset the loss of ability to alter the policy settings in response to shocks? The practical operation of rules, with rolling targets and ranges for the monetary growth rates, demonstrates some compromise in the light of this cost–benefit question;[19] the formulation of contingent rules would go much further in the direction of discretion.[20]

Where expectations are not 'rational' there may be a case for applying the monetary target regime in a gradualist way, though whether this is so or not depends on the character of expectations formation, the slope of the short-run Phillips curve and the nature of the penalty on unemployment appearing in the government's utility function.[21] This version of monetarism, though expressed here without reference to the openness of the economy, differs little in its internationalist version. The main difference is that, for an open economy, the exchange rate is a significant part of the transmission mechanism and problems may arise for the trading sector and the balance of the economy if foreign exchange markets mark up the exchange rate on news of a tighter monetary growth rule while labour market behaviour continues to display a high component of autoregression. This '1925 problem' has haunted the operation of monetary growth targets in Britain and Europe in the 1970s.[22]

It suggests that the labour market does not operate in the manner assumed by the classical theory. It is indeed clear that there are important differences between auction markets like those in foreign exchange and securities, where prices are free to jump, and the labour market, where contracts are implicitly or explicitly set for a period and where wage relativities play a powerful role. To the extent that much of Keynesian theory derives from an assumption that the labour market is significantly different from other markets, the awkward experience of operating monetary growth rules promises the revival and renewed strength of more traditional demand management approaches. The experience also suggests that the rationalisation of pursuit of monetary targets in terms of minimising informational error may be too heavy and that a lower-level rationalisation is more appealing: monetary rules bring inflation down by deflating demand, and causing unemployment.

But the comfort to be derived from this by demand management activists is limited. The prediction that inflation can be cured by using only one instrument (demand deflation) at the inevitable cost of unemployment may be secure, but where is the necessary extra instrument of policy? New searches are on for an optimal incomes policy, but the objectives of such a policy are, it seems, twofold. It must be capable of internalising the 'public goods' character of wage restraint, and so of assisting the control of inflation without penal unemployment in the transition. But this alone does not allow any employment objective to be chosen in the long run unless the policy can also supervene on real wages, and thus on the distribution of welfare between union and non-union members and between employed and unemployed workers.

Nevertheless, if the applicability of natural rate doctrine to the short-run is rolled back, the scope for demand management policy is revived; if an incomes policy can be devised which will also supervene on the natural rate in the long run, then the monetarist counter-revolution would be decisively halted. But there must be a great doubt whether, and when, the larger ambitions for incomes policy can be realised, and while that remains the case adventurous demand management policies, especially at the national level, will be handicapped by the encapsulation in current prices of their suspected long-run effects in the foreign exchange and security markets. Unconditional monetary targets make some sense in long-run terms, traditional demand management in the short-run, but effective policy design now seems to require a more subtle blend of policy such that response to short-run shocks is not prevented by rigid adherence to rules that make sense only as between points of long-run equilibrium, and such that effective response to short-run shocks is not held to compromise long-run outcomes. A move towards contingent rules might help policy-makers break out of this impasse. In any event, renewed experimentation with incomes policy seems likely: the earliest advocates of demand management, as we have already remarked, always anticipated that demand management would find its limits in the political problem of wages policy.

Notes

1   This is the usual working interpretation of what Hicks (1974) has called Keynes's 'wage theorem', his habit of working throughout in real terms. The assumption need not be interpreted as literally true, provided that (equiproportionate) changes in wages and prices are treated as orthogonal to the working of the model.

2   These propositions are worked out with some care in Laidler (1971); see also Carlson and Spencer (1975) for an account of traditional crowding-out.

3   See e.g. Mundell (1963).

4   This result is the one associated with the earlier work of Mundell (1962).

5   The full-employment budget surplus is an alternative target here, which does not induce destabilising policy actions.

6   Poole (1970) offers the classic analysis of these cases extended to consider the general case where *both* schedules are stochastic; when account must also be taken of covariances in the disturbances.

7   See Laidler (1972) for a full working out of this case.

8   The recent flourishing of literature in this area owes much to the stimulus provided by Blinder and Solow (1973), but many of the results were foreshadowed by important but neglected earlier contributions by McKinnon (1969), Ott and Ott (1965) and Mackinnon and Oates (1965).

9   The calendar time correlate is in dispute. Some observers see the wealth adjustment processes in question as comparatively quick and certainly significant within the customary time span of short-term forecasting and demand management policy horizons — e.g. the 'New Cambridge' school (see e.g. Cripps, Godley and Fetherston, 1974).

10   For comprehensive surveys of this literature the reader is directed to the papers by Currie (1978, 1981). Artis (1980) provides an introduction.

11   See e.g. Robinson (1937), Worswick (1944), Kalecki (1944).

12   The equilibrium real wage cannot be changed in the terms in which the augmented Phillips curve is usually expressed. Artis and Miller (1979) explore this question in the context of real terms of trade shocks.

13   For a rigorous analytical argument see Buiter (1980).

14   An excellent and accessible survey appears in Portes and Muellbauer (1978); see also Stoneman (1979).

15   Keynes himself (1936) seems to have had this in mind in appearing to subscribe to the view that the economy was always 'on its demand for labour curve' (see Grossman, 1972, for a succinct if combative discussion of the issue).

16   With inelastic labour supplies, the equilibrium real wage would be constant.

17   Dixit (1976) has undertaken such an extension, but he effectively interprets the definition of a small open economy as one which cannot suffer from a shortage of *domestic* demand (since firms can always, by assumption, sell all they want to abroad). The analysis thus collapses to the case analysed earlier (p. 18), where a demand management stimulus simply spills over directly to the balance of payments without affecting domestic output and income. Hahn (1980), Muellbauer and Portes (1978) and Malinvaud (1980) have indicated ways in which this impasse may be avoided, but a convincingly detailed account of the scope for demand management policies in an open economy context has yet to be provided.

18   For, unless public announcement *adds* something, following the rule 'in secret' would be one of the options of discretion. Hence discretion could not be *worse* than publicly announcing a rule, and has extra degrees of freedom.

19   The beneficial effects of the public announcement depend on credibility and therefore, up to a point, on performance. A 'wide bands' growth target reduces the chances of target miss, though at some cost in scrambling the information content of the policy itself.

20   It can, of course, be argued that all rules are contingent, since they would be abandoned in the face of undefined but high enough costs; the contingent rules referred to here would pre-specify (some of) the conditions in which the rule would be abandoned or amended.

21   With linear short-run Phillips curves, adaptive expectations and a penalty on peak unemployment, gradualism is enjoined; however, in these circumstances the integral of unemployment implied by inflation control is unaffected by the speed with which it is desired to go.

22   The '1925 problem' is a reference to the difficulties occasioned by Britain's return to the gold standard in 1925, which involved an over-appreciated exchange rate. The difficulties affecting the conduct of monetary policy in Germany and Switzerland in the 1970s in regard to the level of the real exchange rate are commented upon in Vaubel (1980), whilst those afflicting the United Kingdom in 1979 and 1980 are reflected, *inter alia*, in evidence submitted to the House of Commons Select Committee on the Treasury and Civil Service (1980).

Using the Treasury model to measure the impact of fiscal policy, 1974–79

1. Introduction

In this chapter[1] we put forward estimates of the effects of the fiscal actions undertaken by the 1974–79 Labour administration. However, our principal purpose in providing these estimates is not so much to provide a detailed evaluation of the policies of that administration as to illustrate the application of a method of measuring fiscal policy, using an econometric model which has previously been applied to United States data by Blinder and Goldfeld (1976).

Various summary measures of fiscal policy (e.g. the full employment budget surplus) do of course exist, and versions of them are available for the UK;[2] the measure proposed here, though at first sight distinct from traditional measures, can be seen to be related to the weighted standardised surplus (Blinder and Solow, 1974) as already pointed out by Blinder and Goldfeld and, although it employs a formal econometric model, is a direct successor to the approach pioneered in the UK by Godley and Hopkin (1965) and by Corrigan (1970) in the United States.

In what follows we first review the construction of traditional measures of fiscal policy based on the balance in the budget and some of the criticisms to which these measures have been exposed. We then present the methodology of the Blinder and Goldfeld measure along with some (comparatively minor) extensions to which pursuit of their methodology leads. In section 4, because the estimates obtained are model-specific, we present an outline of some of the principal features of the Treasury model (HM Treasury, 1979) which we have employed. In section 5 we turn to a review of the results obtained in estimating the measures for the period of the

1974–79 Labour government. The final section contains some concluding comments and makes suggestions for the way in which the methodology used in the paper can be further exploited.

2. Fiscal measures

The general motivation for computing summary measures of fiscal policy is provided by the observation that a simple listing of the current setting (or change in setting) of fiscal instruments is an unhelpful method of evaluating fiscal policy and its effects in that it provides no means of weighting the values of changes in different instruments. Summary measures seek to provide such weights.

It is conventional to distinguish between budget balance-related measures and measures of fiscal influence. The former summarise the overall magnitude of a particular tax and expenditure programme in terms of budgetary magnitudes, while the latter provide an estimate of its impact on some policy target, usually gross domestic product (GDP).

Blinder and Solow have critically surveyed most extant fiscal measures. Their main ideas can be illustrated with the aid of the following primitive fix-price IS–LM model:

$$Y = C + I + G \tag{1}$$

$$C = C(Y - T) \qquad\qquad C' > 0 \tag{2}$$

$$T = T(Y, \tau) \qquad\qquad T_Y > 0, T_\tau > 0 \tag{3}$$

$$I = I(R, \alpha) \qquad\qquad I_R < 0, I_\alpha > 0 \tag{4}$$

$$R = R(\overline{M}, Y) \qquad\qquad R_{\overline{M}} < 0, R_Y > 0 \tag{5}$$

All variables are in real terms where Y = aggregate income, C = private consumption, I = private investment, G = government spending, T = income tax revenues, R = the rate of interest, M = the quantity of money, τ = the income tax rate in real terms, α = the autonomous element in private investment.

The expressions $T_Y, \dots$, etc, denote the partial derivatives $\partial T / \partial Y$, $\dots$, etc. Equations 1–5 are, respectively: the National Income Account; the consumption function; the direct tax function; the investment function; and the inverse of the money demand function (the money supply being assumed constant). By substitution:

$$Y = C\,[Y - T(Y, \tau)] + I\,[R(\overline{M}, Y), \alpha] + G \qquad (6)$$

and the linear approximation to this system evaluated at the current level of income has the solution:

$$dY = \frac{dG - C'T_\tau d\tau}{1 - C'(1 - T_Y) - I_R R_Y} \;+\; \frac{I_\alpha d\alpha + I_R R_{\overline{M}} dM}{1 - C'(1 - T_Y) - I_R R_Y} \qquad (7)$$

This expression for the change in equilibrium income in response to (local) changes in the exogenous variables of the model can be used to illustrate the construction of the various fiscal measures. Since interest is focused on the representation given by these measures to *changes* in fiscal policy, we refer to their first differenced counterparts; thus, letting the superscript F denote 'full employment', we can represent these as follows:

$$\text{The actual budget surplus} = dT - dG$$
$$= T_Y\,dY + T_\tau d\tau - dG \qquad (8)$$

$$\text{Leverage}\,[3] = (C'dT - dG)\,(1 - C_Y)^{-1}$$
$$= (C'T_Y\,dY + C'T_\tau d\tau - dG)\,(1 - C_Y)^{-1} \qquad (9)$$

$$\text{The full-employment budget} = dT(Y^F, \tau) - dG$$
$$= T_\tau(Y^F, \tau)d\tau - dG \qquad (10)$$

$$\text{The weighted standardised surplus} = C'T_\tau d\tau - dG \qquad (11)$$

In their survey Blinder and Solow concluded in favour of the weighted standardised surplus (WSS). Referring back to equation 7, the first term on the right-hand side is the change in income due to discretionary changes in fiscal policy (dG and $d\tau$). The attraction of the WSS is that it is just the negative of the numerator of this first term the denominator being the reciprocal of the IS–LM multiplier. Thus the negative of the entire first term in equation 7 can be interpreted as the fiscal impact version of the WSS, equation 11 being a budget-balance-related measure.

These traditional measures have been subjected to a number of criticisms, many of which are discussed in detail in Bean and Hartley (1978). For example:

1. The measures are confined to GDP effects, whereas fiscal policy also influences, in particular, prices, unemployment and the balance of payments.
2. They make unvarying assumptions about other policies. In fact the effects of a specified fiscal action will depend, *inter alia*, on the monetary policy regime and whether an effective incomes policy is in force.
3. They ignore initial conditions and non-linearities in the economy.
4. The time scale is unclear.

While it is possible to defend the traditional measures against these criticisms the measure which we propose is more easily defended. Moreover it has the advantage that it responds to such criticisms in a constructive way. First, however, we set out formally the nature of the measure.

3. The measure proposed

We begin with a large-scale macroeconometric model which can, for convenience, be represented as a non-linear (vector) difference equation:

$$Y(t) = F(G(t), A(t), Y(t-1)) \qquad (12)$$

Here $G(t)$ is the vector of fiscal policy instruments in the model at time t (including appropriately redefined lagged values of these instruments); $A(t)$ is a vector of strictly exogenous variables (including lagged values); and $Y(t)$ is the vector of endogenous variables. For simplicity we will conduct the exposition in terms of one element of $Y(t)$: real income.

To measure the impact of the fiscal policy actions taken in a particular time period ($t = t_0$) we first simulate the model using the actual historical values of $G(t)$ and $A(t)$ to generate a (base) series of estimated values of $Y(t)$; call it $\hat{Y}(t)$. We then construct an adjusted series for G which follows the historical paths of the instruments up to time t_0, remains unchanged at t_0, and then replicates all subsequent *changes* in G. The model is then simulated again to produce another sequence of values for $\hat{Y}(t)$; call it $\{\hat{Y}(t, t_0)\}$. The proposed measure of fiscal impact describing the effect of policy changes undertaken at time t_0, $\{F(t, t_0)\}$, is the difference between the base series and the simulated series[4] or

$$F(t, t_0) = \{\hat{Y}(t) - \hat{Y}(t, t_0)\} \tag{13}$$

Thus in fig 2.1(a) the continuous line represents the base series of $\hat{Y}$ generated by the actual values of G (in this case government spending — also shown as a continuous line in fig. 2.1(b)). The policy action taken at time $t = 4$ is shown in 2.1(b) as $g(4) = G(4) - G(3)$, with the broken line $G(t, 4)$ representing the adjusted series of G purged of this policy action. Simulating the model using $G(t, 4)$ generates a sequence of values of Y determined by the multipliers of the model and shown as the broken line $\hat{Y}(t, 4)$ in fig. 2.1(a). The difference between the two sequences of Y are the measures (F) of the policy action taken at $t = 4$.

In effect we 'undo' a particular set of policy actions taken at a particular time and then work out what would have happened to (say) GDP in the absence of these actions. The difference between this GDP series and the base series is the measure of the influence of the policy package in question. The measure can be seen as equivalent to the fiscal impact version of the WSS; for the simulated values of GDP, and hence the policy measures, are automatically weighted by the dynamic multipliers of the econometric model. *Mutatis mutandis*, similar measures can be obtained of the effect of fiscal policy on variables other than GDP such as prices, unemployment and the balance of payments.

Since the econometric model is dynamic, any fiscal action at time t generates a sequence of effects which in principle is infinite. Though the value of the measure may become negligible or constant in finite time, in practice most macroeconometric models generate deep cycles and do not converge to a steady-state path over the time period for which data are available. As argued by Blinder and Goldfeld, this suggests that the measure must be truncated after an arbitrary number of quarters.

The fact that the model is dynamic also creates a need to distinguish between the effects of a fiscal action taken at time t on subsequent levels of GDP and the total effect on GDP at time t of all *past* fiscal actions. In any quarter the *total* effect of fiscal policy may be defined as the cumulative sum of the effect in that quarter of current fiscal actions, the lagged effect of actions taken in the

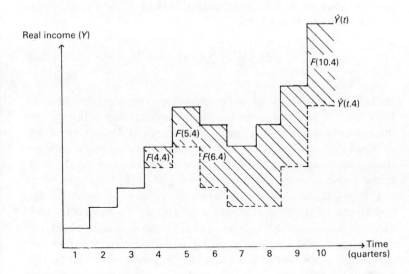

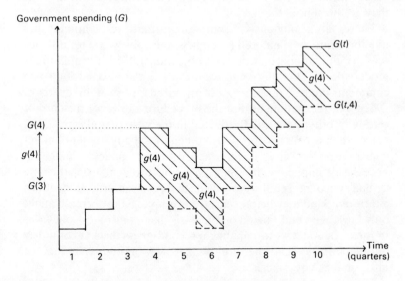

Fig. 2.1   Measuring fiscal impact: an illustration

previous quarter and the longer lagged effects of actions taken in the quarters previous to that:

$$F(t) = \sum_{i=0}^{n} F(t, t-i) \qquad (14)$$

If n is large enough, this would measure the entire agglomeration of fiscal actions since the beginning of government! In practice we are interested in the first difference of this series as descriptive of the change in effect of fiscal policy between any two quarters, and the truncation described earlier will provide a limit on n. Thus the goal of the exercise is the measure $dF(t) = F(t) - F(t-1)$.

The technique described is capable of meeting some of the objections levelled at traditional measures. In particular, this measure is precisely dated; it is not confined to measuring effects on output; it takes account of initial conditions and accepts the specification of other policies actually prevailing, as given by the base period data; and it takes account of non-linearities in so far as they are present in the model.

There are, obviously, some important reservations and qualifications to be entered (even neglecting, as we do for obvious reasons, the rational expectations objection!). First, the measure is model-specific. On this count we include in the next section some comments on the Treasury model proposed for use in this exercise.

Second, the statement that the procedure allows for the current setting of other policies as reflected in the base period is true, but naive when account is (properly) taken of the government budget constraint, for any counterfactual fiscal policy simulation necessarily implies a different financing problem from the one actually encountered. It is also clear that policy interdependence of a different kind may be present: for example, a tax decrease might only have been undertaken on the basis that an incomes policy was in force. In effect we are unable to second-guess this kind of policy interdependence and therefore make the working assumption of independence of policies.

There is a more general issue to be settled which is common to any measurement exercise, and that is the appropriate baseline (or neutral) fiscal policy, deviations from which are used to generate the measure. In the present exercise the baseline fiscal policy is 'no change' in explicit tax rates, allowances, etc, and 'no change' in government spending. While this definition is vulnerable to criticism,[5] it may be argued that, whatever the reason for changes from the chosen baseline, such changes must be financed and hence the zero-change assumption is about the best.

In relation to the use made of this measure by Blinder and Goldfeld in their work with United States data, the present exercise differs from theirs in two principal respects. First, we consider the effects of fiscal policy not only upon GDP but also upon certain other macro-variables of interest to policy-makers. Second, whilst our data period is much shorter than theirs, in concentrating on the policies of a single administration, it seems reasonable to describe the effects of those policies by inspecting the measure of their cumulative effect. This frees us from the need to assume an arbitrary truncation period.

4.   The structure of the Treasury (HMT) model

As implemented here, the measure we propose to estimate requires the use of a full econometric model,[6] and for this purpose we have chosen to use the National Income Forecasting (NIF) sector of the Treasury's Unified Model.[7] The full model includes also a monetary sector and a capital flows sector, the three corresponding analytically to representations of the IS, LM and BB curves of a simple model of an open economy (Mundell, 1963), together with a Phillips curve relation to determine money wages.

Using only the NIF model means that the interest rate structure and the exchange rate are assumed to follow their actual historical values. Analytically this amounts to simulating fiscal policy effects as shocks to (and changes in the slope of) the IS curve, the interest rate and exchange rate remaining unchanged. These assumptions are more appropriate to the pre-1971 than to the post-1974 period for which the present paper reports results and, though they keep the spirit of the exercise closest to that of traditional budget balance measures, do mean that the results can be regarded only as a useful first approximation. This particular configuration of assumptions was dictated simply by the unavailability of the full model at the time the work was carried out, and an extension of the exercise to the whole model would obviously be instructive.[8]

5.   Fiscal policy, 1974–79

To implement our measure of fiscal policy, simulations were

Table 2.1   *Fiscal policy effects, 1974. II–1979.I*

Policy actions taken during financial year	Cumulative effects by				
	1975.I	*1976.I*	*1977.I*	*1978.I*	*1979.I*
(a) Effects on GDP (£ million, 1975 prices)					
1974/75	66·49	−15·19	−23·53	−33·72	−70·60
1975/76	–	281·70	184·71	44·24	−93·97
1976/77	–	–	−414·70	−407·36	−308·26
1977/78	–	–	–	−23·86	−5·58
1978/79	–	–	–	–	32·93
1. Total effect	66·49	266·51	−252·91	−420·70	−445·46
2. Total effect (% of historical GDP)	0·29	1·14	−1·06	−1·72	−1·78
3. First difference of 2	0·29	0·85	−2·20	−0·66	−0·06
(b) Effects on unemployment ('000)					
1974/75	−52·35	−65·26	−46·66	−40·22	−30·72
1975/76	–	−171·70	−188·83	−142·79	−74·61
1976/77	–	–	130·53	214·42	193·79
1977/78	–	–	–	9·75	3·14
1978/79	–	–	–	–	−34·05
1. Total effect	−52·35	−236·96	−104·96	41·16	56·55
2. Total effect (% of the labour force)	−0·22	−1·01	−0·44	0·18	0·24
3. First difference	−0·22	−0·79	0·57	0·62	0·06
(c) Effects on the balance of payments (current account; £ million, current prices)					
1974/75	−6·42	28·16	50·77	46·55	49·50
1975/76	–	−49·24	−80·30	−114·20	−143·99
1976/77	–	–	233·07	333·09	334·59
1977/78	–	–	–	16·69	65·39
1978/79	–	–	–	–	−36·70
1. Total effect	−6·42	−21·08	203·54	282·13	268·79
2. First difference	−6·42	−14·66	224·62	78·59	−13·34
3. Total effect (% of historical GDP)	−0·03	−0·09	0·85	1·15	1·07

Table 2.1   *continued*

Policy actions taken during financial year	Cumulative effects by				
	1975.I	*1976.I*	*1977.I*	*1978.I*	*1979.I*
(d) Effects on inflation (% per annum)					
1974/75	−1·39	0·46	0·04	0·34	0·23
1975/76	−	2·21	0·66	0·90	0·79
1976/77	−	−	0·77	−0·55	−0·28
1977/78	−	−	−	0·92	−0·52
1978/79	−	−	−	−	−0·03
1. Total effect	−1·39	2·67	1·47	1·61	0·19
2. First difference of 1	−1·39	4·06	−1·2	0·14	−1·42

conducted on the Treasury NIF model to remove, quarter by quarter, all changes in rates of taxation and allowances[9] and all changes in government expenditure over the period of the 1974–79 Labour government. The effect of each quarter's fiscal actions, so defined, is then identified as the difference between the relevant simulation run and the base run; a measure of the total cumulative effect in any quarter of all previous and current quarter fiscal actions was then taken as the simple aggregation of such differences.[10] As presentation of the full results on a quarterly basis would be excessively cumbersome, table 2.1 presents them on a summary, fiscal year, basis taking GDP, unemployment, the balance of payments and the rate of inflation in turn. Thus part (a) of the table, for example, shows the cumulative effect upon GDP of the measures taken in successive fiscal years, from 1974/75 to 1978/79, as at the end of each of these years, aggregated to a total cumulative effect at the foot of the table. The final two rows of this part of the table show respectively the cumulative effect re-expressed as a proportion of historical GDP, and the first difference of this series. A similar interpretation, *mutatis mutandis*, applies to the remaining parts of the table.

In terms of the effect of fiscal policy upon output, row 3 of part (a) of the table indicates that the principal feature of the period was the large deflationary turn-round, amounting to more than 2 per cent of GDP, in 1976/77, the middle of the period. Most of this was

Table 2.2   *The fiscal mix: the output effects of changes in taxation and expenditure considered separately*[a] *(% of GDP)*

	1975.I	1976.I	1977.I	1978.I	1979.I
Expenditure changes	0·50	1·70	−2·54	−0·67	−0·17
Tax changes	−0·22	−0·85	0·35	0·01	0·10
Net effect[b]	0·28	0·85	−2·19	−0·66	−0·07

Notes

a   Figures show the differences between the cumulative effect of policy actions (taxation or expenditure) on GDP at the dates shown.

b   Figures in this row equal, up to a rounding error, those shown in the last row of table 2.1(a).

accounted for by measures taken during the same year, although at the same time the net expansionary effect of policy actions undertaken in the previous two years was declining. The output effects of the 1977/78 and 1978/79 measures were relatively small, and, as indicated by the rightmost entry in row 2, by the end of the period, output was some 1.75 per cent less than it would have been in the absence of the fiscal actions accounted for.

It is evident from parts (b), (c) and (d) of the table that the deflationary policies of 1976/77 contributed in correspondingly large measure to an improvement in the balance of payments and a reduction in the rate of inflation, though at a cost — registered with some lag — of a substantial increase in unemployment. By the end of the period, however, the calculations suggest that there was relatively little difference to be found in unemployment or inflation from the values these variables would have assumed in the absence of the fiscal activism of the period.

5.1.   *The balance of policy*

Similar methods can be used to examine the relative contribution of taxation and government expenditure policies to the overall out-turn. Here we concentrate only on output effects, for the sake of brevity. The taxation and government expenditure changes simulated together for purposes of arriving at the results shown in table 2.1 were simulated separately, and the cumulative effects on

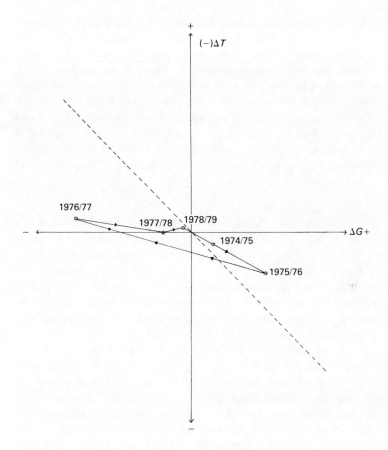

Fig. 2.2 The output effects of taxation (ΔT) and expenditure (ΔG) changes

GDP calculated as before; the differences between these cumulative effects, at the dates shown, are given in table 2.2 and graphed in fig. 2.2. In the diagram the output effects of tax changes are shown along the vertical and the output effects of expenditure changes along the horizontal axis. The 45° line thus represents the locus of neutral fiscal actions where tax increases (decreases) match expenditure decreases (increases) in output terms, points above and to the right of the line representing net expansionary actions and those to the left and below, deflationary actions.

The graph indicates clearly that the fiscal actions examined, over fiscal year intervals, were typically 'mixed' actions with output-expanding tax cuts accompanying output-decreasing expenditure reductions or vice versa; there is no instance where both arms of fiscal policy were pulling in the same direction. It can also be seen that whereas the expansiveness of fiscal policy in the first two years was due to expansionary expenditure policies partially offset by contractionary tax effects, in the subsequent three years, and most notably in 1976/77, the deflationary net out-turns were due to expenditure reductions, only partially offset by net tax reductions.

5.2.   *Stabilisation effects*
It is natural to ask whether, in the light of the estimates of policy effects we have obtained, fiscal policy should be regarded as having been successful in stabilisation over this period. The question may be interpreted in two senses: first, whether policy improved the performance of the economy in respect of output, unemployment, inflation and the balance of payments over the period as a whole; second, whether policy actions succeeded in producing greater quarter-by-quarter stability in these target variables.

Evidence appropriate to answering the first question has already been presented in table 2.1; by averaging over the figures given in row 1 of each part of this table we find that our estimates imply an average loss of GDP of approximately two-thirds of 1 per cent, and an improvement in the balance of payments (as a percentage of GDP) of nearly comparable order. Unemployment (thanks to lags in the GDP–unemployment relationship) was slightly reduced, on average by a quarter of a basis point, with the inflation rate being increased by something under three-quarters of 1 per cent.

The second dimension of stabilisation was examined by computing semi-log regressions (quarterly) for each of the four target variables defined, first, at their historical ('with policy') values, and second, at their hypothetical, 'without policy' values, these being generated by adding back to the series of historical values our estimates of policy effects. This facilitates a comparison of the stability of the trend-corrected series, as measured by the coefficient of variation. Table 2.3 displays the results of this comparison, which suggest that policy had statistically significant effects in stabilising the path of GDP and unemployment, though

Table 2.3 *Stabilisation impact of fiscal policy: coefficients of variation (% of the mean)*

	GDP	Unemployment	Cumulative current account balance$^\alpha$	Prices
1. With policy (realisation)	0·15	2·38	4·23	0·98
2. Without policy (hypothetical series)	0·20	3·28	5·16	0·84
3. *F* ratio of residual variances^b	1·88*	1·97 *	1·44	0·74

Notes

a The stabilising impact on the current account was computed by taking deviations from trend of the cumulative surplus or deficit from the second quarter of 1974.

b Ratio of the trend-adjusted without-policy variance to that of the trend-adjusted with-policy variance.

* Ratios which are significant at the 90 per cent level (indicating that the with-policy variance is significantly smaller than that without policy).

not in respect of either the (cumulative) balance of payments or the inflation rate.

5.3. *Comparison with other fiscal measures*

It is instructive to compare the measures proposed here with some existing ones. For this purpose we have chosen the (unweighted) high employment budget surplus and the weighted budget balance which are regularly estimated by the National Institute (*Economic Review*, May 1980, for example). Its measures are not precisely comparable with ours, for the full-employment measure implicitly assumes an indexed tax structure.[11] Moreover its estimates are of budget measures, and whilst the weighted version takes account of the differential impact which the budget components have on demand, neither version takes any account of the multiplier consequences, in contrast to our (fiscal impact) measures, which included the (dated) multiplier consequences of policy changes.

The National Institute's estimates together with those from the present study are shown in table 2.4. For purposes of comparison

Table 2.4   *Comparison of GDP effect of different fiscal measures (% of GDP)*

	1974/75	1975/76	1976/77	1977/78	1978/79
1. Artis and Green	0·29	0·85	−2·20	−0·66	−0·06
2. Weighted budget balance (NIESR)	1·1	−1·4	−1·3	−1·9	−
3. High employment budget balance (NIESR)	1·6	−0·8	−1·1	−2·7	−

Notes. The rows are defined as follows:

1. First difference of cumulative effects of policy actions in percentage of historical GDP. (Source: table 2.1(a), row 3.)
2. Change in the weighted budget balance with sign reversed (− denotes a decrease in the deficit or increase in the surplus) in percentage of high-employment GDP. (Source: National Institute *Economic Review*, May 1979.)
3. Change in the high-employment budget balance with sign reversed, in percentage of historical GDP. (Source: National Institute *Economic Review*, May 1979.)

the Institute's measures are shown with sign reversed. Thus a positive entry in the table denotes an expansionary fiscal stance and a negative entry a contractionary stance.

All three measures present the same broad picture of expansionary policy followed by contraction over the period as a whole. However, there are some interesting differences in the measures' estimates of the relative size and timing of policy actions. The most marked of these differences comes in the 1975/76 fiscal year. According to the two budget measures, policy began to be contractionary in that year, whereas the present estimates suggest that it was still expansionary. As it was a year in which offsetting changes in taxes and expenditures were particularly substantial,[12] the estimates of the relative magnitudes of the different multipliers would be particularly important in determining the overall impact of policy in that year.

6.   Conclusion

The use of an econometric model to measure fiscal policy appears to be an interesting addition to the stock of existing policy measures. The measures of the impact of fiscal policy during the 1974–79 Labour administration obtained by application of this method to the Treasury model broadly confirm other comparable estimates of fiscal policy effects in this period, albeit with some difference in timing and magnitude. In fact one particular advantage of using an econometric model to estimate such measures is that policy effects are precisely dated and the appearance of different 'vintages' of policy in any given period highlights the importance of taking into account lagged effects when considering the impact of policy changes. In the present exercise this point is particularly evident in the case of the policy changes made in the 1976/77 fiscal year, which continued to exert a strong contractionary impact for at least the following two years. An important limitation of the present exercise is the assumption of fixed interest rates and fixed exchange rates, although this does facilitate comparison with extant measures.

The technique we have used can be extended in various ways, two of which will be indicated briefly here. First, an econometric model can be used to study monetary policy in much the same way as fiscal policy. Whereas there is no generally accepted monetary analogy to the full-employment budget,[13] the counterfactual simulation technique requires only an appropriate definition of monetary policy instruments for it to be used to construct monetary measures analogous to the fiscal measures presented here.

A second application of the technique is in the construction of implicit policy 'preference trade-offs'. Since the measures reflect the dated impact of policy changes, they should directly reveal the policy-makers' preference among alternative objectives — for example, as between inflation and unemployment. It is a relatively straightforward matter to compute a set of implicit valuations of one target in terms of another in the manner suggested by Fisher (1970).

While it must be admitted that the measures obtained by this method are model-specific, this does not seem an unduly serious objection in so far as any formal or informal (even uniform) weighting scheme implicitly embodies a certain view about the effects of policies. In this respect it would be interesting to obtain comparable measures from other econometric models.

Notes

1   This is an abbreviated version of a paper with the same title issued as
     Manchester University Discussion Paper No. 20. We are grateful to
     Paul Ashurst and David Blackaby for research assistance of a high
     calibre and for useful comments. Useful comments on earlier drafts
     of this paper were also provided by Rod Apps, Robin
     Bladen-Hovell, Simon Domberger, Derek Leslie, Peter Middleton,
     David Savage and Graham Smith. Funding for this research was
     provided by a grant from the Social Science Research Council. The
     usual *caveat* applies.

2   See, for example, Ward and Neild (1978) and Price (1978).

3   The concept of leverage is due to Musgrave (1964).

4   Obviously the base series $\{\hat{Y}(t)\}$ will track actual income $\{\hat{Y}(t)\}$ only
     to the extent that the model is a satisfactory representation of the
     economy.

5   The full-employment budget surplus assumes that *failure* to index
     tax rates, allowances, etc, is *policy*. This is broadly consistent with
     the spirit of the Rooker–Wise amendment, which provides for
     automatic indexation of personal allowances. Changes in
     government expenditure are also undertaken for a variety of
     non-stabilisation reasons. However, Price's attempt (1978) to
     disentangle from ministerial statements and programme shortfalls
     and overruns the 'true' discretionary changes in government
     spending generates a set of highly subjective estimates whose precise
     interpretation is unclear. It should be noted that our simulation
     methodology allows for any desired variations in the assumptions
     concerning the baseline fiscal policy.

6   If non-linearities can be neglected, and all tax and government
     expenditure changes expressed as 'first-round deviations in
     aggregate demand', a simple multiplier–accelerator model can be
     applied to these deviations to provide a series describing the output
     effects of the fiscal actions. It was in these terms that the pioneering
     work of Hopkin and Godley (1965) was systematised by Shepherd
     and Surrey (1968) and pursued by Bristow (1968) and by one of the
     present authors (Artis, 1972).

7   The NIF model was made available in Manchester under the terms of
     the 'Bray amendment'. It should be noted that the entire HMT
     model is continually changing. The work reported in this paper was
     carried out on a 1979 version; more recent versions may give
     different results. Moreover it was found necessary to make a variety
     of more or less *ad hoc* technical adjustments to the model to render it
     suitable for the present exercise. Some of these adjustments are
     discussed in the longer version of this chapter referred to in note 1
     above.

8   This set of assumptions does, however, free us from the need to take
     more account of the government budget constraint. The implicit
     financing decision associated with each fiscal policy action is simply

to sell or purchase whatever mix of government debt the private sector wishes to hold at the prevailing set of interest rates.

9   Excluding the 1974 stock relief provision, because no modelling of it appears in the HMT model and no reliable estimates of its effects are, to our knowledge, available elsewhere.

10 It could be objected that this procedure perpetuates an unwarranted assumption of linearity in policy effects. However, it was found that this assumption was in fact approximately justified. The appeal of the present procedure is that it makes possible the ready identification of fiscal 'overhang' effects.

11 See note 5 above.

12 See table 2.2. The National Institute's estimates also show that tax measures were contractionary and expenditures expansionary in 1975/76 (*NIER*, May 1980). In their case, however, the contractionary element was estimated to be stronger than the expansionary element.

13 Although see Hendershott (1968) on the neutralised money stock.

Crowding-out in UK macro-models

1.   Introduction

The effectiveness of fiscal policy in changing the level of output has come under increasing challenge in recent years. Attention has been drawn to the fact that fiscal policy may be blunted in its effectiveness by offsetting changes in private sector behaviour. It has been suggested that in this way fiscal policy may be substantially — and in the extreme — completely 'crowded out'.

The principal purpose of this chapter[1] is to evaluate this 'crowding out' phenomenon by examining the evidence provided by the three major quarterly macroeconometric models of the economy — those of the National Institute of Economic and Social Research, the London Business School and HM Treasury (hereafter, NIESR, LBS and HMT respectively). These models are, of course, essentially models of the 'short run'; by contrast, a large proportion of the existing theoretical literature in this field has been concerned with analysing the long-run or even the very long-run implications of the crowding-out phenomenon. However, in conducting the discussion within the confines of a neoclassical steady-state equilibrium, existing studies are not particularly well suited to resolve the operational questions raised by the debate. To begin with, a time horizon of only a few years is likely to be pertinent, rather than either the impact or long-run steady-state solutions so often emphasised by the literature. Second, in the steady-state solutions entertained in this literature, supply-side considerations assume a far greater degree of significance than seems appropriate for policy-relevant horizons in economies characterised by demand constraints. Moreover, interpretation of the theoretical results must be carried out with great care; for instance, it cannot simply be assumed that crowding-out is necessarily greater in the long-run than in the short-run; as Tobin and Buiter (1976) have shown, complete crowding-out of private expenditure in the short-run because of full employment can, in the long-run, be more than offset by the capital-deepening effects of the initial government expenditure.

The remainder of this chapter is divided into five sections. First we consider the role assigned to fiscal policy in conventional analysis of the short-run, initially within the setting of a closed economy and subsequently for a small open economy operating a flexible exchange rate. This is followed by an examination of the views of the three groups of United Kingdom macro-modellers, the LBS, NIESR and HMT, noting the key respects in which these modellers diverge from orthodox analysis. Section 4 discusses the results of comparative policy simulations conducted for these three models and the implications of the models for the degree of crowding-out in the United Kingdom. Then two aspects of the above simulations are discussed with specific reference to the Treasury model. In particular, attention is drawn to the nature and power of a bond-coupon effect which counters traditional crowding-out arguments, and to the importance of inflation for the crowding-out of government expenditure. The final section contains concluding comments.

2. An analysis of fiscal policy

The standard textbook exposition of the relative efficacy of monetary and fiscal policy is conducted in the context of IS–LM analysis. In the absence of wealth effects of any kind, the relative effectiveness of the two policies depends only on the relative magnitude of the interest elasticities of the private expenditure and money demand functions. An increased expenditure elasticity lowers the absolute effectiveness of fiscal policy, since it increases the extent to which the fiscal stimulus is offset by the induced rise in interest rates, reducing private-sector expenditures: while it raises that of monetary policy by increasing the effect of a given change in interest rates on aggregate demand. A reduced interest elasticity of money demand increases the rise in interest rates that accompanies a given fiscal stimulus and, therefore, lowers the effectiveness of fiscal policy: while it raises that of monetary policy by increasing the change in interest rates resulting from a given change in money supply. Thus the larger the ratio of the expenditure elasticity to the money demand elasticity, the greater the relative efficacy of monetary to fiscal policy.[2]

Utilising this analysis provides the simplest rationale for crowding-out for monetary reasons. An expansionary fiscal policy unaccompanied by monetary expansion induces a rise in interest rates and a fall in interest-sensitive private-sector expenditures, thereby offsetting the expansionary effects of the fiscal stimulus. However, there are two important qualifications. First, the offset to fiscal policy will be only partial, except in the case of either a completely interest-inelastic money demand function or an infinitely interest-elastic expenditure function, neither of which receives any empirical support. The second qualification is perhaps more fundamental in that government expenditure assumes no privileged role in the argument. An increase in consumer spending can crowd out private-sector investment or, in an open economy with less than perfect capital mobility, an increase in exports can have the same effect.

It is for an entirely different set of reasons that traditional theory maintains that the short-run effect of fiscal policy on the level of output in a small open economy operating a flexible exchange rate would be zero (see, for example, Fleming, 1962, Mundell, 1962 and Dornbusch, 1976). This conclusion, however, depends on the satisfaction of a number of fundamental conditions. Specifically it must be assumed that, *inter alia*, the supply of domestic output is perfectly elastic at a given price level and that individuals are subject to money illusion. Further, it must be postulated that there is perfect capital mobility for domestic residents relative to the rest of the world which, together with an assumption of static exchange rate expectations, means that domestic and foreign securities are perfect substitutes across uncovered interest differentials.[3]

Within such a framework the rise in the rate of interest consequent upon a bond-financed fiscal expansion induces a capital inflow and must result in an exchange rate appreciation so as to preserve a zero overall balance of payments, reducing net exports by an amount sufficient to offset completely the initial fiscal stimulus. Moreover, relaxation of the capital mobility assumption and the introduction of imperfect capital flows leaves the broad policy conclusions intact: bond-financed fiscal expenditures remain

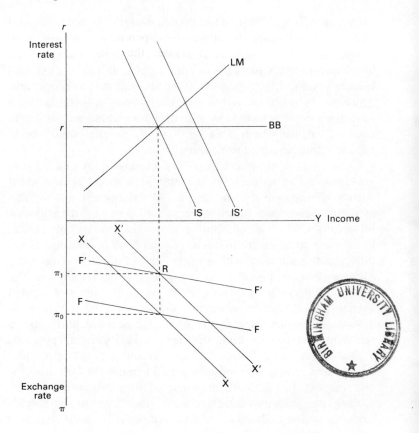

Fig. 3.1 Fiscal policy under fixed/floating exchange rates

impotent, since any divergence from interest parity gives rise to either a higher exchange rate or limitless devaluation. In contrast, money-financed deficits or pure monetary policy are capable of influencing the level of activity by exerting a depreciating effect on the exchange rate, hence stimulating a 'crowding in' of net exports.

These results can be clarified with the aid of fig. 3.1. In the top quadrant IS and LM plot the familiar equilibrium relationships along which, for a given exchange rate, the product market and money market are in equilibrium, while BB describes the external balance condition which, given perfect capital mobility, is dominated by the world level of interest rates.

Of course, if there existed less than perfect (but non-zero) capital mobility, the BB schedule will have an upward slope, allowing both income and interest rates to rise with a fiscal expansion. In the lower quadrant XX plots the internal balance and FF the external balance condition as a function of income and the exchange rate. Thus the IS schedule yields internal balance only for a given exchange rate, represented by π_0 in the bottom quadrant; while the external balance schedule FF applies only for the initial rate of capital inflow (assumed to be zero).

Consider now the effect of a fiscal expansion. An increase in government expenditure shifts the internal balance schedules to IS' and X'X' respectively. At the initial exchange rate, π_0, this increases income and hence the demand for money. To maintain money market equilibrium, interest rates tend to rise, and capital inflows are attracted from abroad. Under *flexible* exchange rates, however, this improvement in the balance of payments causes the exchange rate to appreciate. In the lower quadrant, therefore, the new equilibrium is established at R, where the price of foreign exchange is lower but output unchanged; the increase in government expenditure is offset by a fall in net exports, the IS schedule in the top quadrant being returned to its original position.

Objections can, however, be directed at the particular equilibrium solutions proposed by the Fleming–Mundell analysis, and four specific issues are identified for further discussion.

First, the analysis characteristically posits that in the foreign exchange market equality is maintained between the current and forward exchange rates, interest parity being sustained across uncovered interest differentials. Such an assumption, however, is rather implausible for a world operating under a flexible exchange rate regime, since it requires individuals not to expect the exchange rate to change even though it actually does. Relaxing this assumption introduces the possibility that domestic and world interest rates may diverge, since it is now the expected net return on alternative assets which concerns investors, and arbitrage will occur across the covered interest differential. Under these circumstances some power may be restored to fiscal policy, since, provided the responsiveness of the forward rate to movements in the current spot rate is inelastic, the subsequent rise in the exchange rate is moderated to the extent to which capital inflows are reduced as a direct result of the forward discount generated by the rise. Thus a fiscal expansion which induces an over-appreciation of the currency relative to its expected value will, in principle, provide for a positive output effect at an increased interest rate.[4]

Second, while the results demonstrate independence of the assumed degree of capital mobility, they do not demonstrate a similar independence of the manner in which capital mobility is modelled. Here the traditional assumption was that continuing capital inflows could be attracted into a country by a given, once-for-all increase in the domestic interest rate (differential) relative to the rest of the world. In contrast, recent empirical work favours the stock adjustment principle, capital inflows occurring in response to a once-for-all rearrangement of portfolios in favour of the country increasing the interest rate (see, for example, Beenstock and Bell, 1979). The extent of capital stock adjustment and the resultant capital inflow would, of course, be related to the degree of substitutability of assets of various origins in the portfolio. Further, apart from any natural growth of the portfolio, a continuing capital inflow would require an increasing differential between the world rate and the domestic rate of interest.

Naturally, introducing a stock adjustment principle in the Fleming–Mundell analysis is of particular importance for the behaviour of the exchange rate subsequent to a fiscal expansion and hence for the overall crowding-out mechanism. For within such a system the long-run value of the exchange rate can be thought of as being determined solely by movements in the current account of the balance of payments, and its value subsequent to an expansive fiscal policy will represent a depreciation relative to its initial value. In contrast to the Fleming–Mundell model, therefore, the exchange rate mechanism reinforces the expansive effect of government expenditure and may, in a fixed-price world, give rise to instability.

Third, while the above places the short-run validity of the Fleming–Mundell results in doubt, analysis of the intrinsic wealth adjustment process raises questions about its applicability for the long-run. The short-run equilibrium noted above cannot persist in the long-run, since it requires the existence of a trade imbalance with corresponding changes in private-sector wealth. A balanced-budget fiscal policy, for example, while involving no budget deficit-induced wealth effects, generates an initial foreign balance deficit via an appreciation of the exchange rate leading to a reduction in private-sector wealth. As wealth falls the decline in the demand for money places downward pressure on interest rates, inducing a capital outflow and a reduction in the exchange rate, thus stimulating output through an increase in exports. In the long-run the level of private-sector wealth will be lower, and income higher than initially, in proportions such as to maintain money market equilibrium. Private-sector expenditures decline, but since income increases in the long-run, this crowding out is only partial. Moreover, since the trade account must balance in the long-run (implying a zero change in private-sector wealth), then, despite higher income, the exchange rate must be lower in the long-run than in its initial position.[5]

In contrast, a bond-financed fiscal deficit has the short-run impact noted by Fleming and Mundell: with income unchanged, the resulting budget deficit is equal to the full increase in government expenditure and, since the trade account deteriorates by an amount sufficient to offset the stimulus in demand, the impact equilibrium is characterised by a position where the trade deficit is completely matched by the budget deficit. Hence no wealth adjustment occurs; the short-run equilibrium is equivalent to the long-run equilibrium, with the government deficit entirely taken up by the overseas sector.

The *fourth* and final modification of their model is to amend Fleming and Mundell's assumption of constant prices. In a world of flexible exchange rates the assumption that domestic prices are fixed is rather anomalous; changes in the exchange rate, through their impact on import prices, feed into domestic costs and hence prices and wages. Nor is this the only way in which exchange rate changes are transmitted into the price system. Recent evidence for the United Kingdom (see, for example, Brown, Enoch and Mortimer-Lee, 1980) suggests that, in addition to the important cost–price–wage mechanism, exchange rate changes have a direct effect via 'law of one price' considerations on domestic prices. Of course, in the short-run the dominance of the fixed-price assumption may be justified by appeal to the existence of lags in the adjustment process: empirical evidence, however, suggests that these lags are not particularly lengthy (see, for example, Artis and Currie, 1980).

Incorporating flexible prices and inflation into models which envisage floating exchange rates and wealth adjustment enables us to postulate the existence of yet another, alternative, equilibrium solution, whereby an exchange rate depreciation and associated inflation impose an 'inflation tax' on the private sector, reducing the value of personal assets fixed in nominal terms, and neutralising the expansionary effect of the budget deficit. The balance of payments in this case would be zero and the level of income unaltered, the exchange rate having undergone a once-for-all depreciation. Such an equilibrium is, of course, easier to motivate if the Fleming–Mundell assumption regarding capital mobility is replaced by the idea of capital stock adjustment.

Since the conclusions concerning the effectiveness of fiscal policy are so dependent on specific assumptions, it seems appropriate to contrast the above with the views currently expressed by United Kingdom macroeconometric modellers regarding the working of the economy. In general we find that the points of departure they adopt from the Fleming–Mundell analysis coincide with the modifications introduced above. Thus we discover that the Treasury model specifies the capital account along stock adjustment lines, while all three models incorporate flexible prices and inflation. However, while consensus appears to have been reached regarding the appropriate departures to make from orthodox theory, the manner in which these departures are incorporated varies considerably across models in a number of key respects, with significant implications for subsequent model behaviour.

3. United Kingdom models

The first important issue on which the modellers diverge is in their treatment of the wage–price response to an exogenous shock, in particular a shock originating from the balance of payments. Here the tendency is towards the assumption that exchange rate changes are not very effective in the long-run. Modellers disagree, however, about the speed with which, and the way in which, exchange rate changes are transmitted throughout the system. The National Institute, for example, utilises an augmented Phillips curve to determine average wages, where the long-run coefficient on inflation is 0.8, and pricing relationships based on normal cost procedures; the Treasury incorporates similar pricing functions but employs a hybrid Phillips–real wage resistance relationship to determine average wages. Moreover, in contrast to the National

Institute, the Treasury version of the Phillips curve has a long-run coefficient of inflation of unity, providing for a vertical relationship between unemployment and inflation after two years. On the other hand the London Business School maintains that demand influences on the wage–price response are quantitatively small and favours instead a more direct link between domestic and world prices, while a 'Scandinavian school' view is expressed for wage determination. In the long-run wages and prices are homogeneous of degree one in the exchange rate, or nearly so in the case of the National Institute's model. However, in all models the presence of fixed lag structures in both prices and export volume responses ensures that a continuous depreciation of the exchange rate will improve the balance of payments.

The second departure from the policy conspectus found in the literature follows from the need to incorporate explicitly within the system a specification of exchange rate expectations. Here the Treasury's account of the way in which the exchange rate must move to clear the market, given an incipient disequilibrium, is the most complete.[6] The spot rate moves, relative to its expected value, to a point where, in combination with a highly imperfect capital account, expectations of future movements in the rate are sufficient to attract matching speculative flows to clear the overall balance. In theory the long-run equilibrium rate is provided by a version of the relative money supplies hypothesis,[7] which is consistent with the view that the rate will be that which will clear the current account. Such a view follows naturally from the stock adjustment mechanism incorporated for the capital account. The London Business School adopts a similar view of exchange rate determination, though in its case the short-run behaviour of the model is more directly related to the relative money supplies hypothesis. Finally, in the National Institute model the exchange rate is expressed as a reduced-form specification which reflects purchasing power parity considerations directly together with covered interest differentials and speculative flow effects.

One final aspect of the departures of modellers from conventional analysis is provided by the inclusion of an inflation tax effect in the consumption function. This is derived essentially from the hypothesis that in periods of inflation which erode the real value of nominally denominated financial assets the personal sector will save in order to restore the real value of its net wealth. Thus, in all models, the consumption function is specified to provide for a rise in the savings ratio in the face of inflation. The Treasury model, for example, formerly incorporated a liquid assets effect, while the more recent versions may be interpreted as including an explanatory variable defined to be equal to the cumulative sum of past savings appropriately deflated. In contrast the London Business School specifies non-durable consumption to depend, *inter alia*, on the liquid assets/disposable income ratio, while the National Institute has recently experimented with an equation incorporating both explicit inflation and wealth terms.[8]

4. Crowding-out in United Kingdom models

While speculation that fiscal policy will have little or no permanent effect on the level of output has, in recent years, gained considerable force, it is clear that the crowding-out effect is not an all-or-nothing phenomenon but rather a matter of empirical detail. For present purposes the degree of crowding out can be more precisely defined as the ratio of the induced change in the scale of some private-sector activity to the change in the scale of the public-sector economic activity that brought it about. The crowding-out debate, in other words, is about the signs, magnitude and relevant time horizons of the public policy multipliers.

The standard method of investigating the effectiveness of fiscal policy within a large-scale macroeconometric model involves the use of dynamic multipliers calculated for alternative simulation exercises (see, for example, Fromm and Klein, 1973, and Laury, Lewis and Ormerod, 1978). Such multipliers are defined, in any quarter, to equal the ratio of the change in constant-price GDP, measured at factor cost, to the change in the initial government expenditure. Policy effectiveness in such studies is typically assessed as more or less expansionary on the basis of the absolute magnitude of the dynamic multiplier.

However, except in the rather special situation where the dynamic multiplier is zero and crowding-out complete, little information is to be obtained on the relative degree of crowding-out across models from a study of absolute multiplier values. Carlson and Spencer (1975) have suggested that since in a fixed-price, fixed-exchange-rate world crowding-out arises through increases in the interest rate induced by a fiscal expansion when the

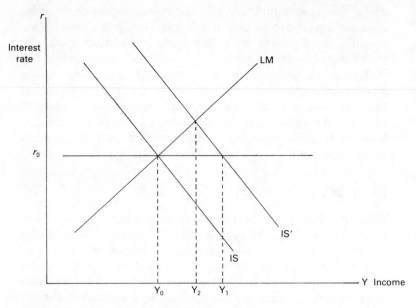

Fig. 3.2   Crowding-out in an IS–LM framework

money supply is constant, an appropriate measure of its effect is obtained from the difference between the value of the fiscal multiplier for a fixed interest rate and the fiscal multiplier derived with a constant money supply, standardised on the former. Such measure is illustrated in fig. 3.2.

In this diagram, product market and money market equilibrium is again shown by the familiar IS–LM relationships, the latter being differentiated according to whether monetary policy is accommodating or not. From the initial equilibrium Y_0, increased government expenditure shifts the IS schedule outwards to the right to IS' which, together with an accommodating monetary policy, will increase income by Y_0Y_1. Under a constant money supply regime, however, income will increase only by Y_0Y_2. In other words the difference in the output response recorded in these two simulations is a measure of the crowding-out effect of higher interest rates on private-sector expenditures. The appropriate measure of the degree of crowding-out in this example is, therefore, found by expressing the change in income levels Y_2Y_1 as a percentage of the potential (constant interest rate) change of

Y_0Y_1. Moreover it is a comparatively simple matter to extend this measure to take account of crowding-out which occurs for other reasons, most notably from changes in the exchange rate or increases in the price level.

Utilising the comparative simulations conducted by Laury, Lewis and Ormerod (1978) for the London Business School, National Institute and Treasury models, we are able to construct the measure discussed above, the results being shown as table 3.1. Here the results are classified according to two alternative interest rate regimes: $K(R)$, a constant interest rate, and $K(M)$, a flexible interest rate response of real GDP to a sustained £100 million increase in public authority current expenditure. In traditional theory the latter response is typically analysed as a constant money supply or bond-financed fiscal expansion. In the models, however, this classification is not appropriate, since money supply actually increases, the increase either reflecting a dampening factor which represents the government's desire to avoid unduly sharp fluctuations in the bond rate, or occurring as a result of short-term borrowing to finance increases in the PSBR.[9] Further differentiation allows us to distinguish between the non-inflationary and the inflationary environment, with simulation exercises being conducted under the alternative fixed exchange rate, exogenous earnings and flexible exchange rate, endogenous earnings regimes respectively. Finally, $C(\%)$ is the Carlson–Spencer measure of crowding-out attributable to higher interest rates induced by the fiscal expansion under each regime, while $T(\%)$ provides a measure of the total percentage crowding-out occurring within the models and allows for the impact of inflation and exchange rate changes on aggregate demand.

Examination of these results reveals little agreement between the models over the significance of crowding-out in the United Kingdom, with some evidence even of a tendency towards negative crowding-out. The latter is most clearly illustrated under the fixed exchange rate, exogenous earnings assumptions which characterise regime I. While the results of these simulations are unable to throw much light on the inflationary impact of money finance, comparison of the two simulations does help to determine the degree of crowding-out due to bond finance. Deficit spending not accompanied by new issues of money results in the floating of public debt issues which compete with private-sector debt in the

Table 3.1 *Crowding-out in three UK macro-econometric models* (Multipliers[a] for standardised increase in public authorities' expenditure calculated against a control solution)

	Regime I			Regime II			Total
	Exchange rate fixed, earnings exogenous			Exchange rate floating, earnings endogenous			crowding out
	1	2	3	4	5	6	7
Quarter	K(R)[b]	K(M)[c]	C(%)[d]	K(R)[b]	K(M)[c]	C(%)[d]	T(%)[e]
			London Business School model				
1	109	109	0·0	106	105	0·9	3·7
4	125	125	0·0	119	106	10·9	15·2
8	115	104	9·6	113	72	36·3	37·4
16	111	104	6·3	122	106	13·1	4·5
24	106	107	−0·9	152	100	34·2	−6·5
			National Institute model				
1	65	65	0·0	66	66	0·0	−1·5
4	84	80	4·8	96	90	6·3	−7·1
8	76	76	0·0	106	106	0·0	−39·5
16	49	48	0·2	80	89	−11·3	−81·6
24	61	61	0·0	47	47	0·0	23·0
			H.M. Treasury model				
1	101	101	0·0	101	101	0·0	0·0
4	111	109	2·0	121	117	3·0	−5·4
8	112	107	4·5	124	108	12·9	3·4
16	109	110	−0·9	112	63	44·0	42·4
24	105	112	−6·7	119	29	76·0	72·4

Notes

a The *i*th period multiplier is defined as $(\delta Y_i / \delta G) \cdot 100$, where δY_i, δG are the deviation-from-control values of GDP and public authorities' consumption, respectively.

b $K(R)$ is the constant interest rate multiplier.

c $K(M)$ is the flexible interest rate multiplier.

d $C(\%)$ is the measure of interest rate-induced crowding-out calculated as $\{(K(R) - K(M))/K(R)\} \times 100$ within each regime.

e $T(\%)$ is a measure of total crowding -out calculated as $\{$(column 1 − column 5)/column 1$\} \times 100$.

Source. Laury, Lewis and Ormerod (1978).

financial markets. The consequent upward pressure on interest rates reduces any private expenditure which is interest-elastic, in particular on private house-building and private non-residential investment. This response, however, is offset in all three models by the operation of a positive bond coupon effect arising from the need to refinance maturing debt at increasing coupon rates, these higher debt payments feeding through to personal income and hence consumption.[10]

Initially it would appear rather strange that bond financing should lead to higher levels of consumption via this channel than financing by increases in the money supply. Indeed, it would seem that the effects of private-sector financial wealth on consumption are probably not being systematically captured in so far as they ignore revaluation effects induced by changing interest rates. In technical terms the presence of this effect means that the IS schedule can be viewed as dynamically swivelling in a clockwise direction after its initial fiscal policy-induced shift, becoming more interest-inelastic as the proportion of debt refinanced at high coupons increases. Naturally, as an extreme, the IS curve may become positively sloped, thus reversing the conventional goods market relationship between income and the interest rate. Moreover this effect is not recognised in the theoretical literature, where, characteristically, bonds are considered to be perpetuities. The bond coupon effect of Blinder and Solow (1973) was of a different variety and related to service costs of additional debt rather than the increased cost of existing debt.

Relaxing the assumption of fixed exchange rates and exogenous earnings allows inflation to be incorporated in the simulations. From table 3.1 it is clear that allowance for these effects significantly alters the results produced by the London Business School and Treasury models. In the LBS model, for example, the slight tendency towards 'crowding in' has been reversed, and after two years 36 per cent of the initial stimulus has been eroded. The main impact of allowing the exchange rate to float is to induce sharp inflationary pressures in the domestic economy which operate, via their impact on personal sector asset holdings, to reduce personal consumer expenditure. Furthermore, with flexible interest rates, fixed investment expenditure is reduced as a result of increased rates of interest which respond via the authorities' reaction function to both a worsening of the current account and a depreciation exchange rate. We also find in the London Business School model that while the need to finance the public-sector deficit at higher rates of interest leads to an increased PSBR, the subsequent rise in the money supply results in greater leverage being applied to the exchange rate, augmenting inflationary pressures and further eroding the value of private-sector net wealth and reducing consumption.

In contrast the National Institute model maintains that crowding-out under either regime is small and displays a slight tendency to become negative. Thus, with a fixed exchange rate and exogenous earnings, we discover that crowding-out is negligible and that, after thirty quarters, 7·6 per cent crowding-in occurs. That the National Institute should find such a strong tendency towards negative crowding-out is itself significant, if somewhat surprising. To appreciate it more fully, it is useful to consider the Institute's formulation of the two-stage process by which bond-financing deficits induce higher interest rates and, consequently, lower levels of expenditure. At the first stage, with a constant money supply, interest rates are obtained by inverting the model's money demand equation. The nature of this function would, *ceteris paribus*, suggest a high degree of crowding out, since the relatively low interest elasticity (-0.56) and high income elasticity of 2.5 both favour a large interest rate response to a fiscal expansion. This is blunted, however, by the small response of expenditures to changes in interest rates, which are channelled predominantly through cost-of-capital effects in prices and disincentive effects in the housing market. At the same time the bond coupon effect noted earlier comes into operation, with higher debt service payments feeding through via higher property income to increase consumption throughout the simulation period. Finally, the National Institute finds no evidence of strong and significant wealth effects operating in either the expenditure or the money demand functions.

The most dramatic response to the removal of the fixed exchange rate–exogenous earnings assumption occurs in the Treasury model. Here the fiscal deficit and consequent deficit on the current account of the balance of payments induce a major depreciation in the spot exchange rate which, together with higher earnings because of increased activity, creates strong inflationary pressures within the domestic economy. The increase in prices implies that, in nominal terms, the fiscal deficit is larger than under regime I and, consequently, requires that interest rates increase by a greater amount for a given money supply. The long-run implication of bond financing under regime II, therefore, is a severe deflationary impact on fixed investment. Moreover, with higher domestic interest rates and a fixed world rate, both the short and long-term uncovered differentials increase sufficiently to generate substantial net capital inflows. The exchange rate, therefore, is prevented from falling by the amount necessary to preserve United Kingdom international competitiveness in the face of higher domestic inflation. This combines with a rise in the savings ratio because of the impact of inflation on personal sector asset holdings to produce a crowding-out mechanism which is more pervasive than those contained in the other two models, operating mainly through the trade balance and inflation mechanism.

To complete the discussion of the evidence on crowding-out available from comparative simulations conducted on the major UK macro-models, the measure $T(\%)$ indicates the degree of crowding-out after allowance is made for the impact of fiscally induced variations in the interest rate, exchange rate and prices. In other words, $T(\%)$ is a comparison between the dynamic multiplier response of column 1 and column 5. Examination of this measure provides additional evidence for the existence of considerable disagreement between model builders on the question of crowding-out in the United Kingdom. Thus we discover that after four years the results range from the 42 per cent crowding-out proposed by the Treasury model to a massive 82 per cent crowding-in for the National Institute model.

In part these differences reflect alternative resolutions of conflicting forces in the crowding-out process; in particular, the depressive effect of higher interest rates on fixed investment and the stimulative influence of a fiscally induced depreciation on the trade balance and hence aggregate demand. Thus the slight tendency towards crowding-in observed in the Business School profile is explained by the stimulative effect of a depreciation outweighing the reduction in fixed investment, while in the Treasury model higher interest rates, by stimulating capital inflows, prevent the exchange rate from depreciating sufficiently to maintain trade competitiveness, with a higher degree of crowding-out as a result. Finally, the $T(\%)$ measure emerging from

the National Institute model and the marked tendency towards
crowding-in reflect a comparatively inelastic response of fixed
investment to higher interest rates and an improvement in trade
competitiveness resulting from the depreciation. Here the
crowding-out in quarter 24 comes about as a result of a sharp
decline in consumer expenditure.

The models do agree, however, that the once orthodox view that
higher interest rates induced by a fiscal expandion reduce
private-sector   investment   expenditure   is   comparatively
unimportant in a fixed exchange rate, zero inflation world. Indeed,
simulations of a fiscal stimulus conducted with a 'constant money
supply' demonstrate a clear tendency towards crowding-in in the
models when earnings and the exchange rate are assumed fixed. As
indicated, this arises from the operation of a positive bond-coupon
effect on personal consumption. Further, two of the models
indicate that inflation has a significant role to play in the
crowding-out process. In the next section, therefore, an attempt is
made to quantify these two effects, using evidence obtained from
the 1979 version of the Treasury model currently available in
Manchester.[11]

5.   The bond-coupon effect, inflation and the Treasury model

Some idea of the significance of the bond-coupon effect can be
obtained by conducting comparative dynamic simulations on the
Treasury's National Income Forecasting model and noting the
response of the system to changes in the interest rate term
structure. The basic technique of such an analysis consists in
comparing the response of aggregate demand and its components
to interest rate changes when the bond-coupon effect is
incorporated with the response of aggregate demand when the
bond-coupon effect is suppressed. The suppression is achieved by
the comparatively simple device of severing the link between
interest payments and personal income, interest payments being
treated as exogenous and so maintained at their historical values
during the simulation runs. Finally, in so far as any feedback from
expenditure and income to monetary variables is neglected, the
simulations should be treated only as partial equilibrium solutions
and, since the NIF model is concerned with determining product
market equilibrium, are analogous to analysing the slope of the IS
schedule in a simple model. Table 3.2 shows the response of the

Table 3.2 Response of GDP and expenditure components to a one percentage point rise in $2\frac{1}{2}\%$ Consol rate; earnings and exchange rate exogenous (£ million, 1975 prices)

Quarter	Bond-coupon effect incorporated					Bond-coupon effect suppressed				
	Consumption	Fixed investment	Imports	Exports	GDP	Consumption	Fixed investment	Imports	Exports	GDP
1	-2	0	-1	0	-2	-2	0	-1	0	-2
4	-1	-33	-12	0	-27	-7	-33	-14	0	-31
8	-7	-57	-25	-1	-45	-16	-56	-28	-1	-50
12	2	-35	-13	-1	-17	-12	-34	-17	-1	-25
16	11	-3	6	0	12	-4	-2	2	0	4
20	13	0	6	0	9	-5	0	0	1	-1
24	17	-8	3	0	4	-7	-7	-5	1	-10

system to an upward shift in the term structure of interest rates, differentiated according to whether the bond-coupon effect is operating or not; for concreteness, the 2·5 per cent Consol rate is allowed to rise in this simulation by one percentage point, while other rates of interest rise in association with this by amounts which were calculated from a separate simulation conducted on the Treasury monetary model.[12] The exchange rate and earnings are kept constant at their historical base values throughout the simulations.

In the first simulation the upward movement in interest rates feeds through to reduce the level of aggregate demand via their effects on fixed manufacturing investment and, because of the higher cost of borrowing, though lower consumer expenditure. However, the decline in total consumer expenditure experienced during the early part of the simulation is comparatively minor and more than offset in subsequent periods by higher non-durable spending induced by higher interest payments. Further, with reduced aggregate demand, imports are lower than they initially were in the base run, though once the stock adjustment process in fixed investment is complete the buoyancy of consumption is such as to worsen the trade balance. The result is that gross domestic product declines during the simulation.

Suppressing the bond-coupon effect in the Treasury model produces a marked change in the behaviour of consumer expenditure, with both durable and non-durable expenditure falling throughout the period. The result is that, with the removal of the bond-coupon effect, GDP is reduced by a greater amount than in the previous simulation. Similar results are also obtained when the interest rate shock is introduced via the Treasury bill rate, though, of course, the profile of individual expenditure components does differ somewhat.

The second issue highlighted by the discussion concerns the pervasive nature of inflation in United Kingdom macro-models. The mechanism visualised in this process involves higher rates of inflation imposing an 'inflation tax' on the private sector, reducing the real value of personal assets fixed in money terms and so inducing higher levels of saving as individuals attempt to rebuild their asset holdings.

In the Treasury model this effect is currently captured by the inclusion of an inflation term in the non-durables consumption function. Consideration of this function provides some idea of the magnitude of the effect of inflation on the private sector. The equation may be written as:

$$\dot{c} = \sum_{i=0}^{3} a_i \dot{y}_{t-i} - 0.0285\ddot{u} - 0.2055\dot{p} + 0.1213 \ln (Y/C)_{t-4} \qquad (1)$$

where

$$\sum_{i=0}^{3} a_i = 0.456$$

and c = consumer expenditure on non-durables, y = real personal disposable income, u = percentage unemployment in the United Kindom, p = retail price index. Dots above variables indicate rates of growth.

Postulating a steady-state growth path along which

$$\left. \begin{array}{c} \dot{c} = \pi_1 \\[4pt] \dot{y} = \pi_2 \\[4pt] \dot{p} = \pi_3 \end{array} \right\} \qquad (2)$$

then, since the system is stable, we may eliminate lags and substitute equation 2 into 1, obtaining

$$\pi_1 = 0.456\pi_2 - 0.2055\pi_3 + 0.1213 \ln (Y/C) \qquad (3)$$

which simplifies to

$$C = Y \exp. \left\{ -8.26\pi_1 + 3.77\pi_2 - 1.67\pi_3 \right\} \qquad (4)$$

Since, in steady state, $\pi_1 = \pi_2$, then

$$C = Y \exp. \left\{ -4.50\pi_2 - 1.67\pi_3 \right\} \qquad (5)$$

Equation 5 describes the long-run consumption function for which, given zero growth and inflation, consumption of non-durables and real disposable income are equal. A 1 per cent rise in the rate of inflation, however, will in the long-run lead to a reduction in consumption of 1·68 per cent. Mechanical calculation using equation 1 shows that after four quarters a 1 per cent rise in the rate of inflation will lead to a reduction in consumption of 0·38 per cent, which, at 1975 levels of non-durable expenditure, corresponds to a decline of £14 million in consumer expenditure from inflation alone.

6. Conclusion

Traditional economic analysis provides grounds for concern regarding the ability of central authorities effectively to stimulate the level of domestic aggregate demand using conventional tools of demand management. The chapter began by reviewing that analysis, drawing attention to the particularly restrictive assumptions underlying the orthodox view of crowding-out in open economies. It was demonstrated that fiscal policy could, under certain conditions, exert some leverage on the economy and that many of the departures from orthodox analysis required for this have been incorporated into United Kingdom macro-models. However, while agreement appears to have been reached regarding the appropriate departures to make from the traditional theory of the 1960s, the manner in which the departures are incorporated varies considerably across models.

The result is considerable disagreement between models regarding the importance of crowding-out for the United Kingdom. Not only is there a lack of consensus concerning the quantitative significance of crowding-out but, even where its existence is not in dispute, the time horizon over which it becomes relevant differs.

On a more positive note, all three models concur that crowding-out is not an important phenomenon in the constant price/fixed exchange rate world, all models registering a slight tendency towards negative crowding-out. The evidence from the alternative regime, however, is somewhat more confused. The problems of stimulating the economy under flexible exchange rates and endogenously determined earnings appear to be larger, and, in particular, the inflationary response of the economy to devaluation is significant. Such simulations also indicate that, in an inflationary environment, increases in interest rates induced by the initial fiscal expansion assume a far greater weight. While this reflects the need for interest rate changes to be larger during inflationary periods to provide sufficient finance for a now larger (nominal) budget deficit, it also demonstrates the potential difficulties associated with the running of a tight monetary policy in association with an expansive fiscal policy.

Finally the chapter has presented crowding-out as if it were a feature specific to fiscal policy. It should be remembered, however, that government spending assumes no privileged role in any of the above arguments. In traditional theory an increase in consumer spending can crowd out private-sector investment, or, in an open economy with less than perfect capital mobility, an increase in exports can have the same effect.

Notes

1   Based on chapter 3 of my PhD dissertation, 'Significance of wealth effects for the operation of monetary and fiscal policy'. Comments, criticism and advice from Mike Artis and Chris Green are gratefully acknowledged.

2   This result is, of course, well known. See, for example, Laidler (1971) for a rigorous exposition.

3   This assumes an absence of risk aversion, otherwise financial assets denominated in different currencies cannot be perfect substitutes.

4   See, for example, Dornbusch (1976). If, however, the model were characterised by elastic exchange rate expectations, a fiscal expansion would produce the perverse result of a fall in output. For in this case a forward premium is generated by the rise in the current spot rate following the capital inflow, and the exchange rate appreciation, reinforced by speculative inflows, is sufficient to reduce the equilibrium level of output, domestic interest rates falling below the world rate.

5   This, of course, ignores any revaluation effects on wealth which may arise from changes in the exchange rate. See Frenkel and Rodriguez (1976).

6   A complete specification of this model may be found in Lomax and Denham (1978).

7   An exposition of this is given by Bilson (1979).

8   See, for instance, 'Monetary and fiscal policy in the National Institute model' (1979), National Institute of Economic and Social Research (mimeo).

9   This latter effect is particularly relevant for the flexible interest rate simulations conducted on the London Business School model, where money supply actually increases more than in the fixed interest rate case.

10   Such an effect is also found to exist in the CEPG model (see, for example, Fetherston, 1977) and in the Cambridge Growth Project model (see Barker, 1976).

11   The Treasury model was made available to Manchester under the Bray amendment.
12   For a more detailed analysis see Spencer and Mowl (1978). The simulations conducted on this model involved shocking the interest rate term structure by a one percentage point rise in the $2\frac{1}{2}$ per cent Consol rate and, subsequently, the Treasury bill rate.

Labour supply

Labour supply in the UK: a review

1.   Introduction

In the 1950s and 1960s unemployment averaged 1·6 per cent. The 1970s were in marked contrast to previous post-war experience, with unemployment averaging 3·6 per cent and in fact never falling below 5·0 per cent from 1976. These figures have provoked widespread disillusion and scepticism among economists and policy-makers, many of whom have concluded that traditional demand management can no longer regulate economic activity. The economy can be characterised in a simple and stylised manner as $y_t = b\bar{y}_t$, where y_t is actual output and $\bar{y}_t$ is the target level of full employment output, and traditional Keynesian demand management is used to make b as near to unity as possible. Although long-run policy has been criticised because $\bar{y}_t$ did not grow as fast in the UK as compared with its competitors, policy-makers could as least take pride in the fact that in the 1950s and 1960s they achieved high levels of b. With the high levels of inflation experienced in the 1970s, the notional target level of full employment income was, at best, revised downwards; at worst b was left to take care of itself because of the overriding concern with inflation.

A defence of the view that the UK economy now has a higher 'equilibrium' level of unemployment comes from the monetarist counter-revolution, part of which embodied the famous natural rate of unemployment hypothesis developed by Friedman (1968, 1975) and Phelps (1970). A discussion of the controversies surrounding stabilisation policy would take us far beyond the scope of this study and they are reviewed elsewhere in this volume. Two points of importance do emerge from this discussion. First, at its zenith, Keynesian demand management tended to ignore the labour market. At its crudest level the labour market was consigned to a simple aggregate production function, and a proper understanding of the goods and money markets was all that was required for a successful demand management policy. Suitable fiscal-monetary packages, with periodic doses of incomes policy to take care of inflation, were all that was required. Through its link with output via the aggregate production function the labour market would, in effect, take care of itself. The monetarist counter-revolution, with its emphasis on expectations as a generator of inflation, obliged economists to take more note of labour market behaviour and revitalised interest in labour market theory. Furthermore, critiques of the monetarist approach to the inflation process were themselves firmly based on alternative analyses of labour market behaviour, of which Hicks (1974) was perhaps the classic exemplar.

A second feature of the decline of the supremacy of demand management was the search for alternative policies to reduce the high levels of unemployment, which from the then Labour government's viewpoint were politically very damaging. The unusual feature of these policies, which incidentally were not unique to the UK, was the attempt to intervene directly in the labour market to mitigate the unemployment problem by the use of selective employment subsidies. In August 1975 the Temporary Employment Subsidy was introduced and was quickly followed by other schemes. At the time it seemed that, with every announcement of rising unemployment, yet another employment scheme was introduced or an old one modified and extended. These included the Community Industry Scheme, Jobs for Unemployed School-leavers Scheme, Job Release Scheme, Job Creation Scheme, Youth Opportunities and the Work Experience Programmes, Youth Employment Subsidy and the Small Firms Employment Subsidy (see various issues of the Department of Employment *Gazette* at the time for a description of the schemes).

By the end of 1978 around 260,000 people were covered — though at the peak over 300,000 were covered at any one time — and the gross cost was then estimated at over £900 million, a not inconsiderable amount. It is, of course, a complete fallacy to conclude from these figures that at the end of 1978 unemployment would have been 260,000 higher in the absence of these employment policies. Many of those covered by the schemes would have undoubtedly found employment anyway, despite the lack of subsidy. (For a discussion of employment subsidies, often described as supply management to contrast with traditional demand management, see Layard and Nickell, 1980.)

In a wider context the Trades Union Congress has advocated a more general supply management approach in economic affairs (TUC, 1978). It argues for a general programme of work-sharing through a thirty-five-hour week, earlier retirement and longer holidays as a threefold method of reducing the length of the dole queue. We appear, therefore, to have moved full circle, with governments now counselled to manipulate the labour market directly as a form of economic management. Undoubtedly it is now the labour market and how it is thought to behave and how it ought to be regulated that has become the battleground over which debates between and among economists, policy-makers and pressure groups such as the CBI and the TUC are fought.

The purpose of this introduction has been to show the importance and relevance of the labour market as a topic for both theoretical and empirical research, and indeed there has been a considerable growth in interest by economists in this area. Like all markets, the labour market consists of a supply side and a demand side. A knowledge of both sides of the market is necessary to understand observed behaviour and to evaluate policy. Indeed, it is a truism to say that a full general equilibrium approach which takes account of every possible feedback in all markets, not just the labour market, is preferable. For some purposes the general equilibrium approach is very fruitful; for example, the new macroeconomics of temporary equilibrium is an instructive and illuminating way of analysing the reasons for unemployment. For other purposes, however, it is an extremely useful simplification to compartmentalise and examine in detail one aspect of one particular market, and much research in economics proceeds on this basis. The present survey does just that, by examining the supply of labour, which is one side of the labour market, and this itself is one part of a larger system. Like all living and dynamic subjects, there is much in labour supply that remains controversial and much that is not fully understood. On the other hand, recent empirical work has given us plenty of new and useful information, as section 4 will show. Section 2 examines the methodology used and some of the problems and puzzles that arise. Section 3 develops in some detail the standard model of household labour supply, and the final section examines some recent work specifically about the UK labour market.

2. Labour supply: an overview

Consider the labour supply decision of a typical male and a typical female over their respective life cycles. Up to the age of sixteen there is limited opportunity for economic activity because until then there is a legal requirement to remain at school; before 1972 the compulsory school age was fifteen. At this point the individual has to make his first big economic decision. He or she must decide whether to remain at school or whether to join the labour market. (A fortunate few of independent means may choose to become economically inactive, and an unfortunate few who are chronically sick or disabled will of necessity become economically inactive. Both categories are, however, very small.) The behaviour of males and females at this decision point is, contrary to what many believe, very similar. In 1971 69 per cent of boys chose to remain at school and 68 per cent of girls. (The source of these data and what follows is the 1971 Population Census.) The decision to remain at school is, for many, a rational economic calculation trading off the opportunity costs of further education in the expectation of future higher earnings. Those who undertake further education hope to supply labour of higher quality later. The decision to leave school should not be regarded as terminating all human capital development, since much additional training will take place on the job, outside the classroom. Indeed, it is often difficult in practice to say where training ends and work begins. Among early school leavers there is a broad division, as about 35 per cent will enter apprenticeships or other approved formal training schemes and about 45 per cent will enter the general unskilled occupational category. At this early stage, therefore, society effectively filters early leavers into two categories. There are those who are destined to reach the top echelons of the manual profession and a second group who are destined for most of their working lives to fill the lowest occupational categories.

As one would expect, there is a steady decline in the number of full-time students in older age groups. Of twenty-one-to-twenty-four-year-olds 7·1 per cent of males remain in full-time education and 4·0 per cent of females. It is only at the very highest levels of post-school education that males dominate.

For those of prime age, i.e. twenty-five to fifty-four, there is a marked difference in behaviour between males and females. Virtually all prime-age males will be economically active, as will most single women. Married females, however, are a separate category, because of their special role in society associated with the home and child-rearing. Not surprisingly, economic activity among this group is much lower compared to other categories, though it has risen dramatically since the war. The economic activity of married females is also strongly age-related. Of twenty-five-to-twenty-nine-year-olds 32 per cent are economically active, and the percentage rises steadily until for forty-five-to-forty-nine-year-olds 57 per cent are economically active. This presumably reflects the falling-off in the responsibility for child-rearing in older households.

Above the age of fifty-five the retirement option becomes increasingly viable. Whereas 95 per cent of fifty-five-to-fifty-nine-year-old males are economically active, from then on there is a steady decline in activity until for the over-sixty-five-year-olds only 19 per cent are economically active and the majority of these will be in part-time employment. (The 1971 Population Census does not distinguish between full-time and part-time employment as far as economic activity is concerned.)

This brief snapshot of the economy in 1971 demonstrates the obvious proposition that economic activity is a state that an individual passes into and out of at various points throughout the life cycle. At its most basic level the labour supply decision can be split into two interconnected components. The first is the *quantity* decision, i.e. over any given period the number of man hours the individual would wish to supply. The second component is the *quality* decision, already mentioned in the context of school leaving. The individual must make a decision on the amount of time and expense he must devote to supply units of labour service of a certain quality or efficiency. This review discusses in the main the former dimension, since the literature on labour supply is compartmentalised along this broad line of division. Strictly speaking, however, it should be recognised that both decisions are interdependent and jointly determined. For a discussion of the quality decision, more often described as the economics of human capital, see Blaug (1970) or Ziderman (1978). For an alternative view, which sees investment in qualifications or signals as not necessarily productivity augmenting, see Spence (1973).

Labour services are two dimensional, consisting of a labour (stock) dimension and an hours of work (flow) dimension, and the empirical literature on the quantity decision tends to follow this convenient distinction, treating each component of labour services separately. The literature on activity rates discusses the former stock dimension and the literature on the supply curve of hours discusses the latter dimension. Strictly speaking, neither gives the true picture of labour supply as a whole, since the former ignores the flow dimension and the latter considers labour supply *conditional* on the fact that the individual is already a participant in economic activity.

At this stage it is useful to make more precise the notion of economic activity, or an activity rate (sometimes called a participation rate or ratio). The economically active population is the number willing to supply labour at some particular time and the activity rate is the ratio of this number to the total population under discussion. Note that it does not refer to man hours willing to be supplied, but to the numbers willing to supply labour. The economically active population, therefore, consists of those who are in employment and those who are unemployed, since this latter group might reasonably be assumed to be actively seeking work and hence willing to supply labour. Broadly speaking, six factors determine whether an individual will be economically active, though it is often difficult to decide where one factor ends and another begins. They are:

1. *Economic circumstances*. Economists, being what they are, regard these as perhaps the most important influence on labour supply! The next section develops the household model of labour supply, so discussion of this point is postponed until then. However, although this survey emphasises economic variables, not all problems necessarily have an economic origin. The other factors discussed in what follows may have an equally important influence on labour supply.

2. *Personal characteristics:* such things as the age, sex, racial origin, marital status, family responsibilities and educational attainments of the individual. Some personal characteristics such as

age, sex and racial origin are immutable, whereas others such as educational attainment and family size are to some extent mutable. Mutable characteristics, often called signals, may be based on rational economic calculation. Thus it turns out, not surprisingly, that married women with small children are less likely to work. Can one, therefore, say that it is this personal characteristic, rather than economic circumstances, that determines labour supply? Not necessarily, if the choice of family size itself is an economic decision (see, for example, Becker and Tomes, 1976).

3.   *Government legislation.* An example of this influence would be the raising of the compulsory school age in 1972. This reduced the size of the economically active population at a stroke, as would legislation on the retirement age for entitlement to a State or private pension. It is possible, however, to exaggerate the influence of legislation on economic activity, as in many other areas of economic life. For example, in 1901 34·7 per cent of thirteen-to-fourteen-year-olds were economically active and 67·5 per cent of fourteen-to-fifteen-year-olds, and at a formal level the fact that no one of these ages is economically active today is due to compulsory schooling. On the other hand, even without legislation it is probable that the numbers who would be economically active in this age group would still be very small, because rising living standards obviate the need for households to send their children to work. Social legislation is very often a reflector of society and as such validates current economic circumstances rather than acting as a leader.

4.   *Arbitrary convention.* This factor includes a variety of statistical conventions concerning what is to be counted as economic activity and what is not. (For a thorough review of statistical sources and conventions surrounding British activity rates see Bowers, 1975.) For example, household work is by convention treated as inactivity, since it involves no market transaction. Some would argue that household ' work is an important component of overall labour supply and to neglect it is seriously misleading (see Gronau, 1973). The definition of what constitutes unemployment provides an additional problem. In the UK many people, particularly women, do not bother to register as unemployed even though they are actively seeking work. In this context the data from the Population Census on unemployment are regarded as a superior measure compared to the DoE figures, since

the former are based on a response to the question 'Are you seeking work or waiting to take up a job?' The unemployment rate revealed by the census is about one and a half times as large as the registered unemployed stock, reflecting the non-registered unemployed (see Hays *et al.*, 1971, for a fuller discussion).

A further problem arises with the treatment of part-time work. Should one treat only full-time workers as economically active, and, if not, at what point should one cut off part-time workers? The Population Census does not distinguish full-time from part-time work, though it treats as economically inactive all those below the compulsory school age even though they may hold part-time jobs. The Census of Employment, another valuable source of information on economic activity, also has its own arbitrary conventions. (See the DoE *Gazette* of January 1973 for a description of the survey.)

5. *General health and morbidity of the population.* This factor requires little comment, since improvements in medical techniques and standards allow many who would otherwise be unable to work to be economically active. For example, in years past a large number of the mentally ill were locked away in institutions, whereas today most are treated quickly within the community and without much disruption to their economic lives.

6. *Custom and social convention.* At the end of the day this factor may have an important influence, irrespective of economic or other influences. Social convention exerts strong pressure on males of prime age to work, and at another level work may fulfil a deep psychological need rather than representing a purely commercial market transaction. Action may be based on the need to conform to the *mores* and ethics of the society that an individual finds himself in at a particular time. It is only the strong and unusual personality who can resist such pressures.

Females face a different set of social conventions and customs. It is perfectly acceptable and respectable for women to remain at home, even those without family responsibilities, and no social ostracism will result. In other societies and in other times social convention may dictate a different response. The fact that it is the male who is 'expected' to be the breadwinner and the female who is 'expected' to be the custodian of the house at a fundamental level does not have an economic basis, though economic circumstances may impinge upon it. It should also be pointed out that observed patterns of labour supply which may appear to have as an explanation social convention may in fact have an economic basis (see later, when the geographic distribution of female labour is discussed).

Having overviewed labour supply in general, we now focus more directly on the economic aspects of labour supply with a discussion of the standard household model of labour supply.

3. The household model of labour supply

In the model labour supply is treated as a standard problem in consumer choice theory and has its antecedents in Becker's (1965) theory of time. A somewhat terse exposition of the model is to be found in Ashenfelter and Heckman (1974), and this exposition will to some extent follow that framework and uses their terminology. The framework is the same as the Hicksian consumer choice problem in which the consumer allocates a given income between commodities in order to maximise a given utility function. The novel feature of the labour supply model is that, instead of coming to the market with a fixed income to spend in any period, the household comes to the market with a fixed amount of time to trade which is allocated between commodities and leisure. It is important to recognise that it is the household and not the individual which is considered to be the basic unit supplying labour. The theory is general to the extent that it allows for the household to contain any number of persons, but the typical household will contain a male member and a female member who are potential suppliers of labour. The theory emphasises that the supply decision is one that is jointly determined, as will be seen. For the typical household, or family unit, the supply decision can be viewed as solving the following constrained optimisation problem.

$$\text{Max. } U = f(L_m, L_f, X) \tag{1}$$

$$\text{s.t. } W_m(T - L_m) + W_f(T - L_f) + Y = PX \tag{2}$$

U is a twice differentiable household utility function whose arguments are L_m, male leisure, L_f, female leisure, and X is a composite bundle of consumption goods which can be identified as total household income. Equation 2 gives the budget or time constraint, where T is the total available time the male and female each has to trade in the period. W_m and W_f are male and female wage rates, Y is unearned income and PX total expenditure on commodities. The budget constraint says, in effect, that total earnings of the male and female in market activity plus unearned income equals total expenditure on commodities.

Even at this level of generality the framework is fairly restrictive. The model is static, and little can be said directly about labour supply over the life cycle. Secondly, no distinction is made between household work and leisure. Thirdly, the utility function embodies a separability assumption, in that commodities are grouped together as a composite and relative price changes within this composite have no influence on labour supply. In effect a two-stage maximisation process is assumed. In the first stage, considered here, the household makes an allocation between leisure and total income, i.e. the size of X. In the second stage, not considered here, the household becomes a Hicksian consumer and allocates its income between various commodities. Gronau (*op. cit.*) develops a model which includes household work as well as leisure, and Abbot and Aschenfelter (1976) and Blundell and Walker (1980) develop frameworks which relax the separability assumption discussed above.

Figure 4.1 shows this two-stage optimisation process, where, for illustrative purposes, it is assumed that the household contains just one adult supplying labour. The right-hand quadrant shows the allocation between income and leisure (the vertical axis, labelled 'Income', represents total expenditure on commodities). The budget constraint is shown as OAE, with OA representing unearned income and the slope of AE giving the hourly real wage. The household maximises utility at B, supplying OC units of labour in return for BC total income, of which BD is earned income. The left-hand quadrant illustrates the second stage of optimisation, where again for illustrative purposes there are just two commodities with their relative price indicated by the slope of the budget constraint RS. The position of the budget constraint is clearly determined by the household's total income, i.e. GS = BC. The consumer allocates his income between x_1 and x_2, choosing GF of x_1 and GH of x_2. The separability of the decision-making process is illustrated by the fact that if the relative price of x_1 and x_2 were to alter, but the real wage remains the same, the household will not

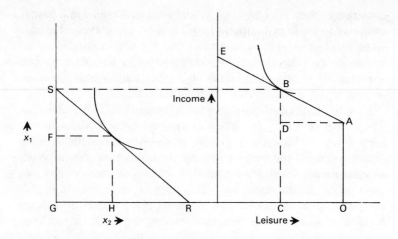

Fig. 4.1   The income–leisure trade-off

alter its allocation between leisure and income.

Figure 4.1 can be used to illustrate other possible solutions. The household might choose to locate at A, supplying no labour, and hence be economically inactive. Another possibility is that the household is willing to supply OC hours at the going real wage but cannot find employment. This might arise from a classical unemployment mechanism, with two high a real wage, or from a Keynesian demand-deficient mechanism. (For a simplified diagrammatic exposition distinguishing classical unemployment from the new macroeconomics of temporary equilibrium see Stoneman, 1979.)

Two further intermediate positions are possible where demand constraints attenuate the simple supply-determined solution. The individual might be a leisure preferrer in that he would ideally like to locate at B but because of contractual obligations is obliged to work for longer hours than OC. Such an individual might finesse this demand constraint by being an absentee for at least part of the week. Absenteeism is pervasive in the UK economy and is discussed in more detail in the next chapter. Alternatively the individual might be an income preferrer in that he would prefer to supply more hours at the going wage rate than those the employer demands. Such an individual might finesse this demand constraint by seeking jobs that offer unlimited overtime or by becoming a moonlighter. To the extent that demand constraints do impinge upon the individual supplier of labour, this gives rise to estimation problems (see later).

It is instructive to examine the Slutsky decomposition for a wage rate change, splitting it into a separate substitution effect and income effect.[1] For purposes of illustration this will be shown for a household containing one supplier of labour, since it is an easy matter to generalise the result for larger households once this has been done. It should be noted that the classical optimisation techniques that lead to this Slutsky decomposition assume that all maxima are of the internal type B, illustrated in fig. 4.1. The simplified problem is therefore:

$$\text{Max. } U = f(L,X) \quad \text{s.t.} \quad (T-L)W + Y = PX \qquad (3)$$

where W is the wage rate, L is leisure and the other terms have been already defined. The first-order conditions require

$$(T-L)W + Y - PX = 0$$

$$f_L - \lambda W = 0 \qquad (4)$$

$$f_x - \lambda P = 0$$

where λ is an undetermined Lagrangian multiplier. Equations 4 say that (a) the budget constraint is satisfied and (b) the marginal rate of substitution between leisure and the composite commodity, f_L/f_x, equals the real wage.

To establish the Slutsky decomposition, totally differentiate the first-order conditions to derive

$$\begin{bmatrix} 0 & -W & -P \\ -W & f_{LL} & f_{Lx} \\ -P & f_{Lx} & f_{xx} \end{bmatrix} \begin{bmatrix} d\lambda \\ dL \\ dX \end{bmatrix} = \begin{bmatrix} -(T-L)dW - dY + XdP \\ \lambda dW \\ \lambda dP \end{bmatrix} \qquad (5)$$

The determinant of the matrix of second-order partials, which shall be denoted as $|D|$, is positive from the second-order conditions. Denote the co-factors associated with the elements of D as D_{00},

D_{01}, etc, and setting $dP = dY = 0$, $\partial L/\partial W$ is derived as

$$\frac{\lambda D_{11}}{|D|} - \frac{H D_{01}}{|D|} \tag{6}$$

This is the Slutsky decomposition, where $\lambda D_{11}/|D|$ is the substitution term and $H D_{01}/|D|$ is the income term. (H is simply $T-L$, i.e. hours of work supplied.) To see this, consider first an income-compensated wage change, i.e. $\partial L/\partial W_{|Y}$ with $dY = -(T-L)dW$. (This is Slutsky compensation: exactly the same results prevail with Hicks compensation, i.e. the wage change is compensated such that the individual remains on the same indifference curve.) It follows that

$$\frac{\partial L}{\partial W_{|Y}} = \frac{\lambda D_{11}}{|D|} \tag{7}$$

Now consider a pure income change, $\partial L/\partial Y$, with $dW = dP = 0$. This is

$$= -\frac{D_{01}}{|D|} \tag{8}$$

Hence the wage change is split into its respective substitution and income terms.

$$\frac{\partial L}{\partial W} = \frac{\partial L}{\partial W_{|Y}} + \frac{H \partial L}{\partial Y} \tag{9}$$

This decomposition has been done in terms of leisure, but it is more usual to express it in terms of hours of work. However, since $\partial L/\partial W = -\partial H/\partial W$ it follows directly that

$$\frac{\partial H}{\partial W} = \frac{\partial H}{\partial W_{|Y}} + \frac{H \partial H}{\partial Y} \tag{10}$$

What can be learnt from this Slutsky decomposition? The compensated wage change, i.e. the first term on the right-hand side of equation 10, is always positive. The intuition of this result is simple, namely if the household's income is kept constant and leisure is made more expensive by raising the wage, the household will demand less leisure. Strictly speaking, the income term, the second part of the right-hand side of 10, is indeterminate in sign but is usually assumed to be negative, i.e. leisure is thought always to be a normal good. This seems reasonably plausible in that most people would wish to spend at least part of an increase in income on additional leisure. The income and substitution terms taken together, therefore, lead to the classic indeterminacy of the sign of $\partial H/\partial W$. If the negative income effect dominates, then there arises the famous backward-bending supply curve of effort. It is important to determine whether at higher wage rates the backward-bending supply curve prevails, since a compression of wage differentials through, say, an incomes policy or a restructuring of the tax system would not have an adverse effect on incentives commonly associated with such policies.

This result is easily generalised. The theory implies that, for a household containing two adults, the labour supply of each is related to *all* the exogenous variables, *viz*.:

$$H_M = f(W_M, W_f, Y, P)$$
$$H_F = g(W_M, W_f, Y, P)$$
(11)

where H_M is the supply of male hours, which, *inter alia*, depends on the female wage rate, and H_F is the supply of female hours, which, *inter alia*, depends on the male wage rate.

The Slutsky decomposition follows quite straightforwardly as

$$\frac{\partial H_i}{\partial W_j} = S_{ij} + H_j \frac{\partial H_i}{\partial Y} \qquad \begin{array}{l} i = m, f \\ j = m, f \end{array}$$
(12)

S_{ij} is the income-compensated substitution term, which is unequivocally positive for S_{ii} only. The household model, therefore, gives little *a priori* information on the supply responses of males and females with respect to wage rate changes. Another problem is that the model specifically denies a role for unemployment as an influence on labour supply, since it is assumed at the outset that this state of affairs cannot occur. Households differ in respect of the probability that each member may find himself unemployed. Clearly the supply response of the female in a household where the male faces a high probability of periodic unemployment may be different to that of a household where the probability of periodic unemployment is low (contrariwise for male behaviour). There is empirical evidence that these considerations are relevant to labour supply.

'Imaginative' use of the standard model must be made when applying it to activity rates, since the dependent variable will be the activity rate and not the total number of hours supplied. The decision to participate in economic activity is argued to depend on roughly the same set of exogenous variables as in equation 11 as well as a further set of 'non-economic' intruder variables. Thus, for example, a typical estimating equation for married females might be

$$A_f = g(W_m, W_f, U_m, U_f, Y, Z) \qquad (13)$$

where U_m and U_f are male and female unemployment and Z is a vector of other variables controlling for the personal characteristics of the household. The inclusion of such variables is really an implicit recognition of the fact that the static framework of the household model is not really adequate. The shape of the household preference function, equation 1, can be thought of as varying at different points over the life cycle, and these variables such as age and family size control for this feature. In addition, other personal characteristics such as racial origin attempt to control for different underlying preferences independent of the life cycle. The dependent variable can be interpreted as the probability that the female will participate in economic activity given any set of values of the explanatory variables. One difficulty is that the dependent variable is constrained to lie between zero and one, and certain values of the explanatory variables could imply a value of the dependent variable outside this range. This potential difficulty can be obviated by expressing the model in LOGIT form (see Kmenta, 1971, pp. 461–3, for details).

In empirical work there are further difficulties in attempting to estimate an equation such as 13, particularly in the measurement of household income. W_m and W_f should be *net* real earnings after all deductions have been made, and in practice this as well as unearned net income Y is difficult to measure. Recent empirical work in this area has concentrated, *inter alia*, on devising 'cleaner' measures of household income. It could also be argued that net real earnings are not strictly the correct measure, since it is the social wage, which includes services provided by the state, that is the true measure of household income. Incidentally, although $\partial A_f / \partial W_f$ and $\partial A_f / \partial W_m$ are indeterminate from the model on household labour supply, it is usually found to be the case that the former is positive and the latter negative in sign.

The role of unemployment in household labour supply centres round the concepts of the 'discouraged' worker and the 'added' worker. A high probability of unemployment may cause some members of the household not to participate in economic activity. This is the discouraged worker effect. On the other hand if the main breadwinner faces a high probability of unemployment, other members of the household may participate in economic activity to maintain or augment expected family income. This is the added worker effect. As far as married females are concerned a positive sign associated with $\partial A_f / \partial U_m$ may indicate an added worker effect, and a negative sign associated with $\partial A_f / \partial U_f$ may indicate a discouraged worker effect. These two effects may equally well apply to other members of the household — for example, the school-leaving decision may be influenced by unemployment in the same competing manner.

4. Empirical studies on labour supply: some UK evidence

Recently there has been an outpouring of empirical literature on labour supply, specific to the UK labour market. This brief review can only outline the barest details of this work, but for a more comprehensive and longer review readers are referred to the survey of Greenhalgh and Mayhew (1979).

The literature can be classified along several broad lines of division, the first of which is between the literature on activity rates and that on hours of work, though recent work combines the two. Further subdivisions can be made according to whether the study is cross-section or time series or whether it uses aggregate data or disaggregated data with observations from individual households. Altogether, therefore, there is a rich menu from which to choose and we shall endeavour to examine an example of each 'type' of study, commencing with work on activity rates.

Early aggregate time series work for both male and female activity rates is to be found in Corry and Roberts (1970) and updated estimates in Corry and Roberts (1974). Their study is addressed to a limited question, namely the relationship between activity rates and the level of unemployment. Corry and Roberts estimate variants of the following equation for both males and females, using annual data over the period 1951–70:

$$A_{it} = a + bU_{it} + cT + v \tag{14}$$

where A_{it} is the activity rate of the ith group at time t. U_{it} is the unemployment rate, T a time trend and v a disturbance term. They find tentative evidence for the discouraged worker hypothesis dominating for both male and females. The coefficient associated with unemployment for females implies a 1·0 per cent fall in activity for a 1·0 per cent rise in unemployment, and for males it is smaller, with a value of 0·36. (These figures are taken from table 11 of the 1974 study, where the estimates are corrected for autocorrelation.) These estimates must be viewed with caution, since the unemployment data used refer to *registered* unemployment and one cannot be sure whether the movements implied are out of the labour force or into unregistered unemployment. Corry and Roberts also confirm the growth in female participation and a fall in male participation, reflecting primarily an increase in the numbers of those of younger age staying in full-time education beyond the compulsory school age. It should be noted that the use of a time trend in these regressions is essentially *ad hoc* and in no way constitutes a theory of activity.

Two examples of aggregate cross-section work for married female activity rates are Greenhalgh (1977) and McNabb (1977). Both use data from the 1971 Population Census; Greenhalgh employs data for 106 towns, whereas McNabb uses data for sixty-three sub-regions. (For a similar study on male activity rates see Greenhalgh, 1979. Since male activity rates are virtually 100 per cent, except for the youngest and oldest age categories, showing little regional variation, the results are not terribly interesting.) McNabb estimates by OLS a linear version of the following basic equation:

$$PM = f(HEMF, HENF, HEMM, UM, UF, \\ FIN, EDUC, IM, CHO) \tag{15}$$

where *PM* is the proportion economically active and the explanatory variables are, in order, average hourly earnings of manual women, average hourly earnings of non-manual women, average hourly earnings of manual men, male unemployment, female unemployment, a measure of industrial structure reflecting female-intensive industries, a measure of educational attainment, a measure of the number of 'New Commonwealth' immigrants in the region, and finally the number of households with no family responsibilities.

McNabb's results are easily summarised. The elasticity of participation w.r.t. female earnings is 1·25, male earnings are insignificant and the elasticity w.r.t. to female unemployment is −2·5, which McNabb interprets as the discouraged worker effect. The elasticity w.r.t. to male unemployment is about 1, which is interpreted as the added worker effect. Overall, therefore, the discouraged worker effect dominates.

Greenhalgh's estimating equation contains a somewhat expanded set of explanatory variables, and — of particular interest — she includes two alternative proxy variables to measure unearned income. The first is the median income of taxable units, which turns out to be insignificant, and the second is the proportion of houses with basic amenities, which does turn out to be significantly negative. However, as a proxy for wealth it is extremely tenuous, and one advantage of disaggregated data is that the investigator can use better, if still not ideal, measures of this variable. Greenhalgh's female wage elasticity is very similar to McNabb's, and unlike McNabb she finds that the proportion of those from the 'New Commonwealth' does have a significantly positive effect on participation. Male earnings also have a strong significantly negative effect. One difference between the findings of McNabb and Greenhalgh is the role of unemployment. Greenhalgh finds a significantly *negative* coefficient associated with male unemployment, though she does not include female unemployment in her regressions. Unlike McNabb she interprets the male unemployment variable as reflecting a discouraged worker effect, and she includes additionally a deficient demand unemployment variable to capture the added worker effect. This turns out to be significantly positive, and unlike McNabb the added worker effect dominates the discouraged worker effect. We shall return to this debatable issue when examining disaggregated studies.

Both McNabb and Greenhalgh recognise that female participation rates are strongly age-related, and they both run regressions for individual age cohorts. Of interest is the fact that they both report poor results for the youngest age category, sixteen-to-nineteen-year-olds. This is hardly surprising, since the decision to be made at this age is essentially different from the decision at prime age. For younger age groups this is the school-leaving decision, which is clearly different from the 'work/don't work' decision. Blackaby and Leslie (1980) have examined the school-leaving decision, using the same data source, and report much better fits than either Greenhalgh or McNabb.

Disaggregated studies offer several advantages over aggregate studies, useful as they are. The first is obvious in that the model of labour supply is itself a disaggregated model at the level of the household and it is clearly better to test it against disaggregated data, where coefficients have a direct interpretation and the aggregation problem is obviated. Other advantages are that, in general, sample sizes are much larger and there is much greater variation in the observations, particularly data on the personal characteristics of the household. A richer set of hypotheses can therefore be tested.

Two recent examples of disaggregated studies of married female participation and their annual hours of work are Greenhalgh (1980) and Layard, Barton and Zabalza (1980). Both use individual household data from the General Household Survey, the former for the year 1971 and the latter for 1974. (The Family Expenditure Survey also offers another valuable source of information for the UK labour market and has been analysed by Elias, 1980.)

There are two fundamental problems that must be faced when using disaggregated data. The first is that the budget constraint is in practice a lot more complicated than the simple structure considered in section 4.2, and secondly it is possible that the marginal tax rate is endogenous, simultaneously determined along with hours of work and earnings. These problems are illustrated in fig.4.2, where a simple piecewise linear budget constraint is considered. OA represents net unearned income, which for a married female would typically consist of her husband's net income plus other unearned income. (Since the cross-substitution effect is in practice small, Greenhalgh argues that it is valid to treat the husband's earnings as exogenous.) At B the budget constraint is

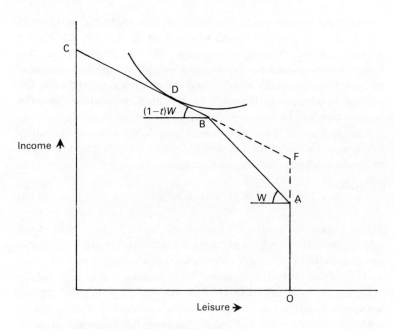

Fig. 4.2   Linearisation of the budget constraint

kinked, as beyond this level of earnings income tax is payable at the rate t. Thus, under the assumption that the individual locates somewhere beyond B, the budget constraint can be written as

$$E = OA + K + (1 - t)(WH - K) \qquad (16)$$

where E is earnings, K is the earned income allowance, H is hours of work, W is the gross wage rate and t is the marginal tax rate. The suggested solution is to linearise the budget constraint and write it in equivalent form as

$$E = OA + tK + (1 - t)WH \qquad (17)$$

In effect the individual is treated 'as if' he has a linear budget constraint FBC, shown in fig. 4.2, paying a constant rate of tax, t, on *all* earnings and receiving an implicit lump-sum subsidy of tK, equal to AF in fig. 4.2. Thus in the labour supply function unearned income is 'corrected for' the implicit subsidy element tK and one would expect the coefficient associated with tK to be the same as the coefficient associated with OA, i.e. in theory it is just a pure income effect. Although illustrated for a simple case, this linearisation procedure can be applied to any piecewise linear budget constraint of any degree of complexity. This is the procedure adopted by Brown *et al.* (1976) in an article on hours of work which will be discussed later.

The possibility of simultaneous equation bias can be easily illustrated. Consider the following labour supply function based on the previous linearisation procedure:

$$H = f(W (1 - t), E + S, Z) + U \qquad (18)$$

Here labour supply is a function of the net wage rate, total non-labour income which includes the implicit subsidy S due to the linearisation of the budget constraint. Z is a vector of other factors and U is the disturbance term. Unfortunately with a generally progressive tax structure neither the net real wage nor the implicit subsidy S is independent of the disturbance term. This can be seen with reference to fig. 4.2 again. Suppose the expected value of equation 18 for a given value of Z placed the individual at point B. With a positive disturbance the individual would locate to the left of B, with a correspondingly lower net real wage and larger S, and contrariwise for a negative disturbance. The upshot is that the net real wage and the disturbance will be negatively correlated and the implicit subsidy positively correlated. (The presence of overtime premiums would give rise to similar problems.)

The solution offered by Greenhalgh and Brown *et al.* is essentially pragmatic and exploits their knowledge of the special characteristics of the British tax system. Suppose it is known that most participants lie in a single linear segment of the budget constraint: then it is clear that the degree of correlation with the disturbance will be minimal. For the UK, at least before the introduction of the 25 per cent income tax band and the possibility of separate taxation for husband and wife, this is definitely true, with most paying the standard rate of tax. For example, 93 per cent of Greenhalgh's sample fell into this category, and her supply function is estimated by ordinary least squares using gross female wages without any adjustment to the budget constraint. Although strictly speaking it is misspecified, she argues that this will not be serious for the reasons given.

Greenhalgh finds a positive own wage elasticity with respect to participation of 1/3 and a larger elasticity with respect to hours of 2/3, thus giving a total elasticity of unity. These results are very similar to the reported elasticities of Layard *et al.*, who use a somewhat different estimation procedure for the year 1974. Greenhalgh combines husband's earnings and other income and finds a negative elasticity w.r.t. participation of about −1/3. Again this is similar to the Layard *et al.* elasticity w.r.t. husband's earnings, though the two are not directly comparable because Layard *et al.* enter unearned income and gross hourly earnings of the husband as separate variables. Their income effect turns out to be very low.

Both studies find that ethnic background and location influence labour supply, but of major importance are family responsibilities as measured by the age and number of children. Only Layard *et al.* consider unemployment directly by including unemployment of the husband as a separate variable. This variable represents an amalgam of the added worker and discouraged worker, and overall they find a strong discouraged worker effect — wives with unemployed husbands are 31 per cent less likely to work. They speculate — and it *is* pure speculation — that the peculiar way the supplementary benefit system operates in Britain may be in part responsible. There is an incentive for wives to cease work, as the family loses supplementary benefit pound for pound for any earnings of the wife when the husband is unemployed.

Finally we consider empirical studies specifically on hours of work of those in employment, and as before we shall discuss both aggregate and disaggregated studies. Two examples of the former type of study are Metcalf *et al.* (1976) and Leslie (1980). Brown *et al.* (*op. cit.*) is an example of the latter type. All these studies refer to male workers.[2] However, the Greenhalgh and Layard and Zabalza studies do have some interesting comments on female hours, and again this shows the advantage of using disaggregated data.

Metcalf *et al.* is a cross-section study with ninety-six observations of inter-industry variations in hours for the point of time 1966, and the Leslie framework is similar, with 122 observations for the year 1971. With an aggregate study there is an immediate identification problem, since the investigator does not know whether he is estimating a supply or demand equation if a single equation estimation technique is used. The Metcalf solution is to specify a demand and a supply equation, with hours and average hourly earnings endogenous, and to estimate both equations using a simultaneous equation estimation technique. Of interest is the supply equation, and this is specified as

$$H = f(W, Z) \qquad (19)$$

W is average hourly earnings and Z is a vector of exogenous variables. When W is entered linearly the estimated elasticity at mean values is positive, with a value of $0 \cdot 30$. Metcalf reports another estimate in which W is entered non-linearly to allow for the possibility of a backward-bending supply curve. It turns out that this specification is significant, and the authors conclude that it demonstrates the existence of the elusive backward-bending supply curve of labour. Leslie, however, has criticised this finding on the grounds that a non-linear estimate which is significant does not necessarily prove the existence of a backward-bending supply curve. A backward-bending region can be inferred by invalidly extrapolating the curve beyond observed values, and, since only a very small proportion of the industries considered by Metcalf lie in the backward-bending region, this is in fact what Metcalf and his co-authors have done. Leslie finds no evidence of a backward-bending supply curve, though his results are tentative.

The study of Brown *et al.* is based on an analysis of a specially commissioned interview survey of married males carried out in autumn 1971. This gave a usable sample of 434 married males, and they report an estimate of this full sample and several further estimates where the sample is restricted on various criteria, one reason for which is given below.

On the assumption that workers *willingly* supply the hours that they work there is no identification problem and a single equation estimation technique is appropriate. However, demand constraints might operate in that the employer might specify a minimum number of hours that must be worked and a maximum number of hours that can be worked and the worker is forced to locate other than at points such as B on fig. 4.1. The resultant bias, if OLS is used, is shown in fig. 4.3. Suppose the true supply curve is upward-sloping, as shown, with the crosses indicating actual

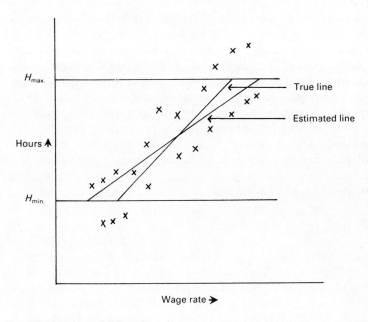

Fig. 4.3 Truncation bias

observations on hours and wages. However, because of the maximum and minimum cut-off, crosses outside this range will not be observed, and these points will be constrained to lie on the $H_{max.}$ and $H_{min.}$ lines. It is clear that this will impose a negative bias on to any estimated regression line and *Tobit* analysis would be a more appropriate estimation technique. Layard *et al.* in fact use this technique in their study because a similar problem arises with non-participants in economic activity where their hours of work are constrained to be zero. Brown *et al.*'s solution was more direct: to eliminate from the sample those whom they considered to be constrained in their choice of hours.

Brown *et al.*'s specification was

$$H = a + bW + cW^2 + dI + eI^2 + fI.W + gY \qquad (20)$$

where W is the marginal wage rate, I is the implicit subsidy from linearisation of the budget constraint and Y is other income, which could include the wife's earnings if she works. In order to account for variation in the preference function of individual households the equation was estimated for various sub-samples as well as the whole. In addition two intruder variables to measure job satisfaction and household need were included in some estimates. Of particular interest is the non-linear specification of the supply function, and it turns out that the coefficient c attached to the quadratic wage term is consistently positive. This implies a somewhat peculiarly shaped supply function — something the authors do not comment on. The implied shape is the opposite of Metcalf *et al.*; hours of work fall as the wage rate increases and then increase beyond a minimum point. *A priori* it is a most peculiar shape and few commentators would find this result acceptable.

5. Conclusion

It is hoped that this survey has given the reader a flavour of contemporary research on labour supply in the UK labour market. It should be remembered that the survey is a limited one: for example, it has ignored work on the US labour market, nor has it dealt with the problems of forecasting labour supply. On the whole, although great progress has been made in recent years, we are still a long way from a reliable forecasting model of labour supply. Layard *et al.* perhaps the best of recent studies, cannot explain all the observed growth in female participation. For those who wish to pursue an interest in this topic there is much interesting and important work to be done.

Notes

1   Readers unfamiliar with comparative static analysis can skip to equation 10, provided they can accept its derivation on trust.
2   In addition Leslie attempts unsuccessfully to explain female hours. The reason for failure is that with aggregate data there is little variance in female hours and consequently little left to explain.

Absenteeism in the UK labour market

1. Introduction

Doherty (1979) has pointed out that over the last decade about 300 million working days were lost on average each year owing to certified sickness. Days lost through certified sickness will considerably underestimate the total amount of absence, since many more days are lost owing to people, for a variety of reasons, not bothering to turn up for work. Far more working days are lost each year as a result of absence, which includes certified sickness, than through unemployment. Furthermore, about a hundred times more days are lost through absence than through strikes. Yet, whereas absence is widely recognised as pervasive in British industry, virtually nothing has been written by economists on the problem, compared with the voluminous literature on strikes and unemployment.

Part of the reason for this seeming lack of interest is simply the unavailability of suitable data. There are just four sources of information, and none of them gives an adequate coverage. The first is *Social Security Statistics,* published annually by the Department of Health and Social Security. It gives detailed information on certified sickness but has the drawback that no industrial or occupational breakdown is given; secondly it does not, for obvious reasons, record absentees other than those certified as sick.

The second source of information is the *New Earnings Survey*, published annually by the Department of Employment. One question relates directly to the problem of absenteeism, asking the employer whether the employee was absent for one of five reasons during the particular pay period, which for most manual workers would be weekly. The five reasons for absence were (a) certified sickness, (b) uncertified sickness, (c) voluntary absence, (d) late arrival or early finish, (e) holidays or other approved absence. These data, therefore, give some qualitative information on the extent of absenteeism, and in 1970, the last year for which a detailed response has been published, it was found that 15·9 per cent of male manual workers fell into one of the five categories. If categories (a) and (e) are excluded, the figure was still an extremely large one at 10·6 per cent. In some industries absence was much greater than these average figures; in shipbuilding it was 31·8 per cent and in mining, again a notorious area, it was 31·1 per cent. Among the female manual labour force the figures were even larger than those recorded for males, with 23·8 per cent absent for reasons (a) to (e), and in manufacturing, considered alone, it was 30·1 per cent.

Whilst the *New Earnings Survey* after 1970 continued to ask similar but less detailed questions relating to absenteeism the responses are not published — an obvious failing for those in the business of attempting to analyse data! A second disadvantage is that the data are qualitative, though some tentative but hardly reliable quantitative information can be derived from the statistics. A third disadvantage is that it gives a snapshot picture for one particular week, whereas one would prefer data on the total number of working days lost over a longer time period.

The third source of information is the *General Household Survey*. The survey asks employees a question relating to absence, and the responses are given by age, sex, region, occupation and industry. Again the information is qualitative and only a limited amount of quantitative information is published, though the survey does ask respondents the question 'During the whole of this period of absence how many working days were you away?' A second problem is that some employees may be reluctant to admit to absence other than for 'genuine' reasons such as sickness.

The fourth source of information is the best, but unfortunately it is available only for one particular industry where absenteeism is notorious, namely coal mining. Since 1947, following nationalisation, the Coal Board has published an annual series recording authorised and unauthorised absences. These data, since they are the best available source of information, will be analysed more closely in section 3.

Some commentators distinguish 'absenteeism' from 'absence'. 'Absenteeism' refers to avoidable or non-excusable absence, which management would regard as unjustified. 'Absence', on the other hand, refers to any non-attendance whether or not it is permissible (Jones, 1971). Thus 'absence' would include sickness whereas 'absenteeism' would not. On the other hand the *New Earnings Survey* reveals a strong correlation between certified sickness and other types of voluntary absence for individual industry categories, which would lead one to suspect that much certified sickness is disguised absenteeism. (For 1970 the correlation coefficient was 0·53, which is easily significant.) The fact that there has also been a strong upward trend in recorded sickness since the war is also enough to arouse one's suspicions. Doherty (*op. cit.*) has made a study of the DHSS data and tentatively concludes that there is evidence of a 'moral hazard' problem arising from the increase in the ratio of sickness benefit (identical to unemployment benefit) to income. However, as Doherty points out, care is required before proclaiming evidence of social security scroungers and malingerers, because higher benefits may mean that people can afford to remain off work whereas previously, because of financial necessity and fear of dismissal, they returned before recovery was complete. In what follows all the data will refer to absence and no attempt will be made to distinguish avoidable from unavoidable absence.

Section 2 discusses the relationship between absenteeism and overtime, where it is shown that the wage payment structure should influence the extent of absenteeism. Section 3 reports the results of a study of absence rates in the coal mining industry over a six-year period 1974–79.

2. Absenteeism and the overtime decision

Absenteeism is a *supply* response on the part of an individual employee, where his own desired hours in any given period are less than those demanded by the employer. What, then, influences the desired hours of the employee? An economist abstracts essentially two factors which determine this quantity. The first is the individual's welfare function, whose arguments are income and leisure. An economist would not have much to say as to what determines the precise shape of this welfare function; that surely is a proper subject for industrial psychologists. The latter group have written extensively on the issue, and the general emphasis is on the nature of the workplace and the characteristics of the employee as the major explanation of absence rates. The purpose here is to show that this approach ignores an important second element: the wage structure offered by the employer. In this analysis the shape of the welfare function is taken as *datum*.

The employer has many options open to him, ranging from a simple straight hourly wage with no overtime to a more complicated structure consisting of a range of fringe benefits and a selection of overtime premiums for work beyond established normal hours. Variation in the wage structure, whilst at the same time guaranteeing a certain level of income in return for a certain number of hours worked, would in general alter the number of desired hours that employees would like to offer. Differing wage structures would therefore lead to different rates of absenteeism. Given that employees will not, in general, have identical utility functions for income and leisure, it follows that the wage structure the employer offers must be a compromise, and the hours he demands are unlikely to correspond with what individual employees would like to supply. In an analysis of moonlighting, Moses (1962) distinguished two types of worker. The first he denoted as 'income preferrers', those workers who for the given wage structure would wish to work longer than those actually contracted. The second type of worker he described as 'leisure preferrers', those who prefer fewer hours than those actually contracted. It is the latter category of worker that would be identified as absentees.

It is now shown that, compared to a straight hourly wage, a wage structure that incorporates an overtime element will reduce the number of leisure preferrers and hence the degree of absenteeism. Suppose in fig. 5.1 the firm wishes to demand AH hours of work per week. Suppose also that the firm establishes that in return for AH hours of work it must pay an income of OG. The employer must now decide between two wage structures, the simple straight time hourly wage represented by AE (passing through C) and a wage structure represented by ABD (again passing through C) which incorporates an overtime payment for working beyond some set standard hours AF. Under the wage structure AE, leisure preferrers would have an indifference curve tangential somewhere along the boundary AC and income preferrers somewhere along

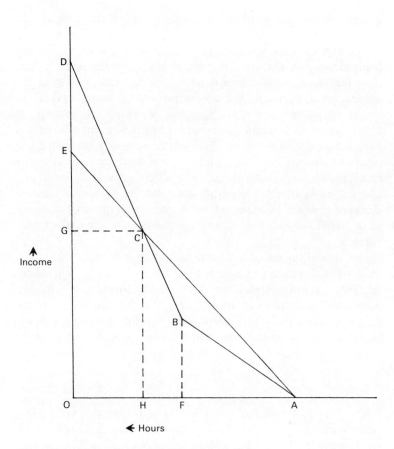

Fig. 5.1 Absenteeism and the overtime decision

CE. Now change the wage structure to ABD. It is impossible to convert income preferrers to leisure preferrers (i.e. an individual who has an indifference curve tangential along CE cannot have an indifference curve tangential along ABC). However, it is possible to convert former leisure preferrers to income preferrers (i.e. an individual who has an indifference curve tangential along AC could have an indifference curve tangential along CD). Hence one motivation for a firm to schedule overtime on a regular basis for regular attenders is that it would tend to lessen the degree of absenteeism. Thus it has been demonstrated that the wage structure influences the amount of absenteeism and that, *inter alia*, a negative association between overtime and absenteeism should be observed.

The hypothesis is, however, not that straightforward. Given that firms recognise that the wage structure influences the absence rate, then the more likely a firm is to experience absenteeism in the absence of an overtime-type wage structure the more likely it will be to introduce such a system, thus lessening the amount of absenteeism. So it might be that when overtime is not offered it is because there is little risk of absenteeism occurring, and when it is offered there will be little absenteeism around anyway! Thus the predicted correlation between *ex post* observed overtime levels and absence rates is not necessarily clear-cut. However, a negative correlation would be expected to the extent that firms are unaware of the relationship between the wage payment system and absence rates.

The model suggested here contrasts sharply with an alternative analysis of absenteeism suggested by Ehrenberg (1970). Ehrenberg suggests a positive association between the absence rate and the amount of overtime. Crucial to his result is the idea that there are fringe costs, which are independent of the number of hours worked, payable on each man employed, *irrespective of whether he attends work or not.*[1] The firm's cost function is given by:

$$\frac{W_0}{\alpha} A + W_2 A \bar{H} + W_2 b (H - \bar{H}) A \tag{1}$$

where W_0 are fringe costs and $\alpha < 1$ is the exogenously given attendance rate. A is the number of men who attend work each week and hence $(W_0/\alpha)A$ gives total fringe costs. W_2 is the wage rate for normal hours $\bar{H}$, and b reflects the overtime premium payable in respect of overtime hours $H - \bar{H}$, where H is actual hours. Going through the standard comparative static exercise of cost minimisation, it turns out that

$$\frac{\partial H}{\partial (1 - \alpha)} > 0 \tag{2}$$

i.e. hours are positively related to the absence rate $1 - \alpha$. This model assumes an exogenous, known absence rate, and in the UK, where certain industries are consistently absence-prone, such would seem to be the case. An inspection of the *New Earnings Survey* data confirms this, and the data for the mining industry show a similarly predictable pattern. Coal-mining regions with high

Table 5.1 *Sickness and voluntary absence, by range of overtime hours: full-time manual workers in all industries and services*

Range of overtime hours	% losing pay from sickness[a] or absence[b]
Nil	23·9
0·1 to 2·0	16·0
2·1 to 5·0	11·8
5·1 to 10·0	11·4
10·1 to 20·0	8·9
20·1 and over	4·4
All workers	14·9

Notes

a Absences from different causes in the survey week are counted separately.

b The figures relate only to a single week and are therefore affected to some extent by the lack of opportunity to work overtime among those who were, for example, away sick; but this effect must be small. For example, only 2 per cent were absent for the entire week and had no opportunty for overtime, and a further 3 per cent worked for thirty hours or less.

absence rates tend to have consistently high absence rates from one year to the next.

The difference in result from these two contrasting models arises from the fact that the Ehrenberg model is purely demand-determined. The former concentrates on the supply responses of the employee and suggests that by offering overtime firms could reduce the absence rate. The available evidence, which is admittedly piecemeal and sketchy, favours the view of a negative association between absenteeism and overtime levels.

The first piece of general evidence comes from the National Board for Prices and Incomes, which produced a special report on overtime and shift working (1970). The Department of Employment carried out a special analysis of the 1968 *New Earnings Survey* for that report. The results, which are striking, are shown in table 5.1. Firms which offer high and regular amounts of overtime suffer less absenteeism.[2] The conclusion of the NBPI was that 'There is on the basis of national statistics a reduction in the rate of absence of full-time manual workers as the amount of overtime they work increases.' One problem with these data is that they present a purely static picture for one particular week. It is possible, therefore, that the result is spurious, because individuals who lose pay might work overtime the following week to make up. Thus the static one-week picture may not reveal the true pattern that would emerge if a much longer time period were considered. Against this interpretation, however, is the evidence that absenteeism is not distributed generally among the work force; rather, a small core of individuals are responsible for most of it.[3] Yolles *et al.* (1974) have stated that 90 per cent of all absenteeism is caused by 10 per cent of the work force, a finding that has been supported by Garrison and Muchinsky (1977), though less strongly.

The second piece of evidence comes from the mining industry, where, as has been mentioned, absence rates are recorded and published for public scrutiny. Since the war there has been an upward trend in absence from 12·4 per cent in 1947 to 17·6 per cent in 1978. (Note the similarity in this finding to the upward trend in certified sickness rates.) In a discussion of these absence rates Handy (1968) has noted that:

Overtime has fluctuated quite considerably in coal mining since nationalisation. But the behaviour of absence rates in relation to fluctuations in overtime during the post-war period does not suggest that overtime in itself provoked increased absence; overtime was greatest when absence was lowest (1950–54) and [overtime] declined most rapidly (late 1957–59) when absence rose sharply.

A third piece of circumstantial evidence is provided by Nicholson *et al.* (1977). In a survey of ninety-five employees of a northern steel mill they found that 'Nearly all the employees worked overtime and the evidence suggests that there is an inverse functional relationship between absence and overtime and absence and total hours worked.'

3. Absence in the coal industry

From 1974 to 1979 absenteeism in the coal industry was fairly constant, the figures being 17·9 per cent, 16·0 per cent, 16·7 per cent, 17·3 per cent, 17·6 per cent and 17·1 per cent for each respective year.[4] The absence rate is measured basically as the ratio of man shifts not worked to the number of possible man shifts that could be worked (excluding overtime man shifts). It includes authorised absences, mainly sickness and injury, plus unauthorised absences, but excludes time lost from meetings such as trade union activities, holidays, strikes and other stoppages of work. Despite the recent relative stability of national absence rates, there is considerable *regional* variation. In 1979, for example, it ranged from a high of 23·1 per cent in the Doncaster area to a low of 13·5 per cent in the South Midlands. Indeed, Handy (*op. cit.*) has pointed out that there is even considerable variation in absence rates among different types of worker within the same pit.

The data for this study use the absence rates for six years from 1974 to 1979 for each of twelve mining regions, giving seventy-two observations altogether. Prior to 1974 the method of calculating the absence rate was slightly different, and the area statistics were published in a different form, so 1974 represents the earliest starting date for which a consistent series can be obtained.[5]

Given the lack of data availability, only a limited analysis could be carried out. Four variables were used to explain the incidence of absenteeism across the twelve mining regions. The variables used were as follows, and the details of the construction of each variable are listed in the appendix. The variables are (1) real earnings per man shift, (2) labour wastage, (3) strike incidence, (4) colliery size.

1. Although both *real earnings* and absence rates have risen steadily since the war, caution is required before one infers a positive causal relationship between the two. In time series analysis extreme care is required when correlating two variables which are highly trended, since any right-hand-side variable with a trend element will turn out to be significant. In testing the influence of earnings on absence rates a cross-section approach is clearly preferable. This study uses pooled data for each of twelve mining regions. Over the years of observation absence rates were on average fairly constant, and secondly, on average, real earnings rose between 1974 and 1976 and then fell between 1976 and 1978 before rising sharply in 1979. It is unlikely, therefore, that the earnings variable will be reflecting any spurious trends in the data.

Given that absence in the mining industry is high, regular and institutionalised, there is considerable discretion on the part of the individual as to how many shifts to attend each week. An increase in earnings would have both an income and a substitution effect. If leisure is a normal good, the former effect would induce more absence and the latter less. Additionally many individuals who as a matter of 'conscience' would be regular attenders would be unaffected by such considerations. All in all, therefore, it is difficult to predict the effect of earnings on absence rates. In his study of the coal industry Handy recognised the problem of spurious correlations between time series of absence and wage rates. In a detailed analysis of non-face workers he found evidence that higher shift rates deterred absenteeism. In general, however, his conclusions on this matter were tentative.

2. It might be suspected that collieries which suffer from a high degree of *labour turnover and wastage* would have correspondingly higher absence rates. Until recently the mining industry has been characterised by a slow and inexorable post-war decline. Since 1947 over 700 collieries have closed and the labour force has declined from 700,000 to just 240,000, and it would be surprising if an industry suffering from low morale as a result of steady decline did not experience high absence rates. However, over the period of this study the average labour force has declined only very slowly, and indeed on average absence rates have been marginally lower. Decline has continued in some regions, for example in Scotland and the North-east, whereas in other regions, such as the South Midlands, manpower has actually increased.

Given this discussion, a positive sign would be expected between wastage rates and absence. High wastage and absence rates are both indexes of discontent.

3. *Strike activity* is but one way of expressing discontent at the workplace: in his book on strikes Hyman (1972) has emphasised that a strike is just one manifestation of industrial unrest and absenteeism is, *inter alia*, another. Where there is strong dissatisfaction, revealed by organised conflict such as industrial action, this discontent is likely to be expressed in complementary form in other ways, of which absenteeism is an important example (go-slows, overtime bans, work-to-rules, industrial sabotage are others). A positive relationship between strike activity and absence would, therefore, be expected. Absence and strikes are essentially complementary activities.

4. There is considerable evidence that individuals prefer to work

Table 5.2 *Dependent variable absence* (t *statistics shown in parentheses*)

Regression No.	Constant	Earnings	Wastage	Strike	Colliery size	R^2
1	26·35 (5·79)	−0·0064 (2·83)	2·73 (0·36)	157·7 (5·56)	0·236 (2·16)	0·41
2	16·29 (9·41)	−0·0033 (6·48)	0·932 (5·13)	0·119 (1·63)	0·547 (3·82)	0·98

in smaller establishments (Shorey, 1975; Metcalf *et al.*, 1976, and Leslie, 1980). Briefly stated, the hypothesis is that smaller establishments tend to be less formal, less bureaucratic and generally provide a more relaxed and friendly work environment. Small establishments might therefore be expected to exhibit lower absence rates. Such a finding has been found for Australian data by Harkness and Krupinski (1977). Average *colliery size* has therefore been included as a separate variable, and a positive sign would be expected.

The results of the analysis are shown in table 5.2. Equation 1 reports the results when the four regressors are included alone. Although the equation appears to be fairly well formed, with all variables having the expected sign and a reasonable R^2, this was not considered to be the most preferred specification. The residuals of the equation showed that there was still considerable unexplained regional variation in absence rates. This is hardly surprising, because the number of regressors was limited by lack of data. Two obvious candidates not included are age variables — absence rates are highest for those under thirty and decline thereafter — or, in view of the discussion on the relationship between absence and overtime, some measure of overtime shifts worked. Moreover Handy has commented that

Past research would suggest that the reasons for [absence] are as numerous as the variations themselves. Attitudes to work ... are a complex phenomenon to which local, cultural, social and environmental factors as well as the 'human relations', technological arrangements and physical conditions of particular workplaces may be relevant.

Table 5.3 *Elasticities at mean values from regression coefficients in equation 2, table 5.2*

Earnings	−0·39	Wastage	0·01
Strike	0·01	Colliery size	0·34

The second equation of table 5.2 includes regional dummies in addition to the variables included in equation 1. Their inclusion therefore attempts to control for missing variables as well as specific local factors. Equation 2, as might be imagined, gives a much better fit than equation 1 (for brevity the precise values of the individual dummies are not reported). The wastage and earnings variable now increases in significance, whereas the strike variable drops in significance. The earnings variable has a significantly negative coefficent, as Handy in his study suspected it might. Altogether the four explanatory variables have a high partial R^2 of 0·68 (i.e. 0·68 of the remaining residual variance can be explained by the inclusion of these variables). Nevertheless it is the regional dummies, which are essentially an expression of ignorance and data limitations, that account for the very high value of the R^2 in equation 2.

Table 5.3 reports the elasticity of the absence rate at mean values implied by the regression coefficients in equation 2.

4. Conclusion

Economics as a discipline is a social science; as such its practitioners believe that, given information about the characteristics of an individual or a particular situation, they can make reasonable predictions about behaviour. This basic methodology has been applied to a study of absenteeism in this chapter. Since absenteeism is a very personal affair, with absentees offering about as many separate 'explanations' as there are working days lost, it might be thought that to apply such a methodology would be a fruitless exercise. However, this study has shown that some general conclusions are possible. First, a relationship between the absence rate and the wage payment system was postulated and the available evidence was shown to be consistent with the hypothesis. Secondly, this general methodology was applied to a study of absence rates in the coal industry and it was shown that they could be partially explained, given information about the characteristics of individual mining areas.

Absenteeism, with its attendant disruption costs, is an expensive problem for industry. If an individual does not turn up for work his output is zero, whereas the cost of employing him is definitely not zero, despite the employer not being obliged to pay wages for the time lost. Section 2 suggested that firms which offered overtime would limit the extent of absenteeism. For those with high fixed costs associated with labour, this option is well worth exploring.

Appendix List of variables included in section 3

Absence. 'The percentage of authorised absences, mainly for reasons of sickness or injury, plus unauthorised absences in the five-day week to the number of men on colliery books multiplied by the number of days in the period excluding Saturdays and Sundays.'
Real earnings per man shift. Earnings plus payment in kind per man shift, expressed in 1978 prices.
Labour wastage. Total wastage minus recruitment, expressed as a proportion of the labour force (measured in percentage terms).
Strike incidence. Loss of output due to industrial disputes, expressed as a proportion of total salable output (measured in percentage terms). The year 1973–74 was characterised by the national strike, where, of course, loss of output was massive. In order to eliminate these large observations, strike data for 1974–75 were inserted for this period.
Colliery size. Number of wage-earners on colliery books at the end of March, divided by the number of collieries in the region.

Notes

1   As well as hiring and training expenses, which the firm can impute on a weekly basis per employee, fringe costs can include a variety of other terms — the crucial point being that these costs are independent of the number of hours worked. They can include such things as canteen and recreational facilities, private welfare and insurance plans, holiday pay, etc. The Department of Employment carries out a survey of fixed costs every four years, and the evidence suggests that these costs represent a not inconsiderable proportion of the pay packet.

2   For a more detailed breakdown of these figures see the supplement to the NBPI report, tables 4, 5 and 6, pp. 128–30.

3   For example, the young worker below the age of twenty-five is much
     more likely to be an absentee.
4   The source of these data and in what follows is the National Coal
     Board *Statistical Tables*, an annual publication.
5   In fact the Coal Board accounting year runs from March to March.
     1974 refers to March 1973 to March 1974, and so on.

6   R. J. Apps and J. S. Ashworth[1]

The production of an adjusted unemployment series

1. Introduction

It is now widely recognised that the rate of unemployment in the UK has not remained a stable index of the level of excess demand in the labour market, and there is general agreement that this breakdown in the relationship began around 1966. A shift in the unemployment function contributed, therefore, with the changed nature of inflationary expectations and perhaps other considerations, to the breakdown around 1966 of the Phillips curve as originally formulated. The response has been, with very few exceptions, to use alternative measures of excess demand in the labour market in aggregate wage equations, for example vacancies, the rate of capacity utilisation, unemployment minus vacancies. These alternatives have given little improvement to the results obtained from the use of the standard unemployment rate.

Although considerable attention has been paid to the appropriate measure of price expectations for use in a Phillips-type wage equation, comparatively little attention has been paid to the nature of the excess demand variable. A quantity of work has been done on the possible increase in unemployment that is attributable to extended periods of unemployment resulting from increased benefit payments to the unemployed, but scant attention has been paid to other possible sources of distortion in the unemployment figures. The purpose of this chapter is to investigate more fully the nature of the shift in unemployment, to examine more closely the adjusted unemployment series proposed by Sumner (1978) to take account of these shifts, and to put forward a more satisfactory derivation of an adjusted unemployment series.

Section 2 comprises some more specific observations on the

operation of the labour market in the UK since 1966, while section 3 presents a model of unemployment in non-manufacturing industries. Section 4 presents the estimation results of equations explaining unemployment in non-manufacturing and in manufacturing industries, and derives an adjusted unemployment series. Section 5 comprises some concluding comments.

2.   The UK labour market since 1966

The relationship between the unemployment rate and the vacancy rate has frequently been proposed as a check on the reliability and consistency of the unemployment and vacancy statistics. The UV curve, as this relation is known, simultaneously plots two measures of excess demand in the labour market: the rate of unemployment, which varies inversely with excess demand, and the vacancy rate, which varies directly with excess demand. A lowering of excess demand from one period to the next results in an increase in unemployment and a fall in vacancies, and in this manner a curve is plotted out over time; should there be a movement in either or both of the underlying unemployment or vacancy functions it will be reflected in a corresponding shift of the aggregate UV curve. Since the aggregate UV function could also change owing to a shift between the employment of men and the employment of women (due to known large differences in the recording ratios), the UV curve is more meaningful when disaggregated into its male and female components.

In brief, the male UV curve for Great Britain since 1959 has shown marked outward shifts and trends, the shifts occurring most noticeably in the fourth quarter of 1966 and in the first quarter of 1972. The female UV curve, although a looser relation overall, does not exhibit any significant shifts or trends, although results indicate a non-significant trend *inwards* throughout the period 1959–1975.

An earlier paper by Apps (1977) investigated this dichotomy of behaviour further. By relating the change in the unemployment rate and in the vacancy rate to the change in output it was found that the shift in the male UV curve for the fourth quarter of 1966 was attributable to a change in the underlying unemployment function, and that the movement outwards in the first quarter of 1972 was primarily the result of a shift in the vacancy function.

Examination of the male UV curve disaggregated into non-manufacturing and manufacturing revealed a dichotomy here also: between the fourth quarter of 1966 and 1970 the movements in the male UV curve for manufacturing were essentially horizontal — that is to say, there were increases in vacancies but no increases in unemployment. For non-manufacturing industries the reverse was true; between the fourth quarter of 1966 and 1971 there were substantial increases in unemployment, but not in vacancies. Considering UV curves for manufacturing and non-manufacturing for females, where there were no significant shifts, the movements along the curves were consistent with the behaviour of the male UV curves. It should be noted that all the above observations were made after allowing for seasonality. Combined with a number of other pieces of evidence, this behaviour of the UV curve suggested that a major cause of the change in the UV curve was possibly the introduction of Selective Employment Tax (SET), since, as will be seen in more detail later, the tax not only penalised employment in non-manufacturing industries more heavily than in manufacturing, but also penalised the employment of men more than women.

The conclusion that SET was a cause of the shift in UV is not in contradiction to the conclusions of some of the other contributors to the UV debate; it differs in that it attributes the greater part of the shift to the tax. However, it is not sufficient to know the cause or the degree of the shift in the UV curve to produce a series for unemployment that is a consistent index of excess demand in the labour market. For this the underlying unemployment function must be estimated and the influence of those variables causing the inconsistency removed.

As has already been noted, there are no significant shifts in the female UV curve, and there are no offsetting shifts in the unemployment–output or vacancy–output relations to maintain this stability in the UV curve. Thus the inconsistency of unemployment as an index of demand in the labour market appears to lie with the male labour market. Furthermore, since the change in the UV relation for males in manufacturing, after an initial movement in the fourth quarter of 1966, was biased towards increases in vacancies and not unemployment, the greater burden lies with male unemployment in the non-manufacturing sector.

In Sumner's formulation of the unemployment equation the difference between the registered unemployment rate and the adjusted unemployment rate is attributable solely to the influence of the rising unemployment benefit–earnings (B/E) ratio. It may be objected that this proposition is itself untenable, since the number of 'induced' unemployed persons (the difference between the registered and the adjusted unemployment rate) is then approximately equal to the total number of people in receipt of unemployment benefit.[2] In other words, Sumner's equation is suggesting that, on balance, none of those persons in receipt of unemployment benefit would have been unemployed had they not been in receipt of unemployment benefit, which is not acceptable. The adjusted unemployment series presented in this chapter does not suffer from the difficulty, since, as will be seen, in the first place this series does not differ from the registered unemployment rate to the same extent as does Sumner's, and secondly part of the difference is attributable to the influence of SET.

The objective of selective employment taxation, as set out in the White Paper *The Selective Employment Tax* (Cmnd 2891, May 1966), was the transfer of manpower from services into manufacturing industries. Reddaway (1970) describes the White Paper's redeployment objective as an unfortunate mis-representation of the government's true intentions, which were in fact to reduce excess demand in the labour market by increasing taxation. Excess demand can, of course, be reduced either by a fall in aggregate demand or by a rise in supply. If SET did not cause a rise in productivity, employers would either raise prices or lose profits, either of which would cause aggregate demand and incomes to fall. If the tax was offset by a rise in productivity, potential supply would be increased, because labour saved in the services sector could be employed either in that sector or elsewhere to produce a rise in aggregate output. Reddaway (1970) has produced evidence that SET accelerated the rate of increase of productivity in the distributive trades, which probably extended into other areas, from which one can conclude that there was an increase in potential labour supply. It is possible that some fraction of that group of unemployed were subsequently employed in industries suffering from labour scarcity, in particular manufacturing. If it was the case that there were manpower transfers between manufacturing and non-manufacturing as a result of SET, then the analysis of the paper would be incorrect in assuming that unemployment in manufacturing and in non-manufacturing industries can be analysed separately. Sleeper (1970) investigated the extent of manpower redeployment as a result of SET and concluded that the tax had merely increased unemployment, and had not influenced manpower flows: 'Instead [of influencing manpower flows] the tax is likely to have caused a change in the level of unemployment at a given level of economic activity' (p. 296). On this conclusion, the division of male unemployment into manufacturing and non-manufacturing is justified.

The series for adjusted unemployment that is derived in this chapter, therefore, allows for the distorting influences of changes in unemployment benefit payments and for the payment of Selective Employment Tax. The rationale for adjusting unemployment for changes in the B/E ratio is well established; other things being equal, it is hypothesised that a rise in benefit payments will induce people to remain unemployed for longer periods and therefore diminish the supply to the labour market. The rationale for making allowance for the effects on unemployment of SET is not so apparent: the additional unemployed are, after all, seeking employment. However, since these unemployed are from non-manufacturing industries, they will be seeking re-employment in non-manufacturing and not in manufacturing industries. As Sleeper (1970) has pointed out, the unchanged manpower flows indicate that few of the unemployed as a consequence of SET found employment in manufacturing. Additionally, the unemployed as a result of SET were predominantly male; in so far as the male and female labour markets can be separated, the conclusion is that the extra supply of labour was extant only in the male labour market for non-manufacturing industries. SET can consequently be regarded as having led to an increase in *structural* unemployment,[3] and registered unemployment remains a stable index of the level of excess demand in the labour market for only as long as structural unemployment bears a constant relation to total unemployment.

3. Model of unemployment in non-manufacturing

3.1. *Influences*
We first consider the influences on unemployment and postulate that

$$U_t^{nm} = f(U_{t-1}^{nm}, D_t, E_t, \Delta L_t) \tag{1}$$

where U_t^{nm} = average unemployment in non-manufacturing in period t, D_t = discharges from non-manufacturing during period t, E_t = engagements into non-manufacturing during period t, and ΔL_t = the change in the potential labour force in the non-manufacturing sector during period t.

We assume that the major influences on the labour force in a particular sector are the level, and the change in the level, of unemployment which operate as proxies for the perceived difficulty to be experienced by an individual in securing employment. A high level of unemployment would tend to discourage entrants to a particular sector of the labour market, and might also cause some of the unemployed in that sector to depart for retraining, etc. In addition, the change in the total working population is included as an influence on the labour force in a particular sector, acting as an indicator of the overall changes in the labour market. In view of Sleeper's (1970) conclusions with respect to manpower flows, neither the level nor the change in the rate of unemployment in the manufacturing sector is included as a determinant of the labour force in the non-manufacturing sector. Thus:

$$\Delta L_t = g(\Delta U_t^{nm}, U_{t-1}^{nm}, \Delta P_t) \tag{2}$$

where P_t is the working population in period t. We might expect this relationship to be non-linear.

Further, since only limited data exist for both D_t and E_t, a behavioural equation is formulated for $(D_t - E_t)$, the net flow either into or out of the non-manufacturing sector after allowing for changes in the labour force. Discharges will be lower, and engagements will be higher, for any positive change in the output of the sector; the net flows will be influenced by any changes in productivity, with the expected result of an increase in discharges and a fall in engagements. By inducing voluntary quits but, more importantly, by extending periods of unemployment, any increase in the rate of unemployment benefit relative to average earnings will cause a lowering of engagements relative to discharges. An increase in the real wage will be expected to work in the opposite direction by promoting engagements and reducing voluntary quits.[4] Increases in employers' National Insurance contributions, relative to earnings, might be expected to increase discharges and lower engagements. Finally, the effect of the introduction of Selective

Employment Tax will be to reduce engagements and increase discharges in the non-manufacturing sector. Thus:

$$(D_t - E_t) = h(\Delta GNP_t, \Delta Q_t, \Delta(B/E)_t, \Delta(W/P)_t, \Delta NI_t, \Delta SET_t) \quad (3)$$

where GNP is a proxy for the output of the non-manufacturing sector,[5] Q = productivity, (B/E) = unemployment benefit–earnings ratio, (W/P) = the real wage and NI = employers' National Insurance contribution, with SET the variable for Selective Employment Tax.

If we now combine the above equations we have a model for unemployment in the non-manufacturing sector. In view of the expected non-linearities and the nature of the model in terms of flows, then we may derive an estimating equation of the form;

$$\begin{aligned}
\ln U_t^{nm} = {} & \alpha_0 + \alpha_1\Delta \ln GNP_t + \alpha_2\Delta \ln Q_t + \alpha_3 \Delta \ln (B/E)_t \\
& + \alpha_4\Delta \ln (W/P)_t + \alpha_5\Delta \ln NI_t + \alpha_6\Delta \ln SET_t \\
& + \alpha_7 \ln U_{t-1}^{nm} + \alpha_8\Delta \ln P_t + u_t
\end{aligned} \quad (4)$$

It can be seen that the estimating equation may be viewed as explaining the level of unemployment at any particular time in terms of approximate rates of change of variables and a non-linear autoregressive scheme.[6] Thus, while requiring discrete time to derive an adjusted unemployment series, the model attempts to reflect the underlying continuous nature of the system. The error term is viewed as white noise. This clearly imposes assumptions on the nature of the errors in equations 1, 2 and 3, but since there are no overriding reasons for a particular different formulation it was left to the data to determine whether there were any indications to the contrary. The possibility of simultaneity bias due to the presence of the U_t in the equation for ΔL_t is ignored for this preliminary exercise, as the reduced form of the system is being estimated.

3.2. *Data*

The division between manufacturing and non-manufacturing was on the standard Department of Employment lines, which coincided (with very limited exceptions) to the differential impact of SET. The data for the benefit–earnings ratio were the average level of unemployment benefit paid to recipients as a fraction of average earnings.[7] The majority of work using a B/E ratio has utilised the ratio published by the Department of Health and Social Security (Sumner, 1978; Maki and Spindler, 1975; Cubbin and Foley, 1977), though it is far from certain that this is the correct measure. The DHSS ratio is derived by dividing the total unemployment benefit payable (including allowances for dependants, and the earnings-related supplement, which are assumed payable in full) by the average earnings for a male in manufacturing industry taken net of tax where the individual is assumed to be married to a full-time housewife and has two children. The important point about this ratio is that it is hypothetical; it reflects the sum of money that would be payable to an individual, given those conditions. Because it assumes that the individual has been in continuous employment for a sufficiently long period at that wage to be eligible for the earnings-related supplement at the maximum rate, and that the individual is not debarred from any or all of his benefit for any reason, it is also the *maximum* that would be payable in such circumstances.

Since not every claimant receives the maximum, for a variety of reasons (not least of them the possibility that he may have exhausted his earnings-related supplement), it is necessarily the case that the average benefit paid to an unemployed person (at the same level of average earnings) who fulfils the remaining conditions will be less than the hypothetical maximum given by the DHSS ratio; typically, therefore, the DHSS ratio will overestimate the size of the benefit payments. This would not be a serious objection to its use if it were the case that the average size of the benefit actually paid had moved closely in line with the hypothetical DHSS ratio. However. Taylor (1977), drawing on data published in a paper by the Department of Employment (1976) and data obtained direct from the Department, has shown that this is far from being so. Using data on the average total weekly benefit actually paid, (including the earnings-related supplement), Taylor constructed a second, 'actual' B/E ratio (using the same after-tax average earnings denominator) and demonstrated that it behaved very differently from the DHSS ratio — the most noticeable difference being the *absence* of a large increase in the actual B/E ratio in 1966. The reason for the divergence of behaviour in 1966 is that the introduction of earnings-related supplement caused a large increase in hypothetical (maximum) benefits reflected in the DHSS ratio, but only a slight increase in the *average* size of benefits. If the increase in maximum benefits had a noticeable effect we would expect a jump in the pattern of unemployment benefit payments at this point. The fact that the average size of benefits actually paid out did not increase markedly in 1966, when the DHSS ratio showed a substantial increase, provides support for the hypothesis that the introduction of earnings-related supplement did *not* induce substantial voluntary unemployment.

The justification for the inclusion of a variable whose basis is unemployment benefits payable in an unemployment equation is that it will reflect the costs to an individual of being unemployed. The nearer his unemployment benefits to his expected earnings, the longer would that rational individual engage in search for subsequent employment, since his costs of remaining unemployed would be relatively lower. A lengthening of the average period of job search would, of course, cause a rise in the stock of unemployment. Following this line of argument, the measure of unemployment benefit that is relevant here is that which is actually received by the individual, on the assumption that he is going to base his decisions regarding future search behaviour on the unemployment benefit he is expecting to receive, and not on the unemployment benefit he would receive if he satisfied the conditions for maximum earnings-related supplement, etc. The use of the DHSS ratio in this context is thus inappropriate, and would be better replaced by the actual B/E ratio.

National Insurance contributions were calculated as those contributions payable by the employer in respect of a male aged over eighteen, and comprised the weekly flat-rate contribution (including National Insurance, Industrial Injuries, National Health Service, Redundancy Payments Scheme, but excluding SET) and the graduated contribution payable by the employer in respect of a male over eighteen in receipt of average earnings. The resultant series for National Insurance contributions is then taken as a proportion of the same average earnings series.

The Selective Employment Tax was introduced in September 1966, and was payable in full by all industries; manufacturing industries received a refund of their contributions, with 30 per cent added, every three months. In addition there were refunds in some non-manufacturing industries, principally agriculture, mining and transport. When first introduced, the rates per week (payable by the employer) were £1·25 for men, 62·5p for women and youths, and 40p for girls. Slight changes were made in the following years — the 30 per cent premium was withdrawn in 1967 (except for manufacturing in development areas), and rates were increased by 50 per cent in 1968 and a further 28 per cent in 1969. In July 1971 all rates were halved as the first stage of the abolition of the tax pledged by the Conservatives, which was completed in the spring budget of 1973.

At this juncture it is worth noting that SET was payable by employers. Although it is probable that some portion would be shifted to the employees, any reaction to the tax lay solely with the employers. Its effect would be to raise the cost of labour in non-manufacturing industries — particularly male labour — relative to all other inputs. The response would be to reduce the total labour input to equate the marginal cost of all inputs. In view of the known extent of labour hoarding in industry prior to the fourth quarter of 1966, the immediate effect of SET would be to dishoard that portion of labour that was not directly relevant to the production process. This reaction would stem solely from the reduction in the cost-minimising level of hoarded labour in view of the changed costs of holding labour to meet unexpected demand, minimise recruitment costs, etc. In addition, since the fourth quarter of 1966 saw the onset of a long and deep recession which would have entailed some dishoarding of labour, regardless of SET, unemployment in non-manufacturing would be expected to increase markedly.

Since manufacturing industries only received refunds on their payments every three months, it is reasonable to postulate that there would also be some incentive for them to reduce their labour input. In particular, they would be expected to reduce their employment of labour when SET was first introduced, and subsequently re-expand it, in order to minimise the size of the effective loan to the government. The refund received at the end of the first quarter, with 30 per cent added, would be used to finance the re-employment of this labour.

In subsequent periods employers in non-manufacturing industries would be expected to alter their production processes, and change their capital/labour ratios, to take account of the changed costs of labour. The net result would be further reduction of employment in that sector, and thus a further increase in unemployment. In assessing the relative cost of labour, the real cost of SET as seen by the employer is the appropriate measure; that is to say, the nominal SET rate deflated by the wholesale price index.

Thus the effect of the introduction of SET on the male unemployment rate in non-manufacturing industries would be an immediate impact effect as firms dishoarded labour, followed in subsequent periods by further increases as firms adjust their factor input mix. This latter effect would be partially offset by the falling real cost of SET as the wholesale price index rose over time.

When the SET rates were increased (in 1968 and 1969) it is postulated that exactly the same occurred: there is an impact effect, as firms dishoard more labour in order to achieve the new cost-minimising level of hoarded labour, and there is an adjustment over time (which will be additional to the pre-existing adjustment) as firms adjust their factor input mix.

With reductions in the SET rate, as in 1971, and removal in 1973, it might be supposed that the reverse would happen. There would be an impact effect where firms take on labour with a view to hoarding it, followed by an adjustment effect as they adjust their factor input mix in accordance with the new price vector. More realistically, however, firms might be expected to expand employment more slowly — they would not take on labour immediately with the sole aim of hoarding but would expand employment as output increased, then hoard some of the labour when output subsequently fell. Consequently there would not be an impact effect so much as a gradual adjustment.

We would expect the effect of SET on the rate of unemployment in non-manufacturing industries over time to be as shown in fig. 6.1.[8] If we believe that the tax operated on the unemployment function in such a way as just to cause an upward movement, not an actual change in the structural form, then the usual manner of dealing with such an effect is to include a dummy variable. However, it would appear from the above discussion that the usual 0, 1 dummy would be inappropriate. We have therefore constructed a weighted dummy as outlined below.

We assume that the adjustment took place with geometrically declining weights after the initial shock. Thus, if we further assume a weight of unity when the effect has worked its way through the system, we may express the effect of the initial imposition of SET in

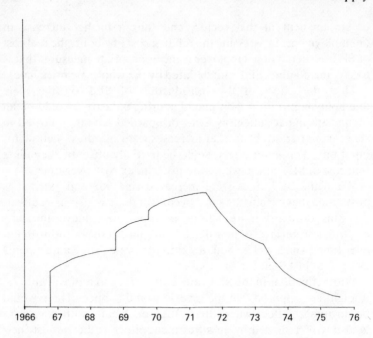

Fig. 6.1   Effect of SET on male unemployment, non-manufacturing

the fourth quarter of 1966 after j periods as

$$\frac{1}{a}[(a-1)+(1-\delta^j)] \cdot \frac{SET_1}{WPI_j} \qquad (5)$$

where $(1/a)$ $(a \geq 1)$ is the fraction of the adjustment to SET which takes place over time as a result of changed production processes, etc, and $(a-1)/a$ represents the fraction that is the impact effect. δ is the adjustment coefficient $(0 \leq \delta < 1)$ and j runs from 1 to n, where the first period is the fourth quarter of 1966 and n is the number of periods that it takes to reach full adjustment. SET_1 is the nominal SET rate for adult males introduced in the fourth quarter of 1966.

The generalised form of the variable up to the second quarter of 1971 is then

$$\sum_{j=1}^{n}\left\{\frac{1}{a}[(a-1)+(1-\delta^j)]\frac{SET_1}{WPI}\right\}$$

$$+ \sum_{j=8}^{n} \left\{ \frac{1}{a} \left[(a-1) + (1 - \delta^{j-7}) \right] \frac{SET_2}{WPI} \right\}$$

$$+ \sum_{j=12}^{n} \left\{ \frac{1}{a} \left[(a-1) + (1 - \delta^{j-11}) \right] \frac{SET_3}{WPI} \right\} \tag{6}$$

where SET_2 is the difference between the SET rate in operation during the period between the second quarter of 1968 and the second quarter of 1969 and SET_1, and SET_3 is the difference between the rate in operation during the period between the second quarter of 1969 and the second quarter of 1971 and $(SET_1 + SET_2)$.

It is clear from this that we impose the retriction that the effects of the three increases (in the first case the introduction) of SET is the same, that is, that a and δ are the same on all three occasions.

When considering the reduction and removal of SET — as we assume that there is no impact effect — the adjustment has just the geometrically declining weights, and the weighting k periods after the reduction is

$$\lambda^k \cdot \frac{SET_4}{WPI_K} \tag{7}$$

where λ $(0 \leq \lambda < 1)$ is the adjustment weight and SET_4 is the nominal tax rate put into operation in the third quarter of 1971. There is a similar term in SET_5, the further decrease which occurred in the first quarter of 1973.

The actual construction of the total value of the dummy applying after the reduction in SET is to take the level of the dummy reached by the second quarter of 1971, add to that the reaction still applying from the series operating through equation 6 (since some SET is still being paid), and subtract the relevant terms of the type shown in equation 7 corresponding to the reductions in SET.

4. Estimation

In the estimation of equation 4 a number of regressions were run in order to determine the lag structure. This was done with a number of different SET variables formed by searching over different combinations of values for the parameters a, δ and λ. By minimising the sum of squares the best-fit equation that emerged has a two-quarter lag on productivity as the only lag on the variables in the equation, and values of 5 for a and 0·96 for both δ and λ in the calculation of the SET variable.[9] That is to say, it was found that the best formulation of the SET variable attributed four-fifths of the total effect to the 'impact' effect, and 40 per cent of the remaining adjustment would be completed within three years. The results of estimation of equation 4 by OLS were (fourth quarter of 1955 to fourth quarter of 1975 inclusive):

$$\ln U_t^{nnn} = -0·1248 - 1·7170\Delta\ln GNP_t - 0·6531\Delta\ln(W/P)_t$$
$$(3·13)(2·17)(0·66)$$

$$-5·1914\Delta\ln Q_{t-2} + 0·6245\,\Delta\ln(B/E)_t + 0·1702\Delta SET_t$$
$$(2·26)(1·17)(2·43)$$

$$-0·0983\Delta\ln NI_t + 0·9927\,\ln U_{t-1}^{nnn} + 0·3259\Delta D63$$
$$(0·85)(39·06)(4·32)$$

$$+1·7447\Delta\ln P_t + 0·2994S1 + 0·1675S2 + 0·2308S3$$
$$(0·58)(9·19)(5·24)(7·15)$$

$$R^2 = 0·965 \qquad h = 1·593 \tag{8}$$

t statistics are given in parentheses beneath each coefficient.

In this formulation a dummy has been included to account for the high level of unemployment associated with the severe winter of 1963. The GNP, SET and productivity variables are all correctly signed and significant at the 95 per cent levels; the benefit–earnings ratio and the population variables both have the correct sign, but are statistically insignificant. The coefficient on employers' National Insurance contributions as a proportion of earnings is, surprisingly, insignificant and incorrectly signed. The equation exhibits marked seasonality in the high level of significance of all three seasonal dummies. Finally the equation shows a high explanatory power (but this is not surprising, owing to the presence of the lagged dependent variable).

This result is in contrast to Sumner's (1978) result, where the real wage was correctly signed and significant, and the benefit–earnings ratio was significant. It may be objected that the insignificance of the coefficient on the B/E ratio in the equation presented here is due to the use of the 'actual' in preference to the hypothetical DHSS ratio; as a check on this, a regression was run, identical to that above but with the actual replaced by the DHSS ratio. The result was that the latter produced both a smaller coefficient and a lower significance level. Further, Sumner's equation, estimated on annual data, has a two-period lag on the real wage, implying that the labour market requires two years to adjust to any discrepancy between the actual and equilibrium real wage. This appears to be an inordinately long lag, which suggests that the real wage may be proxying for some other variable. In addition Sumner includes a time trend, but as this variable proves insignificant it would not appear to be of great relevance.

It must be remembered, of course, that Sumner's equation was estimated for total unemployment, and not just male unemployment in non-manufacturing industries as for the equation presented here. His formulation does, therefore, implicitly assume that the components of total unemployment are all affected by the independent variables. It was noted earlier that central to the explanation of the behaviour of unemployment is the fact that while there have been shifts in the unemployment function for males there do not appear to have been any such shifts in the function for females. Any adjusted unemployment series must, however, include all components of unemployment, from which any influence such as SET and increases in the B/E ratio can be subtracted. Since there do not appear to have been any changes in the behaviour of female unemployment in the post-war period, there is no requirement to subtract the effect of any extraneous influences on female unemployment. There remains the possibility, however, that male unemployment in manufacturing industries was subject to change as a result of the increased B/E ratio and also of SET, since although SET refunds were made to firms in manufacturing they were paid only every three months. It is postulated, therefore, that in order to minimise the 'forced loan' to the government via SET, manufacturing firms would reduce their labour force when the tax was first introduced but subsequently re-expand it in the next quarter when the first refund was received. It would have paid these firms to re-expand their employment levels, since the refund was 30 per cent greater than the original payment. Male unemployment in manufacturing would thus show a rise in the fourth quarter of 1966, followed by a fall in the first quarter of 1967 as a result of SET.

In all other respects it is assumed that the model used for the explanation of male unemployment in non-manufacturing can be extended to manufacturing industries, that is, for male unemployment in manufacturing;

$$\ln U_t^m = \phi_0 + \phi_1 \Delta \ln GNP_t + \phi_2 \Delta \ln Q_t + \phi_3 \Delta \ln (B/E)_t$$
$$+ \phi_4 \Delta \ln (W/P)_t + \phi_5 \Delta \ln NI_t + \phi_6 \Delta \ln SET_t$$
$$+ \phi_7 \Delta \ln U_{t-1}^m + \phi_8 \Delta \ln P_t + v_t \qquad (9)$$

In estimating this equation all variables were defined as previously, except that the SET variable was a dummy which took the value 1 in the fourth quarter of 1966 and 0 elsewhere (and thus of -1 in the first quarter of 1967 upon first differencing). The following result was obtained (fourth quarter of 1955 to fourth quarter of 1975 inclusive):

$$\ln U_t^m = -0.0680 - 3.2648 \, \Delta \ln GNP_{t-1} + 1.6668 \, \Delta \ln (W/P)_t$$
$$\quad (1.51) \quad (2.84) \qquad\qquad (1.06)$$

$$-7.7374 \, \Delta \ln Q_{t-2} \; + 1.4840 \, \Delta \ln (B/E)_t + 0.9630 \ln U_{t-1}^m$$
$$\quad (2.14) \qquad\qquad (1.88) \qquad\qquad (27.36)$$

$$+0.3871 \, D1972 \cdot I \; + 0.4808 \, \Delta SET_t + 0.0392 \, \Delta \ln NI_t$$
$$\quad (3.61) \qquad\qquad (4.58) \qquad\qquad (0.24)$$

$$-0.6608 \, \Delta \ln P_t + 0.2506 \, S1 \; + 0.0720 \, S2 + 0.1890 \, S3$$
$$\quad (0.15) \qquad\quad (5.16) \qquad (1.54) \qquad (3.94)$$

$$R^2 = 0.933 \qquad h = 1.485 \qquad\qquad (10)$$

D1972.I was a dummy added to allow for the effect on unemployment in manufacturing industries of the miners' strike and subsequent power supply disruption of the first quarter of 1972. For the rest of the coefficients, those on GNP, productivity and SET are all correctly signed and significant at 95 per cent; those on the real wage, the B/E ratio and National Insurance are correctly signed but not significant, while the population variable is incorrectly signed but insignificant.

Using the results from these two estimated equations, it is now possible to produce an unemployment series purged of the effects of SET and of increases in the benefit–earnings ratio. Using the coefficients on the B/E ratio and the SET variable in equation 8, the impact of these two variables on the number of male unemployed was calculated, and subtracted from the number registered as unemployed in this category. A similar process was utilised for the number of male unemployed in manufacturing industries, and finally these two adjusted series were summed with the number of female unemployed, which has been assumed to be unaffected by any such influence. This series was then expressed as a rate by dividing by the total number of employees in employment, and is graphed, along with the registered (unadjusted) unemployment rate and Sumner's adjusted unemployment rate, in fig.6.2. It should be noted that Sumner presented his adjusted unemployment rate normalised on the average benefit–earnings ratio that prevailed over his estimation period, so that the averages of the registered and the adjusted unemployment rates were the same; in order to facilitate comparison in fig. 6.2 by having all three series sharing a common base for the first quarter of 1955, the average of Sumner's adjusted unemployment series has been reduced. This amounts to normalising the Sumner series on a much lower value of the benefit–earnings ratio.

As might be expected, the adjusted unemployment series of this chapter does not differ markedly from the registered unemployment rate up to the end of 1966; with only increases in the B/E ratio operating to inflate the registered unemployment rate, the adjusted unemployment rate lies only slightly below the registered unemployment rate, although this difference increases as 1966 is approached. After 1966 the adjusted unemployment rate falls very short of the registered unemployment rate, particularly in 1971 and early 1972, although the two series move in the same direction. The adjusted unemployment series after 1972 moves closer to the registered unemployment series, but they remain as far apart as in the period 1967–70.

With the realignment of his adjusted unemployment series that has been employed here, Sumner's adjusted unemployment series and this chapter's are very nearly coincident up to 1966. The difference between . the registered and Sumner's adjusted unemployment series, it will be remembered, is due wholly to the impact of the benefit–earnings ratio; the low magnitude of his series after 1966 arises from the overstatement of this impact, which may be due in part to the use of the DHSS ratio.

Nickell (1979) has also investigated the effect of unemployment and related benefits of unemployment, this time in terms of unemployment duration. On the basis of cross-section data from the 1972 General Household Survey, the preferred estimates yield

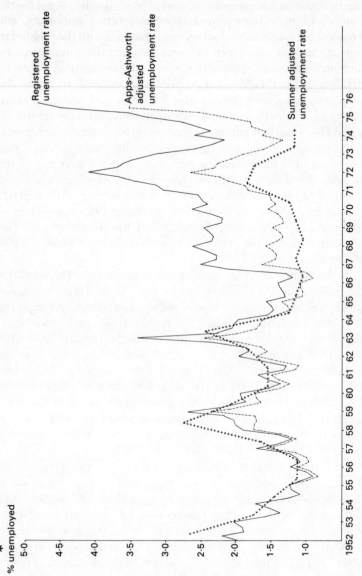

Fig. 6.2. Registered and adjusted unemployment rates, 1952–75

elasticities of unemployment duration with respect to unemployment and related benefits lying between 0·6 and 1·0. Owing to the division in this paper of male unemployment into its manufacturing and non-manufacturing components, to the insignificance of the unemployment benefit terms in both equations and the non-uniformity of the data used, it is not possible to produce elasticities wholly comparable to Nickell's; it is clear, however, that, given reasonable assumptions to overcome these difficulties, the estimated elasticity would lie in the same range as Nickell's estimates and therefore rather different from Sumner's.

5. Conclusion

This chapter has shown that a major cause of the change in the behaviour of unemployment, particularly male unemployment, after 1966 is the employment effects of Selective Employment Tax, which closely supports the earlier paper on the UV relationship. It has further shown that the previous reliance of the benefit–earnings ratio to explain the changed behaviour of unemployment has attributed too much importance to this variable. Finally, it has produced a series for adjusted unemployment that provides a more consistent index of excess demand in the labour market than is provided by the registered unemployment rate, which can subsequently be employed in Phillips-type wage equations.

Notes

1   J. S. Ashworth is at the University of Durham.
2   Reference to fig.6.2 shows that, for example, in the fourth quarter of 1967 registered unemployment stood at 2·5 per cent, while Sumner's adjusted unemployment series yields 1·2 per cent. (Note that, as explained more fully later, in the construction of fig. 6.2 the average of Sumner's series has been reduced such that it is normalised on a much lower value of the B/E ratio than the average value of the B/E ratio employed by Sumner when presenting his series.) The difference, 1·3 per cent of the working population, or approximately 300,000 individuals, represents the voluntarily unemployed as a consequence of unemployment benefit payments. It is known that in the fourth quarter of 1967 the average number of unemployed males in receipt of unemployment benefit stood at 270,000 (Department of Employment, 1976), which is rather less than the 300,000 attributed to the effects of unemployment benefit. Evidence from the UV curve

for females does not suggest that there were many 'induced' unemployed females, and thus the implication is that (at least) all those unemployed in receipt of unemployment benefit would not have been unemployed had the benefit not been payable. The adjusted unemployment series of this chapter attributes only 160,000 of the unemployed of that quarter to the effect of the benefit–earnings ratio, in contrast to Sumner's 300,000; a further 55,000 were unemployed as a consequence of SET. (In addition to the 270,000 unemployed males in receipt of benefit in the fourth quarter of 1967, the remaining unemployed males, approximately 200,000, were in receipt of either Supplementary Assistance (141,000) or no benefit whatever (50,000).)

3   Structural unemployment defined here, as in the usual fashion, to encompass those persons unemployed with skills for which vacancies do not exist. The major characteristic of structural unemployment is thus that it is independent of aggregate demand in the labour market.

4   For considerations pertaining to the inclusion of the real wage in an unemployment equation see Sumner (1978).

5   The choice of GNP as a proxy for the output of the non-manufacturing sector was dictated largely by data considerations.

6   It is clear that if we wish to express the model totally in rates of change then we would impose the restriction that $\alpha_7 = 1$.

7   The data on the average level of unemployment benefit paid to recipients is given as an aggregate, and therefore separate series for manufacturing and non-manufacturing, while desirable, were not available.

8   The diagram is a simplified version of the true representation in that overlapping adjustments are not shown.

9   Although the values of δ and λ were found to be equal, they were not constrained to be so.

Appendix

Adjusted unemployment rate: quarterly observations (%)

1955.	I	1·270	1962.	I	1·951	1969.	I	1·488
	II	0·984		II	1·572		II	1·337
	III	0·840		III	1·669		III	1·356
	IV	0·894		IV	2·020		IV	1·431
1956.	I	1·107	1963.	I	2·405	1970.	I	1·562
	II	0·969		II	1·971		II	1·455
	III	0·990		III	1·720		III	1·529
	IV	1·153		IV	1·668		IV	1·550
1957.	I	1·571	1964.	I	1·638	1971.	I	1·885
	II	1·320		II	1·434		II	1·887
	III	1·155		III	1·240		III	2·111
	IV	1·383		IV	1·171		IV	2·251
1958.	I	1·764	1965.	I	1·318	1972.	I	2·244
	II	1·748		II	1·074		II	2·016
	III	1·710		III	1·065		III	2·274
	IV	1·734		IV	1·095		IV	2·021
1959.	I	2·328	1966.	I	1·101	1973.	I	1·911
	II	1·881		II	0·916		II	1·618
	III	1·643		III	0·984		III	1·499
	IV	1·712		IV	1·159		IV	1·350
1960.	I	1·757	1967.	I	1·621	1974.	I	1·638
	II	1·393		II	1·450		II	1·587
	III	1·242		III	1·439		III	1·793
	IV	1·413		IV	1·506		IV	1·819
1961.	I	1·671	1968.	I	1·604	1975.	I	2·155
	II	1·276		II	1·436		II	2·546
	III	1·222		III	1·361		III	3·548
	IV	1·559		IV	1·387		IV	3·523

Wage determination
and incomes policies

7   M. J. Artis, Derek Leslie and Graham W. Smith

Wage inflation: a survey

1.   Introduction

Theories of wage inflation effectively split into two broad camps, both of which have a long and respectable intellectual tradition. The first asserts the primacy of the market, finding only a limited role for institutional or non-market factors in the process of wage determination. The second asserts the primacy of institutional rules in the process of wage determination, and finds a correspondingly small role for market forces in this process. The former approach has been comprehensively surveyed by Laidler and Parkin (1975), the latter by Addison and Siebert (1979).

It would be misleading to assert that there is only one market theory of wage inflation and even more misleading to assert that there is one institutional theory of wage inflation. Yet reading this survey will tend to give just such a misleading impression, because we have singled out for special attention the expectations-augmented Phillips curve (a predominately market theory) and real wage bargaining (a predominately institutional theory). Our justification is that, in the UK context at least, these theories represent two dominant schools of thought on which considerable empirical research has been done in recent years.

This chapter is split into two main sections. The first of these reviews the expectations-augmented Phillips curve and the real wage bargaining hypotheses, where attention is given to the problem that in practice it may be difficult to distinguish empirically between the two rival hypotheses. The second reviews empirical work on both hypotheses, though it must be stressed that this part of the survey is limited to recent work on the UK economy.

2. The two theories

The essential features of the augmented Phillips curve hypothesis can be described by the following simple three-equation model:

$$\dot{W}_t = f(U_t) + \dot{P}_t^e \tag{1}$$

$$\dot{W}_t = \dot{P}_t \tag{2}$$

$$\dot{P}_t^e - \dot{P}_{t-1}^e = (1-\lambda)\,(\dot{P}_{t-1} - \dot{P}_{t-1}^e) \qquad 0 \leqslant \lambda \leqslant 1 \tag{3}$$

where $\dot{W}_t$ is the rate of change of money wages in the tth period, U_t is the unemployment rate, $\dot{P}_t^e$ is the expected inflation rate, and $\dot{P}_t$ is the actual inflation rate. Equation 1 is the expectations-augmented Phillips curve, which should be familiar. (Friedman, 1975, or most recent intermediate macroeconomic textbooks describe the microeconomic foundations of this equation.) Notice that the coefficient associated with $\dot{P}_t^e$ is assumed to be unity, i.e. no actor in the economy suffers from money illusion and furthermore in this model all actors are assumed to form the same expectations about the inflation rate. Later this assumption will be modified somewhat. The unitary coefficient associated with $\dot{P}_t^e$ is a crucial assumption, since it implies that there can be no permanent or long-run trade-off between the inflation rate and the level of unemployment. This proposition is a cornerstone of monetarist philosophy, and the importance of a unitary coefficient on $\dot{P}_t^e$ will be demonstrated in what follows.

Figure 7.1 shows the relationship between $f(U_t)$ and U_t. Of interest will be the point at which $f(U_t) = 0$, shown as the level of unemployment U_n on the diagram. The diagram can be regarded as a special case of equation 1 showing the short-run trade-off between the rate of change of money wages and the unemployment rate, when the expected inflation rate $\dot{P}_t^e$ is zero. Clearly, equation 1 can be represented more generally as vertical displacements of $f(U_t)$, depending on the value of $\dot{P}_t^e$.

Equation 2 shows the relationship between $\dot{W}_t$ and $\dot{P}_t$, where it is assumed that any money wage inflation is automatically transmitted into a corresponding price inflation. This is a very strong assumption, as one might expect lags in any such relationship, and one might also expect an economy with

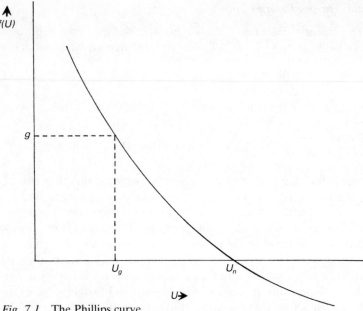

Fig. 7.1   The Phillips curve

productivity growth not to show such a relationship, irrespective of the question of any lags in the transmission of money wage inflation to price inflation. In fact it makes little difference to the conclusion 'no long-run trade-off between inflation and unemployment' — just what is assumed here — and later this equation will be modified to account for productivity growth. No substantive alterations to the analysis are necessary in this case.

Equation 3 shows the relationship between the expected and actual inflation rates. It is assumed that expectations are formed extrapolatively; today's expected inflation rate depends solely on previously observed actual rates of inflation. For the purposes of illustration we have chosen a frequently used extrapolative predictor, namely a first-order adaptive expectations scheme. $\dot{P}_{t-1} - \dot{P}^e_{t-1}$ is the forecast error, and equation 3 says that the expected inflation rate will be adjusted by a fraction $1-\lambda$ of the forecast error. It can be seen that λ is a measure of the adjustment of the expected inflation to the forecast error. In the extreme if $\lambda = 0$, then $\dot{P}^e_t = \dot{P}_{t-1}$ and if $\lambda = 1$, then $\dot{P}^e_t = \dot{P}^e_{t-1}$. Again it makes little difference to the central proposition — 'no long-run trade-off between inflation and unemployment' — precisely what expectations mechanism is assumed; all that is required is some link between the expected and actual inflation rates. In the next section alternative expectation mechanisms will be briefly discussed.

The endogenous variables in this system are $\dot{W}_t$, $\dot{P}_t$ and $\dot{P}_t^e$. The predetermined variables are $\dot{P}_{t-1}$, $\dot{P}_{t-1}^e$ and U_t. Conceptually we can imagine the government adopting a suitable monetary-fiscal package to achieve a target level of unemployment, which will be denoted as $\overline{U}$. Given $\overline{U}$, it follows that $f(\overline{U})$ can be treated as a constant in equation 1, and, since we are interested in the behaviour of $\dot{P}_t$, we will eliminate $\dot{W}_t$ *and* $\dot{P}_t^e$ to derive a reduced form for this variable. (Note there is a one-to-one correspondence between wage and price inflation in this model.) This gives

$$\dot{P}_t = f(\overline{U})(1-\lambda) + \dot{P}_{t-1} \qquad (4)$$

This scheme therefore gives an intentionally simple description of the behaviour of the inflation rate, since 4 is a first-order difference equation in $\dot{P}_t$ (of the structure $Z_t = \text{constant} + Z_{t-1}$). The solution for this equation is

$$\dot{P}_t = f(\overline{U})(1-\lambda)t + \dot{P}_0 \qquad (5)$$

where $\dot{P}_0$ is initial given rate of inflation. Equation 5 demonstrates the central proposition of no long-run trade-off between the inflation rate and the level of unemployment.[1] If $\overline{U}$ is chosen less than U_n, then $f(\overline{U})$ is positive and the inflation rate will increase for ever, as given by equation 5. Only in the case where $f(\overline{U}) = 0$ is there the possibility of a steady-state rate of inflation (which may be a zero rate of inflation). This, of course, is the case when $\overline{U} = U_n$, and for this reason U_n is termed the natural rate of unemployment.

It should be noted that λ, the speed with which the expected rate of inflation adjusts to the actual rate, has *no* influence on the level of the natural rate of unemployment; the latter quantity is determined entirely by the shape of $f(U)$, which ultimately means the special characteristics and institutional structure of labour markets. This is the only role that is allowed for non-market influences in the determination of inflation, hence Friedman's famous dictum that trade unions do not cause inflation. Their fault, in Friedman's view, would be to cause the natural rate to be higher than it would otherwise be. In this context it has been argued that increases in unemployment benefit relative to earnings, a common feature of many economies since the late 1960s, have increased the natural rate by making the opportunity cost of unemployment lower. This argument cannot be invoked to explain the dramatic increases in unemployment observed since 1974, because the benefit–earnings ratio has not increased since 1973! (See Nickell, 1979, for an extensive analysis of this question.)

If this analysis is a correct description of economic behaviour, then it seriously degrades the role of demand management as thought of by traditional Keynesians. If U_n should turn out to be a politically unacceptable large number and the State attempts to set U below U_n, then the policy can be only temporarily successful. Eventually the inflation rate will become so high that the policy will collapse. Nevertheless the State might exercise a less traditional set of policies, which would be to try and influence the shape of $f(U)$, shifting it to the left, thus reducing the natural rate of unemployment. These would be policies that would attempt to make labour markets work more efficiently, rather than trying to heat up the economy artificially and buy temporary reductions in unemployment only at the expense of higher inflation and ultimately even higher unemployment later. It has often been argued that our present problems of high inflation and high unemployment are the result of governments following precisely this latter type of policy in the past.

A suggested way out of the impasse is the use of subsidies to influence the rate of inflation directly and hence reduce inflationary expectations. Indeed, this was a policy that was adopted, albeit half-heartedly, by the 1974–79 Labour government. The argument would go something like this: the government announces that every item in the retail price index will be subsidised to the extent that $\dot{P}_t = 0$. If people believe in the policy, then $\dot{P}_t^e = 0$ and the Phillips curve will reduce to $\dot{W}_t = f(U)$, thus seemingly giving the opportunity of a permanent inflation–unemployment trade-off. However, it is easy to demonstrate that this can be achieved only at the cost of ever accelerating levels of subsidy; there is no steady-state level of subsidies that will permanently maintain the unemployment rate below the natural rate.

A more respectable case for subsidies could be made out, however. Suppose an economy has learnt the lesson of its profligate ways and returns to the natural rate of unemployment, but with a high steady-state rate of inflation that it is wished to 'burn out' of the system. Our model suggests this can be achieved only by going temporarily above the natural rate. However, a system of subsidies, which are progressively reduced, would be sufficient to lower the rate of inflation to any desired target without recourse to setting $\overline{U}$ above U_n. A similar justification could be made for the use of an incomes policy — not as a method of keeping unemployment permanently below the natural rate but as a means of avoiding temporary increases in unemployment above the natural rate by directly influencing expectations.

The whole argument surrounding the natural rate hypothesis depends crucially on the coefficient associated with $\dot{P}_t^e$ being equal to unity. If the coefficient is less than unity, then the whole argument that has been presented so far collapses. That is why it is such an important empirical question to establish what the coefficient associated with $\dot{P}_t^e$ actually is. Indeed, much economic research in recent years has been devoted to answering precisely this seemingly innocuous problem. To see its crucial importance let us suppose equation 1 is in fact of the following form:

$$W_t = f(U) + b\dot{P}_t^e \tag{6}$$

where b is a parameter greater than zero but less than unity. Workers do suffer from some degree of money illusion, depending on the size of b. Now evaluate the reduced form of $\dot{P}_t$ as before. This turns out to be

$$\dot{P}_t = f(\overline{U})(1-\lambda) + \alpha\dot{P}_{t-1} \tag{7}$$

where $\alpha = \{b(1-\lambda) + \lambda\} < 1$, since b is less than unity. Again this is a first-order difference equation, the solution of which is

$$\dot{P}_t = \dot{P} + (\dot{P}_0 - \overline{P})\alpha^t \tag{8}$$

where $\overline{P} = f(\overline{U})/(1-b)$ and $\dot{P}_0$ is the initial inflation rate at $t = 0$. There is now a vital qualitative difference between equations 8 and 5. Equation 8 is stable, since $\alpha < 1$ implies that as $t \to \infty$ so $\dot{P}_t$ will converge to a steady-state inflation rate given by $f(\overline{U})/(1-b)$. Unlike the previous model there is a long-run trade-off between the inflation rate and the level of unemployment. In principle we can achieve any target level of unemployment, provided we are prepared to live with the implied level of inflation, determined by $f(\overline{U})/(1-b)$. Note, as before, λ has no influence on the steady-state rate of inflation, it merely influences the speed at which the economy converges to this steady state. The steady state is determined entirely by the choice of U, the shape of $f(U)$ and the size of b. Other things being equal, the higher b, the higher will be the steady-state inflation rate.

The economy so far described is characterised by zero productivity growth. It has been argued that productivity growth *in itself* is a way of reducing the natural rate of unemployment. The argument is in fact fallacious, but let us see how such a conclusion might be arrived at. Suppose the underlying rate of productivity growth is g, then equation 2 could be modified to read

$$\dot{P}_t = \dot{W}_t - g \tag{9}$$

Thus money wages can rise at a rate equal to g without any resultant price inflation. It follows that the equation, equivalent to equation 5, describing the inflation rate becomes

$$\dot{P}_t = (f(\overline{U}) - g)(1-\lambda)t + \dot{P}_0 \tag{10}$$

It now appears that the natural rate of unemployment, which is that rate which is consistent with a zero or a steady-state inflation rate, has been lowered. A steady-state inflation rate requires, according to equation 10, that $f(U) - g = 0$, rather than $f(U) = 0$. This is illustrated as the point U_g on the diagram, which is clearly below U_n. There is some superficial evidence for this view; after all, West Germany and Japan have until recently been characterised by low levels of unemployment associated with extremely high rates of productivity growth.

The fallacy in the argument is that it assumes that the actors in the labour market are unaware of this underlying productivity growth. Equation 1 embodies the idea that workers anticipate the rate of inflation and that it is taken into account when they make their wage bargains. It would seem highly plausible that workers would anticipate the underlying productivity growth also, and this too would be taken into account in wage negotiations. If the underlying rate of growth were 10 per cent, for example, most workers would want to be compensated for the anticipated inflation rate *in addition* to seeking a real wage increase of around 10 per cent. Workers do not simply bargain to keep their real wage constant. Equation 1, in a world of productivity growth, could therefore be modified to become

$$\dot{W_t} = f(U) + \dot{P_t} + g \qquad (11)$$

It takes little thought to see that equation 11 combined with equation 9 will give precisely equation 5. Thus, to the extent that productivity growth is anticipated, it has no influence on the natural rate of unemployment.

The basic expectations-augmented Phillips curve described by equation 1 can be extended in two further useful directions: explicit allowance can be made for different sides of the labour market and for open economy effects. In this context it becomes important to note that firms sell output produced domestically, by a single homogenous labour input, in domestic and foreign markets. Moreover the underlying money wage deflator differs on both sides of the labour market. Firms, for example, might be considered as deflating the money wage they pay out by the price of their output, whereas households could be viewed as deflating their 'take home' money wage by the price of the bundle of consumer goods purchased. Setting aside the divergence of money wages on both sides of the market, a simple expectations-augmented Phillips curve can be derived.[2] The method is due to Parkin, Sumner and Ward (1976).

Consider an open economy producing a non-traded good with an output price P and a traded good with price $E\pi$, where E is the foreign exchange rate and π is the price of the traded good in foreign currency units. Given a money wage rate W and consumer price deflator P_c, then the excess demand for labour function may be written as:

$$X = F[P, E\pi, W, P_c] \qquad (12)$$

where X is the level of excess demand for labour. Following conventional analysis, equation 12 is assumed to be homogeneous of degree zero in money prices and consequently:

$$X = F\left[1, \frac{E_\pi}{P}, \frac{W}{P}, \frac{P_c}{P}\right] \tag{13}$$

The change in excess demand is given by:

$$\Delta X = F_2 \frac{E\pi}{P} \cdot \frac{\Delta\pi}{\pi} + F_2 \frac{E\pi}{P} \cdot \frac{\Delta E}{E} + F_3 \frac{W}{P} \cdot \frac{\Delta W}{W} + F_4 \frac{P_c}{P} \cdot \frac{\Delta P_c}{P_c}$$

$$- \left[F_2 \frac{E\pi}{P} + F_3 \frac{W}{P} + F_4 \frac{P_c}{P}\right] \frac{\Delta P}{P} \tag{14}$$

Simplifying notation, equation 14 can be written as:

$$\Delta X = f_2(\dot{\pi} + \dot{e}) + f_3 \dot{W} + f_4 \dot{P}_c - (f_2 + f_3 + f_4) \dot{P} \tag{15}$$

where $f_2 > 0$, $f_3 < 0$ and $f_4 > 0$

Money wages are changed, given expectations about $\dot{\Pi}$, $\dot{e}$, $\dot{P}_c$ and $\dot{p}$, to eliminate excess demand, i.e. $\Delta X = -X$, hence:

$$\dot{W} = -\frac{1}{f_3} X - \frac{f_2}{f_3}(\dot{\pi}^e + \dot{e}^e) - \frac{f_4}{f_3} \dot{P}_c^e + \left[\frac{f_2 + f_3 + f_4}{f_3}\right] \dot{P}^e \tag{16}$$

Proxying excess demand by a function of the level of unemployment and defining $\beta_1 \equiv -(f_2/f_3)$ and $\beta_2 \equiv -(f_4/f_3)$ gives

$$\dot{W} = f(U) + \beta_1(\dot{\pi}^e + \dot{e}^e) + \beta_2 \dot{P}_c^e + (1 - \beta_1 - \beta_2) \dot{P}^e \tag{17}$$

where $\dot{\pi}^e$ is the expected proportional rate of change of the foreign currency price of the traded good, $\dot{e}^e$ is the expected rate of change of the exchange rate, $\dot{P}_c^e$ is consumers' inflation expectations and $\dot{P}^e$ is firms' inflation expectations. Equation 17 is an open-economy expectations-augmented Phillips curve, allowing for the differing inflation expectations of households and firms. Since the sum of the coefficients on the expectational variables is unity, the theory predicts that in the long run, when expected and realised changes are equal, wage change is homogeneous of degree one in all other money variables:

$$\dot{W} - (\beta_1[\dot{\pi}^e + \dot{e}^e] + \beta_2 \dot{P}_c^e + [1 - \beta_1 - \beta_2] \dot{P}^e) = 0 \tag{18}$$

If, on estimation, the restriction embodied in equation 18 is not rejected, then, assuming zero productivity growth, that level of unemployment for which $f(U) = 0$ is the natural, or equilibrium, level of unemployment.

Turning now to the second of the two theories, there are several sources of the 'real wage bargaining' or 'real wage resistance' view and accordingly more than one motivation for it. One motivation, of course, is the desire to explain 'stagflation', the phenomenon which defeated the unaugmented Phillips curve; another, the desire to explain how a 'once-over' price shock, like the 1973–74 oil price hike, could result in a process of inflation; and yet another, the belief that realistic descriptions of the wage inflation process should incorporate wage–price responses which are realistically 'economical in computing costs'. Finally, at perhaps a deeper level, there is detectable among at least some advocates of the real wage bargaining view a desire to find a description of wage inflation processes which affords more scope for macroeconomic policy (albeit of a radically 'new' kind) than is allowed by the expectations-augmented Phillips curve approach. It is perhaps not surprising that several variants of the real wage bargaining view are to be found in the literature, some forms of which are capable of the description that they 'merely' afford a redescription of the excess demand term of the conventional Phillips curve, others of which seek, at least, to occupy a distinctively different position from the conventional one. For all this, there is a common basic ingredient to the approach, which has the undeniable appeal of simplicity: money wage inflation is viewed as ensuing from union bargaining, which seeks to close the gap between a 'target' or 'aspiration' real wage, and actual real wages. Supplemented by a mark-up theory of pricing, this basic ingredient immediately yields the prediction that, from any starting equilibrium, both a 'wage push' (upward deviation of the real wage target) and a price shock will yield inflation. To illustrate, the hypothesis may be set out as follows:

$$\text{d} \ln W = \alpha \left(\ln \left(W/P \right)^* - \ln \left(W/P \right) \right) \qquad (19)$$

where d ln W is the rate of change of money wages and $(W/P)^*$ is the 'target' real wage. Equation 19 can be written more succinctly as

$$\dot{W} = \alpha A^* - \alpha \ln W + \alpha \ln P \qquad (20)$$

where A^* denotes $\ln(W/P)^*$. Clearly, here, a price shock of, say, Z or a rise in A^* of Z will promote wage inflation of αZ and a corresponding price inflation in a stationary economy. It would not be unnatural to think of the value of α as approximately unity here, so that – by the computationally economical device of merely consulting the gap between target and actual real wages – this description of the wage process directly affords a degree of security from money illusion. In a dynamic context actual real wages will, of course, be rising at the underlying rate of growth of productivity, but it seems natural to suppose that target real wages will also be following a positive trend path in such circumstances, so the example above can be simply reinterpreted in terms of the additional inflation ensuing from deviations of either target real wages or actual real wages from their trend paths. However, a feature of the example just described is that such shocks precipitate (additional) inflation at a steady rate; but as such inflation stems in the first instance from an attempt to make an additional real gain (or to recoup a real loss), and as the attempt is foredoomed to failure (resulting only in nominal gains), it seems quite possible that realisation of this will provoke further wage push and accelerating inflation. As workers notice that their wage push results in inflation, $\dot{P}$, of Z, this expectation will itself be incorporated in future pay rounds. Thus the additional wage inflation provoked by the initial shock of Z becomes

$$\dot{W}_t = Z + \dot{P}_{t-1} \qquad (21)$$

and inflation becomes

$$\dot{P}_t = Z + \dot{P}_{t-1} \qquad (22)$$

thus *accelerating* at the rate Z per period.

It is interesting to note that the augmented Phillips curve and the real wage hypotheses can lead to very similar predictions. However, the *prescriptions* of both models are very different. The former argues that the government should have a realistic unemployment target, otherwise accelerating inflation is the inevitable result. The latter says that workers should have a realistic real wage target. Furthermore an unrealistic real wage target may be completely independent of market forces, given the peculiar institutional structure of the UK labour market. It is this that places the real wage hypothesis firmly in the institutional camp. Incomes policy is seen as justified by directly breaking down the revision mechanism on which workers through their bargaining agents base their wage claims. Indeed, strong proponents of the real wage model would argue that increasing unemployment could be inflationary, rather than deflationary, because labour productivity is procyclical (see Taylor, 1974, for detailed evidence). Deflation reduces labour productivity, relative to trend, yet workers will continue to press for money wage increases based on previous trend. It is interesting how such a supposedly simple view of the world can lead to very unconventional results.

Models like the one described should not be taken too literally, but rather used imaginatively as an aid to understanding real-world processes. In reality the notion of a target or aspiration real wage is somewhat 'fuzzy': in particular, in empirical work it is difficult to pin down and make precise. Typically researchers experiment with different variants of what might be the target; and models which are flexible can usually be manipulated by skilled investigators to find some plausible fit. This is a worrying feature of the hypothesis. Nevertheless the real wage hypothesis does provide a framework with which to provide an alternative explanation of Britain's inflation in the 1960s and '70s. For example, proponents of the real wage hypothesis have argued that it is the net real wage after all deductions have been paid that is the basis of wage negotiation. From 1964 there has been a dramatic fall in the retention ratio (the ratio of net to gross pay), to the extent that it has seriously reduced the growth of net real earnings. Unions, it was argued, pursued ever escalating wage demands in a fuitless attempt to recoup these tax losses. Note the unconventional implication that tax rises, viewed in this manner, are inflationary. This aspect is emphasised in the work of Johnston and Timbrell (1973) and Jackson, Turner and Wilkinson (1975), and formed an important ingredient in the analysis afforded by Bacon and Eltis (1976). Another aspect emphasised is the oil crisis of 1973, compounded by Britain's deteriorating exchange rate. Those whose sympathies lay with the augmented Phillips curve would argue that this was simply a once-and-for-all change in *relative* prices and should not *ipso facto* be inflationary. On the other hand the real wage proponents argued that the oil crisis generated a transfer problem in that real resources were shifted to owners of oil abroad, and this effectively meant a cut in real wages at home. Again inflation was generated as unions failed to recognise the inexorable logic of events. Finally, whereas the logic of augmented Phillips curve analysis (at least where the long-run trade-off is denied) leaves little scope for macroeconomic policy, the logic of the real wage view is that, since expansion reduces inflation, policy must concentrate on removing the constraint on demand expansion. In the particular case of the British economy this constraint is seen by some proponents (in particular the Cambridge Economic Policy Group) as external, and as justifying resort to a regime of import controls.

Parkin (1978) has noted that 'the most striking thing about bargaining models is the closeness of some aspects of their predictions to those of an expectations-augmented excess demand model'. We have already noted one such similarity and it is perhaps fitting to conclude this section by noting another. In its strongest form the real wage hypothesis explains the rate of change of money wages by the deviation of the real wage from the aspiration real wage and some simple expected inflation proxy such as the current inflation rate. *Prima facie*, therefore, there is a complete difference of emphasis compared to the augmented Phillips curve, since no role is to be found for an excess demand variable in the determination of the inflation rate. However, excess demand might be presumed to exercise an influence in two possible ways. First, a high level of unemployment might exercise a discipline on unions, causing them to revise their aspiration real wage downwards. In some of the variants of the real wage model such a role is allowed for unemployment. Second, a high real wage relative to trend might imply a high level of unemployment, given the assumption of profit-maximising firms and diminishing marginal product. A high real wage is associated with a lower rate of money wage inflation, *ceteris paribus*. (Note, however, that, strictly speaking, this would imply an anti-cyclical pattern of labour productivity, something which is not in fact observed.) A real wage model augmented by a term in unemployment may well be viewed as an elaboration, taken as a whole, of the traditional excess demand model, something adumbrated in Sargan's (1964) earliest work on the subject. From this point of view Parkin's comment has added weight.

3. Recent empirical work in the UK

In testing the expectations-augmented Phillips curve for the UK two issues have received much attention — proxying expected inflation and the excess demand for labour.[3] Relatively little attention has been given to open economy aspects and researchers have usually modelled any natural level of unemployment as constant over the estimation period.

In section 2 we stressed the crucial implications of a unit coefficient on inflation expectations. Empirical estimates of this coefficient are often below unity, but this does not necessarily imply that the 'no long-run trade-off' hypothesis is refuted. Since inflation expectations are not usually observable, some proxy must be used. This means that the 'no long-run trade-off' hypothesis is tested conditional on an auxiliary hypothesis about expectations formation. If the coefficient on an expectational variable in a wage equation is significantly less than unity this could mean that either the 'no long-run trade-off' hypothesis is refuted or the underlying expectations-formation scheme is an inadequate characterisation of that process. Furthermore there are quite compelling reasons for questioning many of the estimates, because they are based on doubtful measures of expected inflation. Some work uses the most recent actual inflation rate, for example Godfrey (1971) and Taylor (1972), which implicitly imposes the restriction that $\lambda = 0$ in equation 3 above; some investigators have assumed an adaptive expectations scheme, for example Parkin (1970) and Henry, Sawyer and Smith (1976), a scheme which is not generally supported by empirical work on expectations formation. (See Carlson and Parkin, 1975, and Smith, 1978.) However, recent work by Parkin, Sumner and Ward (1976) and Sumner (1978) has generally used direct measures of inflation expectations, generated from sample survey data. McCallum (1975) was the first to use a rational expectations framework for the UK.

Parkin, Sumner and Ward (1976) estimated an open economy expectations-augmented Phillips curve which explicitly allowed for the different inflation expectations of households and firms and expectations of tax changes for the period 1956.II–1971.IV. The *a priori* restrictions are not rejected; the restricted estimates are:

$$\dot{W} = 5\cdot911 - 1\cdot997U + 0\cdot503\,\dot{P}^e_w + 0\cdot203\,\dot{P}^e_f + 0\cdot294\,\dot{P}^e_c \ -0\cdot706\,\dot{t}_P$$
$$\quad[3\cdot59]\quad[2\cdot47]\quad\ [2\cdot58]\qquad\ [0\cdot89]\qquad\ [2\cdot58]\qquad [6\cdot18]$$

$$-0\cdot294\,\dot{t}_I + 0\cdot461\,IP(1961\text{–}62) - 1\cdot061\,IP(1966\text{–}67)$$
$$\ [2\cdot58]\qquad [0\cdot29]\qquad\qquad\qquad\ [0\cdot70]$$

$$\overline{R}^2 = 0\cdot432,\quad \mathrm{DW} = 1\cdot689$$

where $\dot{P}^e_w$, $\dot{P}^e_f$, $\dot{P}^e_c$ are the expected percentage rates of change of domestic wholesale prices, export prices and consumer prices respectively; $\dot{t}_P$ and $\dot{t}_I$ are the expected rates of change of employers' National Insurance contributions and of the ratio of take-home to gross pay and IP are incomes policy dummy variables. Since the sum of the coefficients on the expectational variables is not significantly different from unity, the results are consistent with the natural rate hypothesis; assuming productivity growth of 2·5 per cent per annum, the equilibrium unemployment level is 1·7 per cent.

Sumner (1978) developed this model in a way which permits the calculation of average values of the natural level of unemployment over specific periods. He modified the model by relaxing the assumption of constant productivity growth and instead assumed that the actual and expected rates of change of output per man are equal; the expected rates of change of wholesale and sterling export prices are also assumed equal; variables for expected tax changes are omitted, since they were always insignificant in unrestricted estimation in the previous study, and incomes policy variables were ignored in view of the earlier results. Estimating the model for the period 1952–74, using annual data, Sumner found that, provided allowance was made for a changing natural level of unemployment, the expectations-augmented excess demand model was appropriate. He examined the ability of a model estimated over the period 1952–65 to forecast 1966–74; the mean forecast error was small. Moreover he calculated the following estimates of the natural level of unemployment, U_n:

	U_n
1952–54	2·4
1962–64	2·9
1972–74	5·1

Whilst present distribution theory does not permit calculation of confidence intervals, and so it is not possible to establish the extent to which these values are significantly different, informal observation suggests that the natural level of unemployment has been rising and has, perhaps, reached an uncomfortably, if not unpalatably, high level.

McCallum's (1975) expectations-augmented Phillips curve, within a rational expectations framework, was estimated over the period 1956.II–1971.IV. Assuming log-linear labour supply and demand functions, he models (lagged) excess demand for labour as a function of lagged real *per capita* output and a lagged real wage variable. The coefficient on the former is expected to be positive and on the latter negative. Expected inflation is dependent on current and lagged values of monetary expansion and changes in government expenditure, among other variables. His results, whilst not entirely supporting the natural rate hypothesis, lend strong support to it. His preferred results have the proportional rate of change of hourly earnings as the dependent variable. Typically he finds:

$$\dot{W}_t = -0.176 + 0.139 \ln(Y/n)_{t-1} - 0.120 \, [\ln W_{t-1} - \ln P_{t-1}]$$
$$[2.06] \quad\quad [2.48] \quad\quad\quad\quad\quad [2.58]$$

$$+ 0.873 \, \dot{P}_t^e + 0.265 \, H_t$$
$$[2.19] \quad\quad\quad [1.59]$$

$$R^2 = 0.605, \quad DW = 1.88$$

where Y/n is *per capita* industrial production, H_t is the proportion of the working population unionised and the other variables are as previously defined. The excess demand variables are significantly different from zero and correctly signed. The negative coefficient on the lagged real wage is not perverse; it indicates that the higher the real wage the greater the excess supply of labour and the more slowly money wages rise, *ceteris paribus*. The expected inflation variable is significantly different from zero but not significantly different from unity.

Real wage models, in which wage inflation is a function of the gap between an aspiration (target) real wage and actual real wages, subject to conditions in the labour market, have received increasing attention in recent literature. Researchers have been particularly concerned about the extent to which labour market demand, inflation expectations and other variables influence the relationship. Empirical work with these models has not, however, been as rich as one might wish because the target real wage — a variable central to the hypothesis — has usually been proxied by a logarithmic time trend; such a variable describes rather than explains wage inflation.

One of the most generally specified real wage models is described in Sargan (1980a). Money wage changes are hypothesised to be distributed lag functions of real wages, average earnings relative to the wage rate, working days lost by strikes, and the level of unemployment, with the current income tax retention ratio, expected inflation, a time trend and seasonal dummy variables as further regressors. In general he found the coefficients on the level of unemployment, the retention ratio and strikes frequently to be insignificantly different from zero over the period 1952.I–1973.IV. However, work by Sargan (1964) and Henry, Sawyer and Smith found unemployment to be significant in models estimated for earlier periods. Sargan, for example, found for the period 1948.I–1960.IV:

$$\ln W_t - \ln W_{t-1} = -0{\cdot}012 \ln U_{t-1} - 0{\cdot}271 \left[\ln W_{t-1} - \ln P_{t-1}\right] + 0{\cdot}0013t$$
$$\qquad\qquad\quad [2{\cdot}07] \qquad\qquad [3{\cdot}71] \qquad\qquad\qquad\qquad [3{\cdot}69]$$

Henry, Sawyer and Smith (1976) made two main changes to Sargan's basic (1964) model. Instead of real wages, real earnings net of all deductions (calculated with a retention ratio) are used; instead of consumer prices, the retail price index is used. Their preferred model estimated over the period 1948.II–1974.IV is:

$$\ln W_t - \ln W_{t-1} = 0{\cdot}020 + 0{\cdot}476 \left[\ln P_{t-1} - \ln P_{t-2}\right] - 0{\cdot}006 \ln U_{t-1}$$
$$\qquad\qquad\quad [0{\cdot}65] \quad [3{\cdot}17] \qquad\qquad\qquad\qquad [0{\cdot}73]$$
$$\qquad\qquad - 0{\cdot}154 \left[\ln NE_{t-1} - \ln P_{t-1}\right] + 0{\cdot}0009t$$
$$\qquad\qquad\quad [2{\cdot}48] \qquad\qquad\qquad\qquad [2{\cdot}50]$$
$$\qquad\qquad + \text{incomes policy}$$
$$\qquad\qquad\quad \text{dummy variables}$$

$$R^2 = 0{\cdot}498, \quad \text{DW} = 1{\cdot}473$$

where *NE* is net earnings. They consider that their results '...

provide confirmation of the view that pressure for money wage increases from workers in order to reach some target for growth in take-home pay has been a decisive influence in the current inflation'.[4] This is too strong an observation, since it is possible to give an alternative interpretation to their results by attributing different influences to the time trend: it may, for example, be picking up two effects simultaneously: steady growth of expected inflation relative to last period's actual inflation, over a period of generally rising inflation, and a slowly rising natural level of unemployment. On this interpretation, and given that the estimated coefficient on lagged real net earnings is so remarkably similar in magnitude to that on McCallum's lagged real wage variable, their results would appear quite consistent with an expectations-augmented Phillips curve interpretation.

4. Conclusion

Wage inflation is part of the unfinished business of empirical economics. There are many good technical reasons underlying the difficulties experienced by investigators in this field, pertaining, for example, to the quality of available data, the shocks injected into the system by the presence, anticipation and removal of incomes policies, and so on. At the same time, however, views about the underlying determinants of wage inflation differ strongly, and these differences tend to be associated with distinctive philosophies or ideologies, and so with distinctive policy recommendations. This implies that appeal to *a priori* theory and the use of restrictions suggested by economic theory do not command the kind of consensus that, say, the empirical investigation of the demand for coffee might; rather, such appeals tend merely to confirm that the appropriate theory here itself commands no consensus. This certainly does not mean that empirical investigation is useless or that its results are not important, but it does mean that the limitations on the power of statistical tests to discriminate between rival hypotheses permit lively controversy to continue. For example, even within this framework of the augmented Phillips curve itself, empirical economics cannot distinguish between the hypotheses that the coefficient on inflation expectations is unity or less than unity. But, as explained earlier in this chapter, there is a world of difference in the implications for analysis and policy between these two hypotheses. The explanatory power of this approach, more generally, is inevitably limited by the problem of finding a statistical counterpart to the inflation expectations variable, and also by the seeming implication that for this hypothesis to explain current levels of inflation it must be assumed that the 'natural rate' of unemployment has risen steadily and considerably since the mid-1960s, for which convincing independent evidence is difficult to find.

The alternative, real wage, approach discussed in this chapter is in little better shape, however. From the empirical point of view, the slippery component of this approach is the concept of the 'target' real wage, and, whilst many of its advocates are consciously seeking to implement a distinctively different approach from that of the Phillips curve, the question can be raised whether it should not be viewed as a variant on the excess demand hypothesis. Some observers are reported to have welcomed the current policy experiment in the United Kingdom as the nearest economists can hope to get to a laboratory experiment; certainly current data will increase the variances of the series with which investigators work. But the history of the wage equation, and the nature of the issues at stake, suggest that this side benefit will fall long short of a decisive demonstration of the nature of the 'true' wage equation.

Notes

1   Except, of course, in the redundant case when $\lambda = 1$. This is when the expected inflation rate is not influenced by the actual inflation rate in any way.

2   Extension to allow for this would introduce three further expectational variables (changes in the effective rates of employers' and employees' National Insurance contributions and changes in the effective income tax rate) into the wage equation.

3   Shifts in the relationship between unemployment and vacancies and implications for the debate about alternative proxies for excess demand are discussed in chapter 6.

4   Henry, Sawyer and Smith (1976), p. 69.

8   J. L. Fallick[1]

Incomes policies

1. Introduction

This chapter looks at some general and specific supply-side implications of incomes policies. Although, in certain parts of the analysis, reference is made to actual periods of incomes policy, most of the discussion attempts to deal with more fundamental considerations by allowing a broad interpretation of the term 'incomes policy' and considering the problems and potential inherent in this type of State intervention. In order to focus attention specifically on supply-side considerations we have dispensed with the usual discussion of the history of incomes policies. Similarly, the theoretical underpinnings of belief in the efficacy or otherwise of incomes policies are touched on only where necessary to sustain the main analysis. However, these aspects of incomes policies are already very fully documented elsewhere, the former notably by Blackaby (1978) and the latter by Artis (1981), and we hope that emphasis on the supply-side problems will complement rather than replicate existing studies.

Although we have chosen to restrict the coverage, it is appropriate to note that in assessing the supply-side implications we are in effect establishing an implicit criterion (or set of criteria) for the evaluation of such policies. Now, even if one were to attempt to describe the impact of successive real-world incomes policies or outline the possible range of impacts of incomes policies in general, in a purely factual way, it is almost certainly the case that some value judgements would intrude if only as a consequence of the necessary selectiveness of any description. It would therefore seem preferable to adopt some evaluation criteria. However, the question of what are the 'correct' criteria is complicated by the fact that the actual objectives of any incomes policy are difficult to determine, and it seems likely that such objectives as have been set have not remained constant over successive UK policies. Any single criterion or small set of criteria is therefore likely to produce final conclusions which place incomes policies in an unfavourable light. The problem arises essentially because governments have attempted to use incomes policies to control or influence several variables. Although invariably the principal stated objective has been a reduction in the rate of increase in pay,[2] incomes policies often contained specific provisions directed towards low-paid groups, pay differentials in general, income distribution and the make-up of pay. Following Tinbergen (1952), one could argue that these subsidiary variables should be controlled by specific instruments designed solely for the purpose, with fiscal policies being the obvious candidate in the majority of the cases mentioned. The way would then be open for incomes policy to be directed at the control of inflation.[3] As this has not been the case in practice, one must accept that any criterion or criteria finally selected as the basis for an evaluation of incomes policies will inevitably be imperfect.

The rationale for looking at incomes policies from the standpoint of their impact on the supply side of the economy is as follows. Although incomes policies have many objectives, they spring from the twin propositions that inflation is prejudicial to the successful functioning of the economy, and that incomes policies are a way of reducing or even eliminating inflation. If one accepts that inflation is damaging — and for present purposes we need not specify the nature of the damage — one would presumably wish to reduce or eliminate it. The choice of the means of doing so must necessarily include an assessment of the impact on the economy of the policies chosen. Quite simply, there is no point in adopting an incomes policy to combat inflation if that policy is itself likely to be more prejudicial to the successful functioning of the economy than the 'sickness' it is designed to cure. In focusing on the supply-side effect of incomes policies this chapter attempts to raise just that question: on balance, do incomes policies do more damage than the inflation they seek to remove? Because of the complexity of the problems involved, no definitive answer can be given. However, by looking at the impact of incomes policies on many of the institutions and mechanisms which we believe are necessary for the successful functioning of our type of economy, some insights will be gained.

The rest of the chapter is divided into three sections. The first looks at the principal supply-side 'gains' associated with or claimed for incomes policies. Although many of these supposed advantages are the subject of debate and controversy it is convenient to group them together, in the first instance at least, so that a coherent and relatively comprehensive case can be developed in support of incomes policies. The next section presents some of the more important supply-side disadvantages and costs associated with incomes policies, and the final section brings the two viewpoints together and draws some tentative conclusions.

2. Supply-side gains

Beginning more or less conventionally, one can make out a case for supply-side gains which arise from incomes policies based on the real wage resistance view of wage determination[4] and on the expectations-augmented version of the Phillips curve.[5]

The essence of the real wage resistance view of the determination process is the hypothesis that real wages enter explicitly into the wage equation. Although workers bargain for some money wage, they arrive at the desired sum on the basis of a real wage 'aspiration' level which takes into account their desired real wage growth and the income tax retention ratio.[6] If one adopts this view of the labour market, then one is forced to argue that incomes policies can be effective in the long run only if they succeed in reducing real wage 'aspirations' or if, as a result of reduced real wage growth during the period of the policy, events take place on the supply side of the economy which enable it to produce more goods and services and thus sustain higher real wages when the policy restraint is removed. The type of events that would have to take place on the supply side would be a restructuring of investment and/or an increase in the volume of investment, which in each case should lead to higher output. The point to note is that this investment growth would be funded from the greater share of total output going to capitalists as a result of the workers' reduced real wage aspirations and the associated short-term pay restraint.

If real wage aspirations are not permanently reduced, or if the necessary productivity and capacity improvements are not achieved via investment during the currency of the policy, then the removal

Table 8.1 *Increases in gross earnings, prices and net real income from employment: periods with and without incomes policy compared (annual compound rate of increase)*

Period	Gross weekly earnings (a)	Retail price (b)	(a−b)	Net real income[*]	Incomes policy
1948–50	4·30	2·87	1·43	1·15	On
1950–56	7·65	5·26	2·39	2·43	Off
1956–58	3·76	3·33	0·43	−0·74	On
1958–61	5·96	1·63	4·33	3·04	Off
1961–63	4·40	3·09	1·31	1·40	On
1963–65	7·83	3·90	3·87	2·11	Off
1965–69	5·92	4·04	1·88	0·39	On
1969–72	12·23	7·35	4·88	4·20	Off
1972–76	15·64	15·34	0·30	−1·78	On

[*] Gross weekly earnings adjusted for direct tax and price effects. The tax effects are based on the standard allowances for a married man with two children under eleven years of age.

Source. Tarling and Wilkinson (1977), table 2.

of restraint will simply lead to some form of pay explosion as bargaining groups try to recover their lost real wage growth. Leaving aside the vexed question of how real wage aspirations are actually formed in practice, we can usefully examine the evidence on the impact of past UK income policies on real wage growth in an attempt to determine how far aspirations have in fact been lowered, and the extent to which real output growth has been achieved under these relatively favourable supply-side conditions.

While the debate over the general effectiveness of incomes policies in reducing inflation in the long run remains largely unresolved, few would deny that almost every period of incomes policy in the UK has led to a reduction in the rate of increase of real wages while the policy was in operation. Tarling and Wilkinson (1977) show that whereas, on average, over the whole post-war period the annual rate of increase in real gross weekly earnings was 2·3 per cent, in what they designate 'policy on' periods the real increase was just over 1 per cent, while in 'policy off' periods it was over 3·5 per cent.

The first question for those who argue that incomes policies have beneficial supply-side consequences and base their arguments on a real wage resistance approach is whether this reduction in the actual rate of growth of real wages was a result of reduced real wage aspirations or merely of the effectiveness of the government's restraining instruments? The evidence is somewhat conflicting and it is difficult to make generalisations, particularly as the behaviour of organised labour has significantly varied according to whether the government was Labour or Conservative. On the positive side, Tarling and Wilkinson argue that for certain periods, noticeably that of the 'Social Contract' (effectively 1974–78), lower settlements were obtained in return for a commitment by the (Labour) government to introduce a wide-ranging package of economic and social measures such as public control of capital investment, improved social welfare provisions and the repeal of the repressive trade union legislation passed by the previous (Conservative) government. However, even if one chose to interpret this in the most favourable way and argue that real wage aspirations were effectively lowered, such an interpretation could at best be extended only to a very few specific incomes policies. Moreover, if one adopts a broader interpretation of net real income which includes the various non-pay elements and in particular the many State-provided benefits which go to make the social wage, it could be argued that real wage aspirations have not been reduced. What has taken place is simply a shift in the distribution of sources of real income from pay to social welfare provisions. Although this interpretation would require that workers' representatives had undertaken a much more complicated set of calculations involving both money income and benefits to arrive at the desired (or aspiration) *utility* level, it is not entirely implausible, given the way the Social Contract was developed. For other periods of incomes policy the social wage interpretation is not available, and we are forced back on to the question of whether or not real wage aspirations were reduced.

The bulk of the empirical evidence would seem to go against the proposition that real wage aspirations can effectively be lowered by incomes policies. In particular the work of Henry and Ormerod (1978) and Henry (1981) suggests that wage explosions took place immediately after the removal of government restraining instruments, and that a series of 'catch-up' settlements was negotiated as workers sought to regain their real wage target growth path at the point they would otherwise have reached by that date, in the absence of the intervening incomes policy.[7] This interpretation of events is supported by recent analysis of strike activity before, during and after incomes policies. Davies (1979) shows that whilst there is generally a significant reduction in pay-related strikes during a period of incomes policy it appears to be achieved only at the expense of an upsurge in strikes once the restraint is removed, and he goes on to interpret this in a way consistent with the real wage resistance view. Aspirations have *not* been permanently reduced, and the aftermath of restraint is characterised by bargaining aimed at a return to the desired real wage growth path.

If, then, incomes policies appear to offer little hope of reducing real wage aspirations except in conjunction with an explicit commitment by the government to intervene in other areas of social and economic policy (more will be said about these broadly based packages below) the real wage resistance argument for incomes policies must rely on the proposition that they create some form of 'breathing space' in which some of the supply-side problems of the economy can be reduced or eliminated.

In considering this proposition it would again be misleading to generalise too sweepingly. Past policies operated under widely varying real-world economic conditions on both the domestic and the international front. Moreover, even if they had all failed to produce supply-side improvements, this would not necessarily invalidate the general argument that such gains might be realised, though it would obviously cast doubt on it. The evidence that does exist shows, according to Tarling and Wilkinson (1977), that the sacrifice by workers of real wage growth under incomes policies was not turned into increased capacity, productivity and output because 'at some stage during each period of incomes policy, the imminent economic crisis has forced the government to introduce a highly deflationary package, which itself discourages investment'.

They observe that the fall in real consumption relative to output (the real wage reduction) which arose as a result of restraint was translated into unemployment rather than the necessary increase or restructuring of investment. That this happened is of course related to the heterogeneity of objectives mentioned above. As incomes policies have tended to be imposed only at times of general economic crisis, it is perfectly legitimate to argue that the deflation would have arisen (or, more accurately, been manufactured) anyway. In that case incomes policies *per se* cannot be blamed for the lack of restructuring investment. Indeed, in considering the same problem, that of using the 'breathing space' to increase output, Artis (1981) is slightly less pessimistic. He argues that, in periods when incomes policies entailed rules governing price increases, attempts to conform to the rules by capitalists could, and in some cases clearly did, encourage greater productivity and efficiency. Even more important was the role of government agencies set up to monitor and control prices; the National Board for Prices and Incomes in particular demonstrably brought about some supply-side improvements. The example he cites is the NBPI report on bank charges, which 'played some role in stimulating a reappraisal of the nation's banking system and framework of monetary regulation'.

Although such gains have been small compared with the impact of incomes policies on popular consciousness, and certainly too small to provide a justification on their own, the fact remains that the potential is there, and if the supply side is seen as the major constraint on economic growth incomes policies may well offer the 'breathing space' needed to improve supply-side performance. Used in this way, moreover, they could conceivably take on a new role, being used to facilitate periodic realignments of the capital stock and not simply to help deal with a short-term crisis like a balance of payments deficit. This more positive role would depend for success on the willingness and ability of capitalists to respond to the increase in their share of total output with productivity-enhancing investments, and probably also on their willingness to compensate the labour force for its restraint out of the subsequent profits. In this way incomes policies would be seen as a definite *quid pro quo*, with gains accruing to both workers and capitalists and with restraint similarly being shared by both. Although strictly hypothetical, such a role is at least potentially realisable, particularly if one 'breathing space' can be engineered and used to advertise later ones.

Clearly, then, a real wage resistance argument in favour of incomes policies can be made out, but the empirical evidence to date suggests that in practice the benefits are limited and mainly take the form of slight gains in supply-side efficiency rather than the

more far-reaching increase in and restructuring of investment and/
or lowering of real wage aspirations that might have been hoped for.

In somewhat similar vein, some proponents of the
expectations-augmented Phillips curve have argued that incomes
policies may offer a way of reducing the rate of inflation at a lower
cost to the supply side in terms of unemployment than an
anti-inflation package without incomes policy, if inflationary
expectations are lowered as a result. The argument depends for its
force on the fact that, for a given expectations-generating regime, it
can be shown that incomes policies will lower the cost of an inflation
control package against that of a package without an incomes policy
if those responsible for the formation of inflation expectations
believe the policy will be a success and lower their expectations
accordingly. The extent of the resultant saving in unemployment
and lost output depends directly on the slope of the short-run
Phillips curve, and is greatest when the curve is relatively shallow.
As recent evidence for the UK suggests that the short-run Phillips
curve is relatively shallow (Artis and Miller, 1979), the crucial
question is whether or not those responsible for the formation of
inflation expectations feel that a specific incomes policy, or incomes
policies in general, will be successful. Obviously the argument is
dangerously circular, in that if wage bargainers believe in the policy
and reduce their inflation expectations and hence their wage
claims, then the traded goods element in the inflationary process
will be less effective and the policy will stand a good chance of
success. If they do not believe in it, then its chances of failure will
increase dramatically. This uncertainty, coupled with the dangers
of unanticipated internationally transmitted inflation largely
outside the control of the government, would seem to make
incomes policies a risky option. The classic example is the so-called
'threshold payments' of 1973–74, incorporated in stage three of the
Conservative government's incomes policy.[8] In an effort to
encourage restraint and reduce the importance of price
expectations (inflation expectations) in pay bargaining the
government guaranteed to pay 40p a week for every 1 per cent rise
in the retail price index (RPI) after it had risen seven percentage
points above its October 1973 level. It was hoped that settlements
would be based on an implicit 'wage equation' which did not
contain an inflation expectations term on the right-hand side. If this
could be achieved, it was argued, the self-fulfilling element in

inflation would be eliminated. However, the unanticipated rise in the price of oil quickly pushed the RPI well above the 7 per cent threshold. The government was more or less powerless, in the short run, to prevent this, and the anti-expectations clause turned out to be a liability rather than an asset, as none of the exogenous price increases could easily be absorbed through reductions in real wages.

Given the performance of past policies, the task of persuading workers' representatives to reduce their inflation expectations would not appear easy, to say the least. From their point of view such an action would almost certainly guarantee short-term real income losses and at best only offer a less than 100 per cent chance of offsetting real wage gains in the future. An ability to convince them of a policy's likely success, or persuade them that it would be much more likely to succeed with their support, may go far to explain the greater resort to incomes policies under Labour than under Conservative administrations.[9]

Although at first sight the circularity inherent in the expectations-augmented Phillips curve analysis of incomes policies seems to point to a pessimistic prognosis, closer consideration may prove worthwhile. The argument that an agreement to reduce expectations and hence wage claims can slow down the rate of increase of money wages, with at worst only temporary reductions in the rate of increase of real wages and at best no real wage growth losses, highlights an important aspect of incomes policies which is currently underdeveloped. In essence, it underlines the significant 'public good' dimension of incomes policies. Whereas no individual group of workers can benefit by reducing their expectations and/or their pay claims in isolation, clearly if all workers do so the resultant reduction in the rate of inflation is of considerable benefit to each individual group, and also to the economy as a whole. The problem is then a matter of how to advertise this public good element so that the gains can be realised. It can usefully be broken down into two components, which we can think of as the problem of disseminating the information and the problem of obtaining a consensus on what form the policy should take. Of course, the 'information' problem might be eliminated by an enforceable statutory policy with sanctions. Past experience in the UK strongly suggests that such an approach is politically unacceptable and in the long run counter-productive, though again this may have a lot to do with the fact that governments have only resorted to incomes policies at times of general economic crisis and even then have tried to influence a range of variables with this single instrument. Under these circumstances even a statutory policy has only a limited chance of success if the public good effect (i.e. reduced money wage growth) is translated into deflation and higher unemployment, as Tarling and Wilkinson (1977) suggest, rather than into suitably direct and fairly immediate rewards for restraint. For all the attractions to a Chancellor of the Exchequer (and his economic advisers) of increased economic growth three years hence, workers would seem to have a higher discount rate: they want to see the fruits of their sacrifice in a tangible form relatively quickly.

At best, then, even statutory policies seem to offer only restricted scope for starting the ball rolling: if a significant cut in the rate of inflation could be obtained in this way for an initial period, the government might be able to convince people that similar gains were possible in the future under a voluntary policy so long as it was adhered to. An approach like this clearly implies a commitment to some form of permanent incomes policy, perhaps with a target for money pay increases along the lines of the present ones for the growth of the money supply, with the government actively undertaking to discipline expectations. Implausible though it may sound in the UK context, recent West German experience has shown that it can work (Addison, 1981).

Reference to West Germany, or indeed other successful European versions of incomes policy such as that of Norway, leads us to the second component of the 'public good' argument, and highlights the problem of obtaining some sort of consensus on the importance of pay restraint and the form it should take. In the past a consensus has generally been lacking in the UK. Circumstantial evidence suggests quite strongly that what popular support there is for incomes policies derives largely from the feeling that they are fairer to those who have the public's sympathy but no political power, such as the nurses or the 'low paid'[10] (Behrend, 1973).

The public good aspect could, of course, be highlighted by broad economic reform packages implemented in conjunction with an incomes policy, as with Social Contract of 1974–78. How the prospective gains will be passed on can be spelled out in detail *beforehand*, as a way of promoting the consensus on which the success of the policy depends. The scope for this seems relatively wide, though the danger in *a priori* commitments on the government's part is that failure to deliver its part of the bargain would quickly lead to a reciprocal abandonment of restraint by the other parties. For a small open economy with considerable supply-side disadvantages such as the UK the risk of international complications or supply-side problems, either of which would reduce the government's ability to fulfil its obligations, must be high; thus the 'public good' type of package, while attractive, is not without problems.

To conclude this section, we can say that, arguing from either of the principal approaches to the relationship between pay growth and inflation, there would appear to be scope for advocating incomes policies. However, in the real wage resistance view of the world this advocacy depends heavily on three factors. The policy must in some way bring about a reduction in real wage aspirations and/or a restructuring of investment, and the beneficial results must be used to increase output and reward those who ensure wage restraint. Given that it all has to be done in a relatively short time, and that risk and uncertainty can never be fully eliminated, on this view a successful incomes policy needs a great deal of both luck and good judgement. Similarly, the expectations-augmented Phillips curve analysis suggests that if the message gets home that pay restraint can be good for everyone, and some consensus is reached on the form restraint should take, a significant public good element could emerge from incomes policies. Once realised, this would be a powerful and persuasive factor in subsequent periods. For both views the historical evidence is clearly discouraging, although the reason may be that incomes policies have only been used in times of general economic crisis, and have then been expected to perform too many functions.

3. Supply-side costs

Like the general case against incomes policies, the specific one based on their supply-side drawbacks draws on a number of separate sources. Here we will look at three elements relating to supply: the implications of incomes policies for income redistribution and the impact on the allocation of labour; the problems in capitalist and worker decision-making and behaviour arising from the disruption of the normal pattern of pay settlements; and finally the distortions which arise as a result of attempts to enforce and police incomes policies.

Redistribution of income under incomes policies can take two principal forms. In the first instance, if they lower average real wages there is scope for a higher general level of employment under incomes policies than under the 'free market' regime. This constitutes a redistribution from the (previously) employed section of the labour force to the unemployed. In practice, as Tarling and Wilkinson (1977) argue, the gain has not materialised, for various reasons, notably the fall in effective demand brought about by the deflationary measures which have almost invariably accompanied incomes policies. While of interest, therefore, this type of redistribution has seemed unimportant historically, although it is not clear whether the deflation might not have been greater still without an accompanying incomes policy. The second, and far more important, form of income redistribution associated with incomes policies results from the changes in pay relativities among sub-sections of the labour force. Fixed percentage and fixed money increase policies will both lead to changes in differentials. The former will affect money differentials; the latter, percentage differentials. Of course, policies which combine both elements, such as the 1973 £1 + 4 per cent, alter differentials via a complex combination of both effects. As several past policies have included complicated 'exception' and 'special case' provisions covering such items as low pay (e.g. 1965–66 and 1968–69), productivity (e.g. 1962–63, 1965–66 and 1968–69) and labour mobility (e.g. 1962–63 and 1965–66) and in at least one case a cut-off point for eligibility for increases (i.e. the £8,500 ceiling in the Social Contract of 1974), the overall effect of the last twenty years — in which there were approximately eighteen clearly identifiable periods of incomes policy[11] — has been to repeatedly distort the whole structure of pay relativities and differentials. Estimating their movement is fraught with difficulty, but Elliott and Fallick (1979) argue that, while differentials — particularly between skilled and unskilled manual workers, and within the non-manual sector — were compressed by incomes policies to some extent, this was small in comparison with the cumulative effects of changes during 'policy off' periods. Notwithstanding, changes in pay differentials due to incomes policies remain important because of their high profile, the importance traditionally associated with differentials and relativities in Britain, and not least because of the implications for the allocation of labour.

MacKay *et al.* (1971) and others have demonstrated that relative wages play only a limited role in the allocation of labour; but they do still play such a role. Any distortion of differentials and relativities will therefore lead to the misallocation of labour, and particularly where the more highly paid occupations are concerned, this will in turn lead, *ceteris paribus*, to a reduction in human capital investment at the margin. The extent of these effects is practically impossible to estimate, but it clearly amounts to a potential reduction in supply-side efficiency.

Perhaps a more important supply-side consequence of the impact of incomes policies on differentials has been the proliferation of non-wage elements in the remuneration package. Here again quantitative estimates are simply not available, but the unmistakable trend necessitates investigation. The problems inherent in the spread of such payments are considerable. In the first place, they circumvent the spirit if not the letter of incomes policy, assuming that benefits like company cars, expense accounts and so on are obtained over and above the pay increase permitted by the policy. Second, they make the allocation of labour even more liable to inefficiency, since assessment of the rate of return associated with each job offer becomes more difficult and costly. The problem is aggravated if these fringe benefits are kept secret, as they will be when they originate in an attempt to circumvent incomes policy. Since workers have to make job choices on imperfect information and in the face of higher search and information costs, the final allocation of labour will in all probability be less optimal than without these distortions.[12] Third, the ability to obtain fringe benefits varies widely across occupations and industries. The arbitrary element this introduces into the determination of effective pay differentials and relativities is inefficient as well as unfair. The notion of unfairness has come to be of central importance. In particular, the virtual absence of non-wage payments in the public sector, due to superior government monitoring of incomes policies and the simple lack of scope for them in a rigid 'corporate' or institutional structure, has led to a growing feeling that incomes policies restrain the public sector much more than the private. With evidence indicating that even in straight pay terms the former has come off slightly worse in certain periods of incomes policy (Dean, 1981), the further disadvantage *vis-à-vis* private-sector fringe benefits has resulted in considerable feeling against incomes policies among the government's own employees. Given the importance of this section of the labour force, both in economic terms and in terms of their 'psychological' role in attempts to restrain pay, this sentiment and the militancy that goes with it are highly damaging. Whether the public sector's disadvantage is in fact as great as it seems is not the main point. A presumption of unfair treatment is itself enough to lead to disruption and, in the end, to a refusal by negotiators and workers' representatives to support such policies in the future.

Apart from the strictly distributional consequences of incomes policies, but clearly related in practice, is the disruption of the normal pattern of pay settlements which they produce.[13] Before and after a period of incomes policy the number of settlements tends to increase dramatically. Workers try to 'beat the gun' and settle before the legislation comes into force, and/or to catch up on lost real earnings as soon as it is removed. However understandable and even justifiable, such behaviour is damaging to the economy, prejudicial to the success of the policy in question and, once again, liable to generate feelings of unfairness which undermine current and future efforts to obtain a consensus in favour of the concept of incomes policies based on its equality of treatment and 'public good' benefits. Moreover arbitrary variations in different groups' success at this can have long-lasting consequences, introducing a semi-permanent destabilising dynamic force into pay determination. Some attempt has been made to quantify the importance of catch-up settlements. Although certain reservations are expressed about their methodology in Chapter 9, Henry and Ormerod (1978) suggest that they almost completely restore the real wage growth lost under the incomes policy within a period of time approximately equivalent to the duration of the policy itself. Even if such settlements were much less effective in making up for lost ground the disruption caused by a rash of settlements immediately after a policy, and the lingering legacy of related settlements designed to restore some notional 'equilibrium' set of differentials, would in themselves be enough to call the value of the incomes policies into question in the first place.

Finally, mention must be made of the costs of enforcement and policing. Of course, in the end, the cost of enforcing a statutory policy which does not command the support or at least the acquiesence of organised labour may be the complete breakdown of production, or something very close to it. Even where the consequences are not quite so drastic considerable damage may be done to the supply side by reduced worker co-operation, poor motivation and absenteeism. The effect would be difficult to identify, as it would tend to show up in reduced quality as much as reduced quantity, and little is yet known about these concealed costs.

Although many other supply-side losses may be associated with specific incomes policies, the major recurring problems have been touched on, and it only remains to attempt some comparison of the costs and benefits to the supply side of the economy.

4. Conclusions

On an *a priori* basis there would seem to be a strong case for incomes policies. Potentially at least, they offer some limited supply-side gains in the form of reduced wage demands in the short and possibly in the long run, as well as reduced expectations of future inflation rates. The former could conceivably lead to a situation where the short-term reduction in real-wage growth provided enough flexibility in production and investment to realise considerable future gains in real output. These in turn could conceivably be large enough to compensate workers for their temporary transfer of additional resources to the capitalist. Reduced inflation expectations, if sustained, would have a good chance of being self-fulfilling, in that lower wage claims (arising from lowered expectations) would significantly reduce the traded goods element in the overall inflation. Both the aspirations effect and the expectations effect offer significant benefits for the worker and for the economy as a whole; although no individual group would stand to gain from an isolated attempt at restraint, concerted action would yield gains, investing incomes policies with important 'public good' characteristics. The latter offer some hope of economy-wide political and economic support for incomes policies, either by means of a broad package in which consensus is bought, to a degree, by *ex ante* mortgaging of the hoped-for public-good gains, or by somehow coercing workers for a while so that real output and efficiency can be improved enough to produce additional goods and services.

However, the case for incomes policies has tended to founder on practical matters rather than on the weakness of the reasoning behind them. Implementation, and attempts to realise the benefits, have not in general enjoyed the backing of a strong and broad consensus of opinion. Moreover the real gains which could (and should) have been obtained from the limited breathing spaces provided by successive incomes policies have either failed to materialise or been so small as to be negligible. That the reason can be found largely in the fact that incomes policies have tended to be adopted only at times of general economic crisis, and even then have been expected to produce results over a wide range of variables, is of little political relevance. Their record has gradually eroded faith in them, and it seems highly unlikely that workers' representatives will be convinced of the usefulness of lowered aspirations and/or reduced inflation expectations in the foreseeable future. Without broad consensus *and* the necessary faith in them their policy significance can only be negligible.

Notes

1   University of Glasgow.
2   Even this objective was confused. Many early UK policies failed to state explicitly whether they applied to rates of pay or to earnings. The distinction is of considerable importance if one wishes to evaluate incomes policies using their anti-inflation impact as a criterion. Also, it is questionable whether any government actually expected income growth to conform to the target set.
3   Not to mention the fact that it would make the *ex post* assessment of incomes policies by economists far simpler!
4   For detailed discussion of the real-wage resistance viewpoint see Hicks (1974 and 1975), Sargan (1971), Henry, Sawyer and Smith (1976), and, for the results of some recent research in this area, Chapter 9.
5   For detailed discussion of the expectations-augmented Phillips curve see Parkin, Sumner and Ward (1976).
6   However, it is important to note that there are significant differences between many of the authors who espouse this general view; in particular the econometric specification of the wage equation varies considerably. Accordingly the argument presented here is not meant to represent any specific version. The best known is that of Henry, Sawyer and Smith (1976) following Sargan (1971).

$$W = W_{-1} (P/P_{-1})^c [(W/P)^d \cdot (P_{-1}/W_{-1})]^\pi$$

where W = basic wages, P = prices, e denotes the expected value of the variable, d the desired value, and π is a constant. Artis (1981) has produced a simple statement of the general real-wage resistance view as follows:

$$\dot{W} = \alpha \left[(\lambda W/P)^d - (\lambda W_{-1}/P_{-1}) \right]$$

where λ = income tax retention ratio, which brings out the basic point in conceptually simple terms. Note that Artis does not include a price expectations term in his formulation, arguing that the existence of a lagged real net income term on the right-hand side of the wage equation takes changes in the price level into account. This point is discussed more fully in the next chapter.

7   However, see Chapter 9 for a criticism of the catch-up dummy variables employed by Henry and Ormerod.

8   The policy ran from November 1973 until February 1974.

9   Some support for this 'political' element in inflation expectations can be derived from an examination of the expected and actual inflation series presented in fig. 13.2. In March 1974 expected inflation fell quite dramatically. It can plausibly be argued that this was a result of the return of a Labour government under Harold Wilson, which committed itself to an incomes policy or pay restraint policy from the outset. As those surveyed by Social Surveys (Gallup Poll) Ltd (on which the expected inflation series is based) had greater faith in the efficacy of Labour incomes policies, they revised their inflation expectations downwards by almost 10 per cent.

10   In practice, incomes policies may favour these groups only to the extent of ensuring that they get at least the going rate or policy norm. However, as the presupposition is that they are deserving in part because they normally do less well than the average, getting the norm is in fact favourable treatment.

11   See Tarling and Wilkinson (1977) for a short listing of post-war incomes policies, and the appendix to Fallick and Elliott (1981) for a comprehensive catalogue of the nature, provisions and exception clauses contained in UK post-war incomes policies.

12   For a fuller discussion of information in labour markets see, for example, Rees (1966). Of course, much of the impetus to the growth of fringe benefits is tax- rather than incomes policy-induced. Nonetheless incomes policies would seem to have played a part.

13   Strictly speaking, of course, there is no such thing as a 'normal pattern of pay settlements' (Elliott, 1976). However, although there is no fixed pattern or 'pay round', it is possible to argue that the existence of incomes policies disrupts the progress of bargaining and settling pay.

The real wage hypothesis: some results for the UK

1.   Introduction

In the introduction to a volume of the proceedings of a conference that took place in February 1971 H. G. Johnson (1971) noted that a number of participants at that conference sought to explain the shift or disintegration of the Phillips curve in terms of the frustration of rising real income levels:

the argument implies that what the unions are after is the increase in *real* wages that experience has taught them they should be able to get, given the normal rise in productivity, rather than the increase in *money* wages past experience has taught them they can get with a given level of overall pressure of demand for labour. [Page x]

This implies that an important determinant of wage inflation is the time path of the real wage, rather than excess supply or demand as in the Phillips curve system. Not least because of the difficulties of the Phillips curve in providing an adequate explanation of wage inflation after 1971, increasing attention has been paid to the 'real wage hypothesis', as this body of theory has become known. Most contributions to the literature on the real wage hypothesis have been empirical, although there have also been significant analytical contributions, notably from Hicks (1974, 1975) and Jackson, Turner and Wilkinson (1972). It should further be noted that the earliest exposition (Sargan, 1964) antedated the breakdown of the Phillips curve by a number of years.

   The purpose of this chapter is to examine more closely the applicability of the real wage hypothesis to wage inflation in the UK. Section 2 presents a new formulation of the real wage hypothesis[1] and outlines the data series that are used in testing this model. Section 3 presents the results of empirical estimation of the model, and section 4 contains some concluding comments.

2. The real wage hypothesis: a new formulation

The purpose of this section is to present a new formulation of the real wage hypothesis and to test it against UK data. The model comprises two basic equations; the first determines the 'target' wage that unions seek to achieve in any period, while the second determines the rate of wage inflation, using the previously determined target wage as one of its arguments. Thus the target wage, w_t^*, for any period is assumed to be equal to the actual wage paid in the previous period, with adjustments for the desired increase in real net earnings and for price expectations:

$$w_t^* = w_{t-1} \cdot \left(\frac{p_t^{\varepsilon}}{p_{t-1}} \right)^{\beta} \cdot \left(\frac{RNE_t^*}{RNE_{t-1}} \right)^{\pi} \qquad (1)$$

where w = money wages; p = price level; RNE = real net earnings; ε and $*$ superscripts refer respectively to the expected and desired values of the variables; β and π are constants and t is the usual time subscript. Taking logarithms of equation 1 yields

$$\ln w_t^* = \ln w_{t-1} + \pi \ln RNE_t^* - \pi \ln RNE_{t-1} \\ + \beta(\ln p_t^{\varepsilon} - \ln p_{t-1}) \qquad (2)$$

The actual wage in period t, w_t, is assumed to be equal to the wage paid in the previous period, with adjustments for the difference between the target wage in the current period and the wage paid in the previous period, and for prevailing labour market conditions (proxied by the rate of unemployment $\equiv U_t$):

$$w_t = A \cdot w_{t-1} \cdot \left(\frac{w_t^*}{w_{t-1}} \right)^{\alpha} \cdot U_t^{\gamma} \cdot e^{u_t} \qquad (3)$$

Here e is the base of natural logarithms, α and γ are constants, and u_t is a white noise error. Hence:

$$\ln w_t = \ln A + \ln w_{t-1} + \alpha \ln w_t^* - \alpha \ln w_{t-1} + \gamma \ln U_t + u_t \qquad (4)$$

Substitution of equation 2 into 4 yields, after simplification:

$$\ln w_t - \ln w_{t-1} = \ln A + \alpha\pi \ln RNE_t^* - \alpha\pi \ln RNE_{t-1}$$
$$+ \alpha\beta (\ln p_t^\varepsilon - \ln p_{t-1}) + \gamma \ln U_t + u_t \qquad (5)$$

Since incomes policies have been in operation at different times in the post-war period, allowance for the effects of these policies is added to the general model of equation 5. The target wage is assumed to be uninfluenced by incomes policies, which instead have their impact within the model by influencing the rate of wage inflation given by equation 3. In this respect, incomes policies are regarded as operating in a similar manner to the level of unemployment, so that equation 3 is altered to read:

$$w_t = A \cdot w_{t-1} \cdot \left(\frac{w_t^*}{w_{t-1}}\right)^\alpha \cdot U_t^\gamma \cdot F_t^\delta \cdot e^{u_t} \qquad (6)$$

where F refers to the imposition of incomes policies, δ being a constant. Equation 5 then becomes:

$$\ln w_t - \ln w_{t-1} = \ln A + \alpha\pi \ln RNE_t^* - \alpha\pi \ln RNE_{t-1}$$
$$+ \alpha\beta(\ln p_t^\varepsilon - \ln p_{t-1}) + \gamma \ln U_t + \delta \ln F_t + u_t \qquad (7)$$

2.1. *Data*

As in other research, the data source for the dependent variable in the model is taken to be the 'all workers' index of basic weekly wage rates for all industries and services, published by the Department of Employment.

Although price expectations are not as important for the operation of 'real wage' equations as they are for Phillips curve equations — given the existence of a lagged real income term in the 'real wage' equation whereby the price level is taken into account — the role of any price term would clearly be of an expectational nature and specifically not of a 'catch-up' nature. There is a strong case, therefore, for using an expectations variable rather than the simple lagged price change that has been employed in previous estimates of real wage equations. The scheme employed here is the adaptive scheme, whereby

$$\Delta p_t^\varepsilon = (1 - \theta)\Delta p_{t-1}^\varepsilon \qquad (8)$$

where Δp refers to the rate of change of prices and θ is the adaptive parameter. When θ is set equal to unity the scheme reduces to the lagged price change variable of earlier researchers. This scheme is usually integrated into a wage equation by means of a Koyck transformation, from which the parameter θ may subsequently be calculated from the estimated equation. The difficulty with the Koyck process is that the estimating equation derived from using a Koyck transformation includes a lagged dependent variable, which raises econometric difficulties, and further it is not possible to assess the sensitivity of the result with respect to the θ parameter. An alternative method, attributable to Solow (1969), is to generate the adaptive price expectations series outside the model. Reference to equation 8 reveals that in order to generate a series using this scheme outside the estimating equation, in addition to making a choice with respect to the parameter θ, it is necessary to have some prior information about, or make certain assumptions with regard to, expected inflation for one period in order to initiate the system. The procedure adopted here is to assume that actual price change equalled expected price change, which both equalled zero, for the fourth quarter of 1947.[2] The choice for the parameter θ was made for 0·1 to 0·9 in steps of 0·1, resulting in nine separate series. The price series employed was the all-items index of retail prices.

The formulation of the real net earnings variable presents a difficulty in that the only way to proceed is to take a hypothetical individual with a given earnings level and family structure and calculate his income over time. Previous researchers (Johnston and Timbrell, 1973; Henry, Sawyer and Smith, 1976, and Henry and Ormerod, 1978) have utilised an individual in receipt of the average earnings of full-time male manual workers who is married to a full-time housewife with two children. There are two potential difficulties with this procedure.

First, is it the case that a married man with two children is a fair proxy for the whole of the tax structure over time, or was it the case that *over time* single adults (or any other family composition) paid proportionately more in tax? Inspection of the retention ratios (ratios of net to gross average earnings) for six different family structures (single adult, married couple, and married couple with one, two, three or four children respectively) obtained from the Department of Health and Social Security and graphed in fig. 9.1 indicate that there were fairly substantial relative movements in the retention ratios over the period. The trend in the ratios is very much

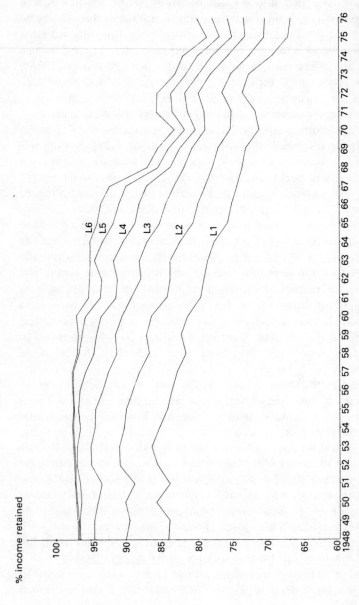

Fig. 9.1 DHSS retention ratios, 1948–76. L1, single person; L2, married couple; L3, married couple with one child; L4, married couple with two children; L5, married couple with three children; L6, married couple with four children.

the same for all family groups, and with only limited exceptions they move in the same direction for any particular year; given that, however, the clustering of families with more than one child at the beginning of the period gives way to a much wider spread by 1976, whilst there is a notable narrowing of the gaps between a single adult, a married couple and a married couple with one child. Since there is no *ex ante* preference for the choice of any particular family structure, the procedure adopted here is to employ all six measures in turn.

The second problem concerns the use of the level of average earnings. Is it the case that for two individuals, both in the same tax position, where one is in receipt of the average level of earnings and the other twice the average level, that the rate of growth of real net earnings was higher for one than for the other — i.e. was there any change in the progressivity of the tax structure? Jackson, Turner and Wilkinson (1972) have shown that there was, with those in receipt of higher-than-average earnings showing a relatively slower rate of growth of real net earnings. In all probability it is safe to assume that this effect balances out, though even this requires the assumption of similar bargaining strength across differing levels of income. In addition, since members of trade unions have varying earnings and thus varying retention ratios which might move in opposite directions, no trade union would be able to react in a specific way to changes in the retention ratio for any one level of income. In any event, it is difficult to see how any adjustment could be made, since the choice of any other earnings level would be equally arbitrary.

Given the objections to the use of a time trend to proxy the level of desired real net earnings over the estimation period, an alternative technique was sought. The approach taken here is that the level of desired real net earnings will not grow at a steady rate from one period to the next over the entire estimation period, and more particularly that the growth of desired real net earnings in any period will depend on the growth of actual real net earnings that was achieved in the recent past. Thus from the identity

$$RNE^*_{t+1} \equiv RNE^*_t + \Delta RNE^*_{t+1} \qquad (9)$$

where RNE = real net earnings, we shall hypothesise that the change in desired real net earnings, ΔRNE^*, is formed in an adaptive fashion using information on the previous growth of actual real net earnings.

$$\Delta RNE^*_{t+1} = (1 - \lambda) \Delta RNE^*_t + \lambda \Delta RNE_t \qquad (10)$$

where λ, the adaptive parameter, lies between zero and one. Substitution of equation 10 into equation 9 yields the expression for the level of desired real net earnings as

$$RNE^*_{t+1} = RNE^*_t + (1 - \lambda) \ \Delta RNE^*_t + \lambda \Delta RNE_t \qquad (11)$$

By adopting a similar procedure to that employed to generate adaptive price expectations, the various series for adaptively formed desired real net earnings were formed outside the estimating equation. The assumptions here are that actual real net earnings equalled desired real net earnings in the fourth quarter of 1948, and furthermore that the *growth* of actual real net earnings was equal to the *growth* of desired real net earnings between the third and fourth quarters of 1948. Nine values of λ were chosen, from 0·1 to 0·9 in steps of 0·1 which, combined with the six alternative real net earnings series corresponding to different family compositions, yielded fifty-four separate series for RNE^*.[3]

The methods employed to measure the influence of incomes policies are necessarily subjective to some extent. The approach taken here is to use a dummy variable for each incomes policy that was considered, *a priori*, to have had some effect on the rate of change of money wages. The choice was based on the summary table of incomes policies presented in Tarling and Wilkinson (1977), and included all those policies which were implemented on a compulsory basis, as well as some that were voluntary but had the support of a wide selection of groups involved in pay bargaining, and/or retained some statutory powers, e.g. of delay. Accordingly, five incomes policy dummies were utilised, which are set out in table 9.1.

Henry and Ormerod (1978), who utilised a real wage equation to estimate the impact of incomes policies on the rate of change of money wages, made use of catch-up dummies for periods after the *removal* of incomes policy controls. With an expected positive sign, the purpose of these dummies is to allow for the rate of wage inflation to be faster after the removal of controls than would

Table 9.1   *Incomes policy dummies*

*D*1	1966.IV–1967.II	Labour government; compulsory pay freeze (stage 2)
*D*2	1967.III–1969.II	Labour government; 'zero norm' policy, with powers of delay (stages 3 and 4)
*D*3	1972.IV–1973.I	Conservative government; compulsory pay freeze (Phase I)
*D*4	1973.II–1974.I	Conservative government; £1 + 4% (Phase 2), 7% or £2·25 plus threshold agreements (Phase 3), compulsory
*D*5	1975.III–1975.IV	Labour government; £6 maximum (Social Contract, Phase 2). Price Commission

otherwise have occurred. It is not clear, however, why these catch-up effects should be separately allowed for; within the real wage hypothesis, the motive force behind money wage increases is the existence of a discrepancy between actual and desired real net earnings increases. If the imposition of an incomes policy forces the growth of real net earnings to fall below its desired level, then unions will seek to increase real net earnings by increasing money wages when the policy lapses; but this is already allowed for in the specificiation of the real wage hypothesis, and the catch-up dummies employed by Henry and Ormerod appear superfluous and in consequence are not employed here.

3.   **Empirical results**

The best-fit results of estimating the equation

$$\ln w_t - \ln w_{t-1} = a_0 + a_1 \ln U_t + a_2(\ln p_t^{\epsilon} - \ln p_{t-1}) + a_3 \ln RNE_t^*$$
$$+ a_4 \ln RNE_{t-1} + a_5\, D1 + a_6 D2 + a_7 D3$$
$$+ a_8 D4 + a_9 D5 + \text{seasonals} + u_t$$

by ordinary least squares over the period 1950.I–1975.IV are given in table 9.2.[4] All variables are in the logarithms of their values, and

Table 9.2 'Real wage' equations utilising adaptively formed desired real net earnings and adaptively formed price expectations; best-fit results for the six DHSS real net earnings variables. Estimation period: 1950.I–1975.IV

	Constant	UR	(a)	(b)	(c)	D1	D2	D3	D4	D5	$\bar{R}^2$	DW
			P6	RNE1*8	RNE1L							
1.	0·0177 (0·90)	−0·0035 (0·84)	1·2034 (10·47)	0·8058 (4·86)	−0·7784 (4·70)	−0·0054 (0·94)	−0·0014 (0·37)	−0·0239 (3·12)	−0·0163 (2·82)	−0·0303 (3·62)	0·6791	1·7793
			P6	RNE2*8	RNE2L							
2.	0·0107 (0·56)	−0·0024 (0·59)	1·2127 (10·74)	0·8374 (5·01)	−0·8116 (4·86)	−0·0053 (0·91)	−0·0010 (0·27)	−0·0227 (3·01)	−0·0148 (2·63)	−0·0309 (3·71)	0·6811	1·7880
			P5	RNE3*8	RNE3L							
3.	−0·0105 (0·56)	0·0024 (0·58)	1·1196 (9·69)	0·3253 (3·05)	−0·3032 (2·83)	−0·0085 (1·40)	−0·0033 (0·84)	−0·0142 (1·84)	−0·0083 (1·45)	−0·0261 (3·00)	0·6380	1·8548
			P6	RNE4*8	RNE4L							
4.	0·0013 (0·07)	−0·0009 (0·23)	1·2414 (10·74)	0·8731 (4·88)	−0·8489 (4·75)	−0·0058 (0·99)	−0·0007 (0·20)	−0·0199 (2·67)	−0·0118 (2·14)	−0·0303 (3·62)	0·6752	1·7799

		P6		RNE5*8	RNE5L						
5.	0·0007	−0·0009	1·2431	0·8674	−0·8428	−0·0056	−0·0013	−0·0179	−0·0096	−0·0341	0·6687	1·7499
	(0·04)	(0·22)	(10·71)	(4·72)	(4·61)	(0·96)	(0·34)	(2·40)	(1·77)	(3·90)	

		P6		RNE6*8	RNE6L						
6.	−0·0056	0·0005	1·2349	0·7648	−0·7418	−0·0073	−0·0022	−0·0157	−0·0078	−0·0279	0·6533	1·7128
	(0·30)	(0·12)	(10·19)	(0·17)	(4·07)	(1·22)	(0·55)	(2·08)	(1·42)	(3·26)	

Notes

UR Unemployment rate.
(a)   The variables $P3$ to $P6$ refer to adaptively formed price expectations where the adaptive parameter takes a value of 0·3 to 0·6 respectively.
(b) $RNE1*8$ refers to the adaptively formed desired real net earnings variable based on a single adult with an adaptive parameter of 0·8: $RNE2*8$ refers to the adaptively formed desired real net earnings variable based on a married couple with an adaptive parameter of 0·8, etc.
(c) $RNE1L$ to $RNE6L$ refer to the six alternative real net earnings variables based on the alternative family structures and lagged one period.

t statistics are shown in parentheses. DW denotes the Durbin–Watson statistic.

are as defined in the previous section. Although seasonal dummies were included, these are not reported. The results provide strong support for the formulation of the real wage hypothesis that is presented in this chapter. In all six equations the desired real net earnings and lagged real net earnings variables are correctly signed and significantly different from zero at the 5 per cent level. Although the choice of family composition gives rise to changes in the size and significance of the coefficients on the real net earnings variables, these changes are not sufficient to undermine the stability of the formulation, and the choice of family composition would appear unimportant. The coefficient on price equations is in excess of unity for all equations, although in only two instances (equations 4 and 5, those for $RNE4$ and $RNE5$) are the coefficients significantly different from unity at the 5 per cent level. The coefficient on unemployment is invariably incorrectly signed, and always insignificantly different from zero. The coefficients on the five incomes policy dummies are correctly signed in all six equations, although the first two ($D1$ and $D2$, corresponding to 1966.IV–1967.II and 1967.III–1969.II respectively) are not statistically significant in any equation. The dummy $D2$, with t statistics consistently below unity, must be regarded as particularly unacceptable. The limited performance of $D1$ is surprising, in view of the fact that the policy to which this dummy relates succeeded in achieving a zero change in the wage rate index for the fourth quarter of 1966; this may be due to the policy's limited success in the later quarters of its operation, or to the fact that the impact was primarily through prices and thence through price expectations such that the dummy understates its influence. The reduction in the rate of wage inflation given by the coefficients on the incomes policy dummies in table 9.2 range from less than 0·32 per cent per annum ($D2$ in equation 4) to about 14 per cent per annum ($D5$ in equation 5). The average reductions for the six equations in table 9.2 are 2·52 per cent p.a. for $D1$, 0·64 per cent p.a. for $D2$, 7·68 per cent p.a. for $D3$, 4·60 per cent p.a. for $D4$ and 12·16 per cent p.a. for $D5$. Even given the limited success of $D1$ and $D2$, these results indicate a greater influence for incomes policies than the majority of econometric investigations have hitherto assigned them.

Reference to equation 7 above shows that the coefficients on RNE^* and $RNEL$ are expected to be equal in magnitude and opposite in sign. Inspection of the results in table 9·2 reveals that the coefficients are opposite in sign, and although the coefficients on the *RNE*L terms are slightly smaller than the corresponding *RNE*[*] terms, formal tests demonstrate that none is statistically different at the 5 per cent level.

It should be noted that the results reported in table 9.2 are not dependent on the inclusion of incomes policy dummies. Although the model recognises that incomes policy dummies should be included, an element of ambiguity remains, since the number and duration of the dummies are open to individual judgement. Although the overall fit declined slightly when the dummies were excluded (as was to be expected) the equations remained very satisfactory in that correctly signed and significant coefficients were produced for the real net earnings terms, and represented an improvement in that the price expectations coefficient lay closer to unity. As an example, the best-fit result for *RNE*4 (married couple with two children) yielded:

$$w_t = 0.0103 - 0.0020 \, UR + 1.0403 \, P8 + 0.9091 \, RNE4^*7$$
$$(0.57) \quad (0.51) \quad\quad (10.64) \quad\quad (4.54)$$

$$-0.8471 \, RNE4L \quad \bar{R}^2 = 0.6384 \quad\quad DW = 1.7429$$
$$(4.46)$$

An important question is whether the formulation of the real wage hypothesis presented in this chapter also applies to other periods than that ending in 1975. In consequence, the equation was estimated over two sub-periods, the first being 1950.I to 1966.IV on the basis that for this period the Phillips curve also provides an adequate explanation of wage inflation, and furthermore that there had not been any of the major disturbances in the labour market that characterised later years. The second period chosen is 1950.I to 1971.IV, when the Phillips curve had run into difficulties but inflation had not reached particularly high levels. The best-fit results for the period ending in 1971.IV are presented in table 9.3 and those for the period ending in 1966.IV in table 9.4.

With reference first to the results for 1950.I–1971.IV in table 9.3, the general conclusion is that the formulation used for the longer period applies well to this sub-period. The coefficients on the desired and lagged actual real net earnings variables are all correctly signed and significant, with the exception of the equation employing *RNE*3. (The coefficients on *RNE*3[*] and *RNE*3L only just fail to reach significance at the 5 per cent level.) The adaptive

Table 9.3 'Real wage' equations utilising adaptively formed desired real net earnings and adaptively formed price expectations; best-fit results for the six DHSS real net earnings variables. Estimation period: 1950.I–1971.IV

	Constant	UR	(a)	(b)	(c)	D1	D2	$\bar{R}^2$	DW
			P6	RNE1*7	RNE1L				
1.	0·0250 (1·38)	−0·0034 (0·90)	0·8302 (5·11)	0·4078 (2·08)	−0·3851 (2·01)	−0·0071 (1·42)	−0·0002 (0·05)	0·2610	1·5652
			P5	RNE2*7	RNE2L				
2.	0·0226 (1·31)	−0·0031 (0·86)	0·8362 (5·30)	0·4492 (2·36)	−0·4246 (2·30)	−0·0070 (1·42)	0·0000 (0·00)	0·2704	1·5734
			P5	RNE3*7	RNE3L				
3.	0·0135 (0·82)	−0·0019 (0·34)	0·7444 (5·05)	0·2031 (1·97)	−0·1890 (1·86)	−0·0076 (1·52)	−0·0002 (0·05)	0·2514	1·6722
			P5	RNE4*7	RNE4L				
4.	0·0196 (1·19)	−0·0028 (0·79)	0·8304 (5·44)	−0·4987 (2·63)	−0·4742 (2·57)	−0·0072 (1·46)	0·0003 (0·09)	0·2789	1·5686

			P6	RNE5*7	RNE5L				
5.	0·0172 (1·04)	−0·0024 (0·67)	0·8049 (5·43)	0·5535 (2·81)	−0·5324 (2·77)	−0·0067 (1·36)	0·0001 (0·04)	0·2756	1·5895
			P6	RNE6*7	RNE6L				
6.	0·0165 (0·99)	−0·0022 (0·60)	0·7845 (5·34)	0·5141 (2·66)	−0·4954 (2·61)	−0·0074 (1·49)	0·0000 (0·09)	−0·2687	1·5737

Notes

UR Unemployment rate.

(a) The variables $P3$ to $P6$ refer to adaptively formed price expectations where the adaptive parameter takes a value of 0·3 to 0·6 respectively.

(b) $RNE1*8$ refers to the adaptively formed desired real net earnings variable based on a single adult with an adaptive parameter of 0·8: $RNE2*8$ refers to the adaptively formed desired real net earnings variable based on a married couple with an adaptive parameter of 0·8, etc.

(c) $RNE1L$ to $RNE6L$ refer to the six alternative real net earnings variables based on the alternative family structures and lagged one period.

t statistics are shown in parentheses. DW denotes the Durbin–Watson statistic.

Table 9.4 'Real wage' equations utilising adaptively formed desired real net earnings and adaptively formed price expectations; best-fit results for the six DHSS real net earnings variables. Estimation period: 1950.I–1966.IV

	Constant	UR	(a)	(b)	(c)	D1	$\bar{R}^2$	DW
1.			P3	RNE1*6	RNE1L			
	0·0610 (3·08)	-0·0108 (2·65)	0·5221 (2·23)	0·1093 (0·51)	-0·1112 (0·53)	-0·0071 (0·93)	0·2365	1·7421
2.			P3	RNE2*7	RNE2L			
	0·0603 (3·13)	-0·0107 (2·73)	0·5685 (2·34)	0·1491 (0·83)	-0·1470 (0·85)	-0·0072 (0·93)	0·2422	1·7399
3.			P3	RNE3*8	RNE3L			
	0·0603 (3·18)	-0·0108 (2·81)	0·5649 (2·56)	0·1199 (1·45)	-0·1226 (1·51)	-0·0072 (0·95)	0·2615	1·8235
4.			P4	RNE4*7	RNE4L			
	0·0570 (2·95)	-0·0100 (2·56)	0·5385 (2·59)	0·2646 (1·44)	-0·2611 (1·47)	-0·0070 (0·91)	0·2560	1·7576

			P4	RNE5*7	RNE5L			
				RNE6*6	RNE6L			
5.	0·0579 (3·01)	−0·0103 (2·63)	0·5549 (2·67)	0·2963 (1·61)	−0·2928 (1·64)	−0·0067 (0·88)	0·2027	1·7578
6.	0·0617 (3·16)	−0·0109 (2·72)	0·4864 (2·52)	0·3083 (1·48)	−0·3112 (1·51)	−0·0065 (0·86)	0·2587	1·7460

Notes

UR   Unemployment rate.

(a)   The variables P3 to P6 refer to adaptively formed price expectations where the adaptive parameter takes a value of 0·3 to 0·6 respectively.

(b)   RNE1*8 refers to the adaptively formed desired real net earnings variable based on a single adult with an adaptive parameter of 0·8: RNE2*8 refers to the adaptively formed desired real net earnings variable based on a married couple with an adaptive parameter of 0·8, etc.

(c)   RNE1L to RNE6L refer to the six alternative real net earnings variables based on the alternative family structures and lagged one period.

t statistics are shown in parentheses. DW denotes the Durbin–Watson statistic.

parameter employed in the desired real net earnings variables takes a value of 0·7 for the best-fit equations for this sub-period, as against 0·8 for the whole period, which may be accounted for by the greater variability of real net earnings in the later years, although it may also be attributable to the increased frequency of settlements during the 1970s — an individual who receives settlements more frequently is in a position to make more use of recent data on which to base his wage claim. Additionally, more rapid inflation (in particular) may have given rise to faster computing generally during the 1970s. The adaptive parameter employed in the price expectations variable is either 0·5 or 0·6, which is identical to the results for the whole period; the coefficient, with an average value of 0·8, does, however, suggest less than complete compensation for expected price change. Only two incomes policy dummies are applicable to this sub-period; the first, $D1$ (1966.IV to 1967.II), is always correctly signed, but insignificant with a t statistic of around 1·4. The second, $D2$, was always very close to zero. Overall it is clear that the formulation of the real wage hypothesis employed here also provides a satisfactory explanation of wage inflation for the period ending in 1971.IV.

Turning now to the results for the estimation period 1950.I to 1966.IV in table 9.4, it is apparent that these results are much less supportive of the real wage hypothesis. In the first place, unemployment is always correctly signed and significantly different from zero at the 5 per cent level, providing a measure of support for the Phillips curve; additionally, although the desired and lagged actual real net earnings terms are always correctly signed, they are not statistically significant, and the t ratio lies below unity on occasion. As regards other aspects of the equations, it may be noted that both the coefficient on price expectations and the adaptive parameter employed in the construction of those price expectations variables are lower than those for the longer estimation period, but would be consistent with the relatively low levels of inflation experienced prior to 1966.IV.

A severe test of any wage equation lies in its ability to forecast the rate of wage inflation for observations lying outside the estimation period, and we turn now to examine the ability of the equations estimated over the period 1950.I to 1975.IV, as reported in table 9.2, to forecast the rate of wage inflation for the two years 1976 and 1977. In making the forecasts it was assumed that the incomes policy dummy for the third and fourth quarter of 1975 applied throughout 1976 and 1977. Owing to the close similarity of the equations in table 9.2 the prediction results given in table 9.5 and discussed here are for only one representative equation, that of *RNE*4. It is apparent that the equation underpredicts for the first three quarters and overpredicts for the remaining five. However, these figures yield an average actual value of the quarterly rate of wage inflation of 2·43 per cent, and a forecast value of 2·12 per cent, leaving an average underprediction of 0·31 per cent. In view of the marked changes in the actual rate of wage inflation, an average underprediction of 0·31 per cent must be considered a very satisfactory result.[5]

It should be noted that we have assumed that the incomes policy that applied for the last two quarters of 1975 also applied for 1976 and 1977, whereas this is not strictly the case; the £6 maximum of Phase 2 of the Social Contract gave way to the 5 per cent (with a minimum of £2·50 and maximum of £4) rule of Phase 3 during 1976. Although these were both voluntary policies, they were sufficiently distinct to merit separate incomes policy dummies in an estimating equation extending to the last quarter of 1977. There is a possibility, therefore, that taking these policies as being the same is giving rise to some of the overall underprediction and, more especially, to the pattern of the errors; on this basis, the coefficient on the incomes policy dummy *D*5 in the estimated equation (based as it is on only two observations) is overstating the impact of Phase 2 of the Social Contract and generating the underprediction for the first three quarters of 1976 evident in table 9.5. In consequence Phase 3 of the Social Contract would be regarded as particularly effective, since use of the coefficient on *D*5 in the estimated equation generates an overprediction of the rate of wage inflation in those quarters.

4. **Conclusion**

In summary, therefore, we may conclude that the specification of the real wage hypothesis employed in this chapter, incorporating adaptively formed desired real net earnings, provides a stable and robust explanation of the rate of change of the index of money wage rates for the UK for data periods ending in 1971 and 1975. For the data period ending in 1976 the support for the specification

Table 9.5   *Forecast rates of change of money wages using RNE4 equation,*
1976–77 (quarterly percentage rates of change)

	Actual value	Forecast value	Forecast error
1976.I	6·07	2·73	3·34
1976.II	3·52	2·09	1·43
1976.III	2·98	1·75	1·23
1976.IV	0·69	1·80	−1·11
1977.I	1·82	2·58	−0·76
1977.II	1·59	2·45	−0·86
1977.III	1·45	2·06	−0·61
1977.IV	1·32	1·49	−0·17

employed is less marked, and, given the success of previous
empirical estimates of the real wage hypothesis (e.g. Sargan, 1964,
1971, Gillion, 1968), thereby represents a worsening of explanatory
power, although this latter group of results was also supportive of
the Phillips curve hypothesis. Thus these results — though not
unambiguous — would not be inconsistent with the view that over
the post-war period the determinants of wage change have altered,
the influence of 'market forces' (excess demand/supply inherent in
the Phillips curve) becoming weaker and bargaining power a more
important influence. In this sense they support the view that the
inflation of the late 1960s and onwards represents something 'new'.

Notes

1   For a survey of the more important theoretical and empirical
    contributions to the literature on the real wage hypothesis see
    chapter 7.
2   Since observations prior to the first quarter of 1950 are not
    employed, by the very nature of the adaptive expectations scheme an
    assumption of any reasonable positive rate of expected inflation for
    the fourth quarter of 1947 would have very little impact on
    observations for the first quarter of 1950 and following.
3   As with the generation of adaptive price expectations, any error
    introduced by assuming $RNE = RNE^*$ and $\Delta RNE = \Delta RNE^*$ for the
    fourth quarter of 1948 would have been rendered insignificant when
    the first quarter of 1950 was reached.

4   All regressions reported in this chapter were run at the University of Manchester Regional Computer Centre, using the ordinary least squares package REGRESS, written by E. J. R. Horler.

5   A formal test of parameter stability using the actual future values of the regressors for the k quarters after the end of the estimation period is given by

$$z(k) = \sum_{t=T+1}^{T+k} (f_t/\hat{\sigma})^2$$

which would be distributed as χ^2 if the parameters of equation 4 in table 9.2 remained constant, where f_t = forecast error in period t, $\hat{\sigma}$ = standard error of the residuals and T = last quarter of the estimation period (see Davidson *et al.*, 1978, p. 674). Calculating $z(k)$ for the forecasts for the eight quarters of 1976 and 1977 made by equation 4 of table 9.2 leads to a value of 17·52, which is slightly in excess of the critical value of $\chi^2(8)$ of 15·51 (at the 5 per cent significance level). This leads us to reject the hypothesis of parameter stability with respect to those observations; in the light of the comments in the following paragraph in the text regarding adequacy of the incomes policy dummies, however, this should not be considered particularly damaging. The test is not able to reject the hypothesis of parameter stability at the 1 per cent level.

Prices and inflation

Pricing behaviour — a survey

1.   Introduction

There has been considerably less theoretical and empirical work on the proximate determinants of prices than of wages. Indeed, much research on price formation has been empirical, with relatively little attention being given to developing the underlying theory. In view of this we feel it is useful to review two broad areas. The first part of this survey is concerned with the relationship between market structure and pricing behaviour. It discusses how models should be specified to test both the influence of concentration on price–cost margins and on the price adjustment process, and this is followed by a critical examination of some representative pieces of econometric work in this area. The second part is primarily empirical and discusses some attempts to model the price equation for UK manufacturing industry. Within the framework of mark-up models the effect of demand on price–cost margins is examined. We also review empirical tests of the expectations-augmented excess demand model.

2.   Pricing behaviour and industrial market structure

The impact of market structure on the behaviour of prices has been hotly debated by economists for nearly half a century. Central to the debate has been the well known 'administered prices' hypothesis first promulgated by Gardiner Means in the 1930s. In its original formulation the administered prices hypothesis was about price rigidity. Means (1935) noted that in the US during the 1930s a large number of industrial prices changed relatively infrequently and also displayed marked stickiness in the downward direction.

Means labelled such prices 'administered', as opposed to 'market dominated', but the inherently tautological nature of this definition has been the source of much confusion ever since.

During the 1950s the hypothesis re-emerged in an entirely different form when it was suggested that administrative pricing behaviour in the US was responsible for inflationary pressures. In a recent restatement Means (1972) went further to claim that underlying the phenomenon of simultaneous inflation and recession is the perverse, i.e. counter-cyclical, behaviour of administered prices. This administered inflation hypothesis, as it has come to be known, is outlined by Means (1959) as follows:

In the beginning of a demand inflation market dominated prices tend to rise more rapidly while administration dominated prices lag well behind. Then, in a period of readjustment, market dominated prices fall back while administration dominated prices continue·to rise ... [1]

We have already noted the circularity in the definition of administered prices. In his later writings Means suggested that such pricing behaviour was to be found in concentrated industries where firms possessed some degree of market power.[2] Nonetheless the curious behaviour of prices, described in the above quotation, defies conventional theoretical explanations. It does, however, highlight the question of time lags, on which conventional theory is conspicuously silent, and it has been in the context of lags and catch-up processes that the hypothesis has been most commonly discussed. More recently the question of adjustment lags has also been receiving greater attention in the macroeconomic literature. In this context it is now commonplace to distinguish between 'fix-price' markets, in which prices are sluggish and the brunt of adjustment to changes in demand is taken by quantities, and 'flex-price' markets in which prices adjust more quickly than quantities. It is clear, therefore, that the administered prices controversy, which has primarily been the concern of industrial economists, has wider macroeconomic implications.

Although countless statistical tests of the administered inflation hypothesis have been conducted by different authors in several countries and covering a variety of time periods, the results have been largely inconclusive. Moreover conflicting claims have been made on the basis of the different findings and it is fair to say that the fundamental issues remain unresolved. In what follows it will be suggested that much of the confusion surrounding this controversy stems from the lack of an adequate theoretical framework and, associated with it, the *ad hoc* nature of the empirical analysis.

By invoking a theory of oligopoly pricing which is firmly rooted in the neo-classical tradition it can be shown that many, if not most, of the standard statistical tests of the administered inflation hypothesis have been essentially misspecified. It follows that the large number of conflicting results are susceptible to explanation, and this will be illustrated by reference to specific findings. Before doing that, however, we shall examine the theoretical relationship between prices and market structure.

2.1. *Pricing in oligopolistic industry*
It is a well documented feature of the modern industrialised economy that the manufacturing sector is almost entirely oligopolistic in character. The appropriate framework of analysis is, therefore, neither that of perfect competition nor of monopoly but of oligopoly. The problem inherent in such analysis, however, is the thorny question of oligopolistic interdependence and how it should be taken into account in the decision-making process of firms. Fortunately there is a tractable and plausible approach, first suggested by Cowling and Waterson (1976) and subsequently adopted by Hannah and Kay (1977). This approach is based on the Cournot–Nash solution to oligopoly, underlying which is the assumption that firms maximise profits independently of their rivals, i.e. there is no collusion, but take their (profit-maximising) output decisions as given.[3] To examine the nature of industry equilibrium under these assumptions, consider the profit-maximising decision of a representative firm i, whose profits are given by:

$$\pi_i = Px_i - c_i x_i \qquad (1)$$

where π = profits, P = price,[4] x = output, c = unit variable costs.
Deriving the first-order condition for a maximum, we have:

$$\frac{\partial \pi}{\partial x_i} = P - c_i + x_i \frac{\mathrm{d}P}{\mathrm{d}X} \frac{\mathrm{d}X}{\mathrm{d}x_i} = 0 \qquad (2)$$

where $X = \Sigma x_i$ is total industry output.

Setting $dX/dx_i = 1$, which holds in equilibrium, summing over all firms in the industry and rearranging terms yields:

$$PX - \Sigma c_i x_i - PX \left(- \frac{X}{P} \frac{dP}{dX} \right) \Sigma \left(\frac{x_i}{X} \right)^2 = 0 \qquad (3)$$

This can be rewritten as:

$$\frac{PX - \Sigma c_i x_i}{PX} = \frac{H}{\eta} \qquad (4)$$

where

$$H = \Sigma \left(\frac{x_i}{X} \right)^2$$

is the Herfindahl index of concentration,[5] and

$$\eta = - \frac{P}{X} \frac{dX}{dP}$$

is the industry price elasticity of demand. Equation 4 describes a theoretical relationship between the industry average price–cost margin and market structure. It can be seen that the margin is positively related to the degree of seller concentration as defined by H, and inversely related to the price elasticity of demand, η.

This expression defines the static equilibrium result but says nothing about how it is achieved or restored following an exogenous disturbance such as an increase in costs. It may appropriately be viewed as describing the long-run industry equilibrium. To accommodate short-run adjustment behaviour into this framework, we introduce the familiar partial adjustment process, whereby the price change in the current period is given as some fraction of the total change required to restore equilibrium, i.e.:

$$(P_t - P_{t-1}) = \lambda \, (P_t^* - P_{t-1}) \qquad (5)$$

where P_t^* is the equilibrium price in period t and $0 < \lambda \le 1$. Thus the industry equilibrium price is gradually attained over time as firms acquire information relating to costs, demand and their rivals' responses to changes in these variables. This clearly implies that price adjustments are not costless.[6]

To obtain the equilibrium price which is implicit in equation 4 we start by dividing the left-hand side of the equation by $X = \Sigma x_i$, which redefines the price–cost margin as:

$$\frac{P - \Sigma c_i x_i / \Sigma x_i}{P} = \frac{H}{\eta} \tag{6}$$

Now, if we assume constant marginal costs across all firms in the industry so that average costs, c_i, equal marginal costs, then it is clear that the expression $\Sigma c_i x_i / \Sigma x_i$ is simply a weighted mean (weighted by firms' output) of the firms' marginal costs. Denoting this by MC and rearranging equation 6 yields the industry equilibrium price:

$$P^* = \left(\frac{1}{1 - \gamma} \right) MC \tag{7}$$

where $\gamma = H/\eta$. The term $1/(1-\gamma)$ is the multiplicative mark-up on marginal costs. Hence equation 7 bears a close resemblance to the standard mark-up model of pricing except that it specifies a *different* mark-up across industries, depending on structural characteristics of the supply side and the corresponding price elasticity of demand. Substituting equation 7 into equation 5 and rearranging yields:

$$P_t = \lambda \left(\frac{1}{1 - \gamma} \right) MC_t + (1 - \lambda) P_{t-1} \tag{8}$$

Finally, assuming a fixed-coefficients production function with labour and raw materials as inputs[7] enables us to disaggregate MC and write equation 8 as:

$$P_t = \lambda \left(\frac{1}{1-\gamma} \right) \alpha_1 PM_t + \lambda \left(\frac{1}{1-\gamma} \right) \alpha_2 PL_t + (1-\lambda) P_{t-1} \tag{9}$$

where $\Sigma \alpha = 1$ is the sum of the fixed-coefficient weights, PM is a material inputs price index, and PL is an index of unit labour costs.

It can be seen that equation 9 incorporates both the long-run mark-up relationship and the short-run adjustment process. Market structure influences the former through γ and may also influence the latter through the size of λ by determining the speed with which industry equilibrium is restored.[8] What is crucial to note, however, is that in either case the impact of industrial structure on prices operates essentially through the mark-up coefficients, which is also true of the price elasticity of demand, η.

This conclusion would not be altered if we relaxed our assumption of a linear fixed-coefficients production function. For example, if we assume a Cobb–Douglas production function and redefine the partial adjustment process as a multiplicative relationship which, expressed in logarithms, becomes:

$$(\ln P_t - \ln P_{t-1}) = \lambda(\ln P_t^* - \ln P_{t-1}), \tag{10}$$

then equation 9 above would be specified as:

$$\ln P_t = \lambda \ln \left(\frac{1}{1-\gamma} \right) + \lambda\alpha_1 \ln PM_t + \lambda\alpha_2 \ln PL_t + (1-\lambda) \ln P_{t-1} \tag{11}$$

In this equation the mark-up coefficient appears as a constant term, assuming both market structure and the price elasticity of demand to be fixed through time. The structural coefficients on labour costs and input prices are now simply the corresponding weights, α_1 and α_2, of these inputs in marginal costs.

Whatever assumption is made about the nature of the technical input-output relations in the industry, there is clearly an appropriate theoretical specification for testing the relationship between pricing behaviour and industrial structure. The importance of adhering to such a specification is highlighted in the context of cross-section regressions based on a sample of industries, since both equations 9 and 11 indicate that each industry will have a different mark-up over costs so that one is confronted with a varying-parameter model.[9] The empirical tests carried out to date have largely ignored the theoretical considerations outlined above, and this has serious implications regarding the interpretation of the results.

2.2. *Pricing behaviour and market structure: some econometric tests*

Neither the administered inflation hypothesis nor its empirical tests have distinguished meaningfully between long-run equilibri.. relationships and short-run adjustment lags. What researchers have generally done is to relate price movements to measures of concentration over fairly long time periods defined by reference to the trade cycle. This reflects attempts to identify upswings in the cycle and thus to test the impact of concentration specifically in the manner suggested by Means. The usual time period has been four years or even longer, but some experiments with annual price changes have recently been conducted by Lustgarten (1975). The tests spanning the longer periods would, had they been correctly specified, capture the long-run equilibrium relationships, whereas the annual price equations would involve some disequilibrium observations. In this latter case the estimated coefficients would be hybrids of the structural and lag parameters.[10]

The typical functional relation employed in these econometric estimates is as follows:

$$\frac{P_{jt}}{P_{jt-k}} = a_1 + a_2 \frac{PM_{jt}}{PM_{jt-k}} + a_3 \frac{PL_{jt}}{PL_{jt-k}} + a_4 CR_{jt} + e \qquad (12)$$

where *CR* is an index of concentration and $j = 1 \ldots n$ counts over industries. It must be emphasised that this is essentially a combined time series and cross-section regression, in which the ratio of prices in period t to those in period $t-k$ (where k may be one or more years) for a sample of different industries is regressed against corresponding changes in variable costs and the level of concentration, which varies, at a point in time, across industries. It is also evident that equation 12 bears no relationship to the specification derived from the theoretical model.

Specifically there are three separate problems with such an equation. First, it relates price *changes* to concentration *levels*, whereas the analysis indicates that, *ceteris paribus*, a given level of concentration determines a given price level. If we are to relate inflation, i.e. price changes, to market structure, then the appropriate specification calls for these to be related to *changes* in concentration.

Second, it assumes a uniform response to concentration across the entire industry samples, whereas our analysis shows that the impact of *CR* on prices is conditional on the price elasticity of demand η. Thus equation 12 effectively assumes an identical ısticity for all industries, which is hardly tenable. Any estimates of the impact of concentration on prices will therefore be biased.

Finally, the lags in this relationship are not modelled in any explicit way notwithstanding the fact that the equation is fitted to different, pre-selected time periods. Clearly this makes it virtually impossible to distinguish empirically between the long-run equilibrium relationships and the short-run adjustment processes.

We now examine some of the empirical findings which are based on this methodology. Most tests of the administered inflation hypothesis, up to the present, have used North American data. Although there are some findings for the EEC which follow the specification given by equation 12, e.g. Phlips (1971), no such results are available for the UK . Consequently for purposes of evaluation we report in table 10.1 the findings of three different US

Table 10.1 *Pricing behaviour and concentration: some previous results*

Author	Time period	$\hat{a}_4$	Sample
Weiss (1966)	1953–59	0·085 (2·50)	US, unweighted cost variables
	1959–63	−0·013 (0·619)	
Dalton (1973)	1958–63	0·112 (2·29)	US, weighted[*] cost variables
Lustgarten (1975)	1958–59	0·010 (1·000)	US, unweighted cost variables
	1959–60	−0·002 (0·200)	
	1961–62	−0·007 (−0·875)	
	1962–63	0·001 (0·083)	

[*] Weighting essentially involves rescaling the cost variables.

Source: Lustgarten (1975), *t* ratios in parentheses.

studies which have used the same functional form and covered
similar time periods.

The study by Weiss (1966) was the first to use an equation such as
12 which allows changes in costs as well as market structure to
influence prices. Weiss found a positive and statistically significant
impact of concentration for the period 1953–59, but a negative and
insignificant relationship for 1959–63. Dalton (1973) on the other
hand, also using US data and an almost identical time period, i.e.
1958–63, discovered a large positive *and* significant impact of
concentration.

In contrast, Lustgarten (1975) proceeded to test the relationship
for individual years within the 1958–63 time period.[11] Although he
found the impact of concentration to be consistently insignificant,
the coefficients exhibit reversals in sign both at the beginning and at
the end of the period. These results are reproduced as the last four
rows in table 10.1.

The above is but a small sample of the extensive empirical tests
which have been undertaken along similar lines. They serve,
nonetheless, as an illustration of the ambiguities and contradictions
which have bedevilled this methodology. Lustgarten (1975) is
clearly aware of its potential dangers when he states, referring to
the 'administered prices' hypothesis, that:

> ... neither the length of the lag, nor its point of origin are well specified by
> the theory. The result is that in analysing price change over some period,
> one can never be certain, whether the period encompasses the effect of the
> lag the catch up or some combination of both.[12]

Perhaps the most surprising aspect of the debate is the fact that
contradictory findings have been interpreted as being consistent
with the hypothesis. For example, both Weiss (1966) and Dalton
(1973) interpreted their dissimilar findings of the influence of
concentration on price changes during 1958–63 as lending support
to the administered inflation hypothesis.

2.3. *An alternative methodology*

In the previous section we criticised the approach to the analysis of
pricing behaviour and market structure which has evolved through
attempts to test the administered prices hypothesis. Our criticisms
were twofold. First, this approach does not proceed from a

recognisable theoretical framework to derive a link between equilibrium price levels and industrial structure. We argued that such a link can be derived from a theory of oligopoly. Second, the treatment of short-run adjustment lags in pricing behaviour is unsatisfactory because, given this approach, they cannot be separately identified and become enmeshed in the long-run equilibrium relations.

If meaningful empirical results are to be obtained a different approach is required. The long-run relationship between market structure and price–cost margins has been tested within the framework discussed in this chapter by Cowling and Waterson (1976), and their results confirm the prediction given by equation 4. They found a positive and statistically significant relationship between changes in price–cost margins and changes in concentration for a large sample of UK manufacturing industries over a five-year period. The estimated elasticity coefficient was found to be 0·25, which means that doubling concentration would raise price–cost margins by 25 per cent. Assuming the average margin to be 0·15 in the base period,[13] this would imply a rise to 0·188 with a corresponding rise of the mark-up over cost, $1/(1-\gamma)$, from 1·18 to 1·23. Thus a doubling of concentration would raise the price level, holding costs and demand elasticity constant, by some 4 per cent, which is clearly a modest increase. This estimate is supported by the recent results of Hart and Clarke (1980), who found an elasticity of price changes with respect to changes in concentration of 0·045 over a five-year period (1968–73) with UK data.[14] Thus doubling concentration would raise prices, *ceteris paribus*, by only 4·5 per cent.

The next question which needs examining within this framework is the relationship between concentration and the speed of price adjustment. Clearly such a relationship, which would operate through the size of λ, would influence the distribution of price changes over time and not the absolute amount of the change, which is determined by the structural coefficients of the price equations. In chapter 12 we shall consider the influence of concentration on the rate of price adjustment and draw inferences concerning the short-run rates of inflation, exogenously determined by cost increases, under different concentration regimes.

3.   The proximate determinants of prices in the UK

Much of the empirical work on the proximate determinants of UK prices may conveniently be divided into two broad areas: explanations of the price of output and of retail prices. A further distinction can also be made between mark-up models and expectations-augmented excess demand models. The latter distinction is not wholly precise, as often demand variables have merely been added as additional regressors in mark-up models, and since expectational variables have been proxied by lagged values of actual variables (for example, Lipsey and Parkin, 1970) then some mark-up models have an expectations-augmented excess demand interpretation, although there have been few serious attempts to subject that hypothesis to rigorous investigation.

3.1.   *Mark-up models*
Studies of the determinants of the price of firms' output have attempted to answer two main questions. Do output prices respond to actual costs or to normal costs? Given that costs affect prices, does demand exert some additional direct influence other than indirectly through factor prices? Neild's 1963 monograph was the first published study in which the two questions were investigated using econometric methods, and as much of the literature on UK price equations is to some extent based on Neild's work it is helpful to begin with his study.

   Neild was concerned with, among other things, assessing the validity of the Godley hypothesis that '... so long as the long term trend of productivity can be projected, prices can be forecast simply by reference to that trend and to a figure for the change in wages (and a figure for the change in any intermediate inputs into the sector considered)'.[15] It was hypothesised that price was set as a mark-up over prime costs per unit of output, C, plus a fixed absolute amount:

$$P_t = \alpha_0 + \alpha_1 C_t \tag{13}$$

Prime costs comprise only unit labour (W) and materials costs, including fuel (MF). Because of behavioural and institutional characteristics of firms' pricing policies and since aggregate manufacturing was effectively treated as a single firm (in effect aggregating over industrial sectors representing successive stages in the production process). Neild used distributed lag functions of the prime cost variables:

$$C_t = \beta_1 \bar{W}_t + \beta_2 M\bar{F}_t \tag{14}$$

where:

$$\bar{W}_t = (1-\lambda)W_t + (1-\lambda)\lambda W_{t-1} + (1-\lambda)\lambda^2 W_{t-2} + \ldots$$

$$M\bar{F}_t = \mu_0 MF_t + \mu_1 MF_{t-1} + \mu_2(1-\lambda)MF_{t-2} + \mu_2(1-\lambda)\lambda MF_{t-3} + \ldots$$

The estimating equation is therefore:

$$P_t = \alpha_0(1-\lambda) + \alpha_1\beta_1(1-\lambda)W_t + \alpha_1\beta_2\mu_0 MF_t + \alpha_1\beta_2(\mu_1-\lambda\mu_0)MF_{t-1}$$
$$+ \alpha_1\beta_2\{(1-\lambda)\mu_2 - \lambda\mu_2\}MF_{t-2} + \lambda P_{t-1} \tag{15}$$

To provide estimates of labour costs Neild tried three labour productivity measures through three different labour cost variables:

(i) Actual hourly earnings divided by current productivity (measured in man-hours), W_a/Q.

(ii) Standard hourly earnings divided by a compound growth rate, $W_s/(1 + r/100)^{t/4}$, $r = 2\frac{1}{2}$ per cent per annum.[16]

(iii) As an alternative to (ii), an attempt was made to estimate the productivity trend using the approximation:

$$\frac{W_s}{(1+q)^t} \simeq W_s(1-qt) = W_s - qtW_s$$

and introducing the additional variable $W_s t$ into the regression in order to estimate the trend parameter, q.

Neild added the usual error term to equation 15 and estimated the model by ordinary least squares for UK manufacturing excluding food, drink and tobacco for 1950.I–1960.IV and 1953.I–1960.IV. Neild's preferred model was one having the labour cost variable specified as (ii). The results obtained by imposing a given productivity trend were superior to those obtained in attempting to estimate such a trend using (iii). Typical of his results for the period 1950.I–1960.IV is:

$$P_t = 0 \cdot 044 + 0 \cdot 141 \, \frac{W_s}{(1 \cdot 025)^{t/4}} + 0 \cdot 106 \, MF_t + 0 \cdot 065 \, MF_{t-1}$$
$$\quad [2 \cdot 75] \quad [5 \cdot 64] \qquad\qquad\quad [7 \cdot 57] \qquad\qquad [3 \cdot 10]$$

$$-0 \cdot 037 \, MF_{t-2} + 0 \cdot 683 \, P_{t-1} \qquad\qquad R^2 = 0 \cdot 998$$
$$\quad [1 \cdot 95] \qquad\qquad [14.2]$$

Because of significant positive first-order serial correlation in the residuals, Neild added current cumulative excess demand,

$$\sum_{i=0}^{\infty} d_{t-i}$$

in which d_t is the Dicks Mireaux–Dow index of excess demand for labour, directly to equation 15, with $W_s/(1 \cdot 025)^{t/4}$ as the labour cost variable. The regression results were not reported, although it was stated that for 1953.I–1960.IV the estimated coefficient on the demand variable was negative, but insignificantly different from zero, and for 1950.I–1960.IV it was negative and significant.

Rushdy and Lund (1967) criticised Neild's work on two grounds: his interpretation of his results and the way in which he introduced the demand variable into the estimating equation because of autocorrelation. They reformulated the model in price changes rather than price levels.

Rushdy and Lund argued that Neild's preferred labour cost variable, standard hourly earnings divided by the long-run productivity trend, is not defined in a meaningful way because it implies that at any point in time manufacturers are aware of the productivity trend for the entire estimation period and set prices according to the distributed lag of unit wage costs implied by the trend. They showed, using Neild's data, that the level of demand and output per man hour are positively correlated over the cycle. This is implicit in Neild's work. He found that the inertia of businessmen in hiring and firing labour over the cycle will give the labour productivity variable a pattern similar to that of real output over the cycle. Such a pattern will also follow that of demand, and hence productivity could be a proxy for the demand for products.[17] Given this, the use of an exogenously determined productivity trend will implicitly introduce the level of demand into the pricing relationship. If, when demand is high, current productivity (Q) is greater than its trend level, i.e. Q is high, $W_s/(1 \cdot 025)^{t/4} > W_d/Q$ and unit labour costs will be overstated. Similarly, when demand is low and Q is less than its trend level, unit labour costs will be understated. Hence the reason why formulation (ii) is superior to (i) is that the former implicitly includes the level of demand.

Rushdy and Lund also criticised Neild's procedure of simply 'adding on' an unweighted index of cumulative excess demand to the estimating equation. For, if cumulative excess demand is added to the *structural* equation (as in equation 17 below), it should enter the estimating equation in the same weighted way as labour costs, i.e. as

$$(1-\lambda) \sum_{i=0}^{\infty} \bar{d}_{t-i} = (1-\lambda)\,[(d_t+d_{t-1}+d_{t-2}+ \ldots) + \lambda(d_{t-1}+d_{t-2}+ \ldots) \\ + \lambda^2(d_{t-2}+ \ldots) + \ldots]$$

$$= (1-\lambda)\,[d_t+(d_{t-1}+\lambda d_{t-1}) + (d_{t-2}+\lambda d_{t-2}+\lambda^2 d_{t-2}) + \ldots]$$

$$= (1-\lambda)\,[d_t+(1+\lambda)d_{t-1} + (1+\lambda+\lambda^2)d_{t-2} + \ldots] \qquad (16)$$

Thus Neild's procedure (since $0 < \lambda < 1$) amounted to the proposition that excess demand enters the structural equation with *increasing* weights.

Rushdy and Lund considered there were advantages in studying price changes. They were primarily concerned with inflation, and the ranking of models' abilities to predict P_t may be different from that of those predicting P_t-P_{t-1}. Their dependent variable, however, was the first difference. Using first differences rather than percentage rates of change seems questionable, since the level of excess demand is, in general, a trendless variable, whilst the levels of prices, labour costs and the costs of materials and fuel have rising trends. The effect of first differences is to associate a given level of excess demand with, for example, a 5 per cent increase in prices at a specific point in time but only a $2\frac{1}{2}$ per cent increase in prices later in time when prices have doubled. If in fact proportional changes are the appropriate specification, then first differences of levels will decrease the role of the trendless excess demand variable.

Rushdy and Lund used four alternative lag distributions of costs with eight demand formulations. Their estimated coefficients were sensitive to the choice of included variables. They found that the most appropriate demand variable to include with ΔP_t as the dependent variable was d_{t-1}. However, the constant, often having a point estimate of $0\cdot4$, was frequently significantly different from zero, typically for 1950.I–1960.IV:

$$\Delta P_t = 0.581 + 0.159 \, \Delta \frac{W_s}{(1.025)^{t/4}} t - 0.051 \, \Delta \frac{W_s}{(1.025)^{t/4}} t - 1 + 0.072 \, \Delta MF_t$$
$$\quad [3.54] \quad [1.99] \qquad\qquad\qquad [0.615] \qquad\qquad\qquad [3.79]$$

$$+ \, 0.156 \, \Delta MF_{t-1} + 1.207 \, d_{t-1} \qquad \bar{R}^2 = 0.840, \, \text{VN} = 1.039$$
$$\quad [8.21] \qquad\qquad [4.02]$$

Johnston (1967) commented that the use of the cumulative demand variable in a price-level equation might be plausible if it was the only explanatory variable; but since Neild was relating current prices to recent costs, any additional demand influence on the price–cost margin would probably be due to current, or very recent, levels of demand. The cumulative index could be at a high level and declining when excess demand was relatively low, and on Neild's formulation this would be expected to result in a greater profit margin than, say, a much lower level of the cumulative index, even though, at this low level, current demand might be high.

However, Neild, Rushdy and Lund, and McCallum (1970) all consider that the cumulative level of demand is the appropriate form for a price-level equation.[18] Although Rushdy and Lund criticised Neild for entering the demand variable directly into the reduced form equation rather than into the structural equation, they presented no estimates of the more appropriate model. If cumulative demand and the random error enter the structural equation, that is, if

$$P_t = \alpha_0 + \alpha_1\beta_1\bar{W}_t + \alpha_1\beta_2 M\bar{F}_t + \alpha_2 \sum_{i=0}^{\infty} d_{t-i} + u_t \qquad (17)$$

then the estimating equation becomes:

$$P_t = \alpha_0(1-\lambda) + \alpha_1\beta_1(1-\lambda)W_t + \alpha_1\beta_2\mu_0 MF_t + \alpha_1\beta_2(\mu_1-\lambda\mu_0)MF_{t-1}$$

$$+ \, \alpha_1\beta_2\{(1-\lambda)\mu_2 - \lambda\mu_1\}MF_{t-2} + \lambda P_{t-1} \, \alpha_2 d_t$$

$$+ \, \alpha_2(1-\lambda) \sum_{i=1}^{\infty} d_{t-i} + u_t - \lambda u_{t-1} \qquad (18)$$

It is expected that $\alpha_2 > 0$ and the coefficient on

$$\sum_{i=1}^{\infty} d_{t-i}$$

is positive and smaller in magnitude than that on d_t. Clearly it would be useful to have estimates of such a model.

Williamson (1967) has produced estimates of the indirect effect of demand on prices, based on work by Kalecki which considered the price-fixing policy of a profit-maximising firm in an oligopolistic market. Demand enters Williamson's model through the proposition that the height of the demand curve for an imperfectly competitive firm is proportional to the price of goods of competing firms. Williamson follows Neild in assuming the latter's cost structure and obtains an estimating equation which is identical to Neild's apart from the inclusion of a lagged price variable, P_{t-2}, and the exclusion of the constant. Williamson estimates an equation identical to Neild's but with the inclusion of P_{t-2} and finds for two periods, 1950.I–1960.IV and 1950.III–1960.IV, that the constant is insignificantly different from zero, as expected, MF_{t-1} is insignificant at the 5 per cent level and all other variables are significantly different from zero. He typically found, for the period 1950.III–1960.IV:

$$P_t = 0 \cdot 017 + 0 \cdot 083 \frac{W_s}{(1 \cdot 025)^t} + 0 \cdot 117 \, MF_t + 0 \cdot 002 \, MF_{t-1} - 0 \cdot 039 \, MF_{t-2}$$
$$[0 \cdot 739] \, [2 \cdot 52] \qquad\qquad [7 \cdot 31] \qquad\quad [0 \cdot 069] \qquad\quad [2 \cdot 17]$$

$$+ 1 \cdot 099 \, P_{t-1} - 0 \cdot 281 \, P_{t-2} \qquad R^2 = 0 \cdot 998, \text{DW} = 1 \cdot 92$$
$$[7 \cdot 58] \qquad\quad [3 \cdot 02]$$

A problem arises in the interpretation of these results. Parkin, Sumner and Jones (1972) pointed out that Neild's model could be respecified in such a way that it was not possible to distinguish the models on the basis of their estimated coefficients.

Godley and Nordhaus (1972) attempt to test the hypothesis that 'the mark-up of price over normal historical current average cost is independent of the conditions of demand in the factor and in the product markets and is independent of the deviation of actual cost from normal cost'.[19] To test the hypothesis a predicted normal price series is constructed. The predicted normal price variable equals the 1963 mark-up multiplied by historical normal unit cost. The latter is first calculated by removing the reversible cyclical elements from hours worked, earnings, employment and output and allowing for *a priori* time lags between costs and prices which arise from historical cost pricing. The historical value of the normalised labour costs variable is added to the historical values of the other costs (materials, fuel, services and indirect taxes paid by manufacturers) to generate normal historical current average cost. The predicted and actual price series were then compared by regressing the proprotional rate of change of actual prices, $\Delta \ln P_t$, on the proportional rate of change of predicted prices, $\Delta \ln NP_t$, and the first difference of a constructed measure of capacity utilisation, $\Delta \ln (X/XN_t)$, over the period 1954.III–1969.IV.

$$\Delta \ln P_t = 0 \cdot 001399 + 0 \cdot 6248 \, \Delta \ln NP_t + 0 \cdot 000238 \, \Delta \ln \frac{X}{XN_t}$$
$$\quad\quad [1 \cdot 42] \quad\quad [5 \cdot 36] \quad\quad\quad\quad [0 \cdot 66]$$

$$R^2 = 0 \cdot 340, \, \mathrm{DW} = 1 \cdot 83$$

They found the estimated coefficient on the predicted price variable to be significantly less than its expected value of unity on the basis of a t test at the 5 per cent level. The demand variable was insignificantly different from zero. The explanatory power of the model is weak. In total Godley and Nordhaus ran 100 regressions using three measures of factor market excess demand and seven measures of labour market excess demand with ten alternative specifications of the price equation. Only the estimated t statistics on their demand variables are reported for the complete set of regressions, and these are summarised below.

Estimated coefficient on demand variable	*Number*
Significant and positive	1
Insignificant and positive	50
Insignificant and negative	46
Significant and negative	3

This appears to indicate that *current* product market demand does not directly affect current output prices. Although product market excess demand is more appropriate than a labour market measure, the exclusion of possible time lags in the adjustment of prices to excess demand appears to be a serious weakness. Godley and Nordhaus made no attempt to reconcile their results with those of earlier researchers, implying that their normalisation procedure supersedes all previous work on the normal cost hypothesis.

Pesaran (1972), in a study which uses the Godley–Nordhaus

approach to the normalisation of unit labour costs, found that the estimated coefficient on the demand variable was marginally significant. However, the intercept in the model was significantly less than zero on the basis of a *t* test at the 5 per cent level, and he imposed the unit coefficient on predicted normal price without testing that constraint.[20] Pesaran typically finds:

$$\Delta \ln P_t - \Delta \ln NP_t = -0.00144 - 0.01017 \Delta \ln \frac{X}{XN_t}$$
$$[2.14] \qquad [0.34]$$

$$+ 0.05785 \Delta \ln \frac{X}{XN_{t-1}} + \hat{u}_t$$
$$[1.93]$$

$$\hat{u}_t = 0.3621 \, \hat{u}_{t-1} + \hat{v}_t, \qquad \hat{\sigma} = 0.33 \text{ per cent}$$
$$[2.84]$$

Clearly this work, with that of Godley and Nordhaus, merits closer consideration. It is discussed in detail in chapter 11.

3.2. *Expectations-augmented excess demand models*

Solow (1969), McCallum (1970) and Smith (1978) have estimated expectations-augmented excess demand models explaining price changes.

Solow's model has three explanatory variables: a unit labour cost variable (the annual proportional change in wage bill ÷ real GDP), the Paish capacity utilisation index (a labour market measure), and expectations of the rate of change of prices generated by an adaptive expectations model.

$$\Delta P_t = -0.2325 + 0.0812 \, \Delta ULC_t + 0.00243 \, CU_t + 0.8085 \, \Delta P_t^e$$
$$[4.770] \quad [1.630] \qquad [4.844] \qquad [8.113]$$

$$R^2 = 0.8436$$

$$\Delta P_t^e = 0.7 \, \Delta P_t + 0.3 \, \Delta P_{t-1}^e.$$

The capacity utilisation variable, which entered with no lag, was significantly different from zero, as was the price expectations variable. Unit labour costs were insignificantly different from zero. It is not clear why this variable enters the regression, since in such a model it is usually argued that anticipated changes enter through the expectational variables and unanticipated changes through a non-zero level of excess demand. One theoretical justification is that it is a proxy for the expected rate of change of actual unit labour costs. In that case the sum of the two point estimates of expectational variables is approximately 0·9. Solow did not report a test against autocorrelation.

McCallum derives a model in which price changes depend on excess demand and lagged price changes. An expectations-augmented excess demand model would result in an estimating equation similar in form to McCallum's but with a constant included. For the period 1950.I–1960.III, using Neild's data, he found:

$$\Delta P_t = 0{\cdot}2547 + 3{\cdot}775\,d_{t+1} - 2{\cdot}856\,d_t + 0{\cdot}7161\,\Delta P_{t-1}$$
$$[1{\cdot}447] \quad [3{\cdot}595] \qquad [2{\cdot}483] \qquad [6{\cdot}173]$$

$$R^2 = 0{\cdot}6922, \text{DW} = 1{\cdot}81$$

The demand variables and the lagged dependent variable are significantly different from zero, and the latter is also significantly less than unity. However, it is not wise to put too much reliance on these estimates, since no appropriate test against autocorrelation is presented.

Smith's model is derived using the procedure developed by Parkin, Sumner and Ward (1976). It differs empirically from the models of Solow and McCallum in that it uses a product market measure of capacity utilisation (CU) and expectations of price changes (ΔP^e) and cost changes (ΔC^e) generated from sample survey data by a similar method to that described in chapter 13.

$$\Delta P_t = -44{\cdot}284 + 0{\cdot}4621\,\frac{1}{3}\sum_{0}^{2} CU_{t-i} + 0{\cdot}3716\,\Delta P^e + 0{\cdot}7733\,\Delta C^e$$
$$[2{\cdot}574] \quad [2{\cdot}470] \qquad\qquad\quad [2{\cdot}473] \qquad\quad [7{\cdot}420]$$

$$R^2 = 0{\cdot}9120, \text{DW} = 2{\cdot}39$$

All the explanatory variables are significantly different from zero and the sum of the coefficients on the expectational variables is not significantly different from unity. If this latter restriction is imposed, then the implied natural, or equilibrium, level of capacity utilisation is approximately 97·5 per cent.

All these attempts to estimate expectations-augmented excess demand models are potentially deficient in that they model the natural level of capacity utilisation as constant over the estimation period — giving a central role to the intercept, which in some empirical work is merely regarded as reflecting the net effect of omitted explanatory variables. It would be useful if future empirical work allowed for a changing natural level or, better still, modelled its determinants. This might also be investigated within a rational expectations framework — an approach which has not yet been pursued in the context of price determination in the UK manufacturing sector.

Notes

1   See Means (1959), pp. 9–11
2   For example, Means (1975).
3   A useful discussion of the Cournot–Nash assumption and its implications is given in Hannah and Kay (1977), chapter 2.
4   We are implicitly assuming a single industry price and therefore no product differentiation. However, this assumption does not alter the substance of the argument as is suggested by Cowling and Waterson (1976), pp. 267–8.
5   A discussion of the properties and merits of alternative measures of concentration will be found in Hannah and Kay (1977), chapter 4.
6   For example, chapter 13 in Cowling *et al.* (1980) argues that the costs of information and hence the costs of adjustment of industrial prices are inversely related to the level of concentration.
7   The relationship between the production function and the disaggregated cost function has been detailed by Nordhaus (1972) for the linear, fixed-coefficients production technology as well as several others such as the Cobb–Douglas. Note that further disaggregation or addition of factors of production would not change the analysis.
8   Further discussion of this relationship is deferred to chapter 12.
9   The varying parameter model is defined as one in which the parameters, i.e. both the structural and the lag coefficients in equations 9 and 11, vary systematically across the sample of observations.
10   The short run must be defined by reference to a time period during which non-stochastic changes in cost and demand can occur but adjustment to equilibrium is only partially completed. The majority of studies which have attempted to identify lags of price adjustment, generally at a high level of aggregation, have therefore used quarterly data on costs and prices.
11   In total twelve separate annual time periods were examined, from 1958 to 1970. See Lustgarten (1975).
12   Lustgarten (1975), p. 194.
13   This is an estimated average price-cost margin of all manufacturing industries in SIC orders IV to XIX obtained from the 1971 input–output tables for the UK.

14   Hart and Clarke (1980) test the direct influence of concentration
      changes on price changes in a multiple regression framework. Their
      estimate, whilst positive, was not statistically significant at the 5 per
      cent level. For details see their table 6.1.
15   Neild (1963), p. 4.
16   If rates are used rather than earnings, then r will pick up both the
      productivity trend and wage drift and r would be expected to be less
      than the trend in productivity.
17   Neild (1963), p. 31.
18   *Ibid.*, p.20; Rushdy and Lund (1967), p. 366; McCallum (1970),
      p. 149.
19   Godley and Nordhaus (1972), p. 869.
20   Stromback and Trivedi (1976) in a study at the industry level found
      that demand, normal unit labour costs and the cost of materials were
      all important determinants of the price of output. Coutts, Godley
      and Nordhaus (1978), however, find demand not to be an important
      explanatory variable of the price–cost margin. They do not reconcile
      their findings with Stromback and Trivedi's earlier results.

The normal cost hypothesis: a reappraisal

1.   Introduction

The normal cost hypothesis, that price is set as a mark-up over normal costs and that this mark-up does not vary with demand, has received considerable attention over the last two decades. The earlier work for the United Kingdom was directed primarily towards examining the hypothesis for manufacturing industry excluding food, drink and tobacco (for example, Neild, 1963; Godley and Nordhaus, 1972; Pesaran, 1972b), whereas some recent work has been mainly at the industry level (Coutts, Godley and Nordhaus, 1978). Research has often been concerned with two main issues: the method by which costs are normalised, and whether the mark-up is in fact influenced by demand.

Since normal cost is an unobservable variable, some proxy for it has to be found. If that proxy is inadequate, then spurious demand influences will enter the normalised series and that variable will be of no use in testing the normal cost hypothesis. Godley and Nordhaus developed an elaborate normalising technique which has been used by Pesaran and Coutts *et al.* The present chapter accepts this approach to normalisation as the best currently available and, within this framework, the derivation of normal unit costs is discussed. A test of the normal cost hypothesis is then presented. All the work reported here is for UK manufacturing industry excluding food, drink and tobacco. In consequence, the chapter is primarily about the aggregate results reported in Coutts *et al.* and in the first study to use this method for the UK by Godley and Nordhaus. The former work is taken from Pesaran (1972b), but since his results are not accurately reported in Coutts *et al.* references are to Pesaran's own paper.[2]

In what follows relatively little reference is made to the disaggregated study by Coutts *et al.* In that study employment–output relationships were not used to generate time series of normal employment of operatives and of administrative, technical and clerical staff because relationships having satisfactory statistical credentials were not estimated. In consequence these variables were derived '... as the simple log-linear interpolation between the relatively reliable figures given in the three censuses of production (1958, 1963, 1968)'.[3] However, this procedure introduces a potentially serious flaw into their work. In the three census years output was not on its trend path.[4] All their normal employment variables are derived independently of the trend paths of output. Consequently the normal unit labour cost variables which they derive are inconsistent with their definition of the normal value of a variable, with the result that their estimated price equations do not test their normal price hypothesis.

The more important results of this chapter may be summarised briefly. Using the Godley–Nordhaus approach, taking care to specify carefully the models from which the normal unit-cost variable is generated, and paying attention to the relationship between the mark-up and excess demand, then the evidence does *not* support the normal cost hypothesis. The mark-up varies with demand.

The outline of the rest of the chapter is as follows. In the next section the hours, earnings and employment relationships used by Godley and Nordhaus and Pesaran are discussed, and alternative specifications presented. In section 3 tests of the normal cost hypothesis are discussed. Conclusions appear in section 4.

2.   The derivation of normal unit costs

2.1.   *The basic approach*
The normal value of a variable is defined as 'The value that the variable would take, other things equal, if output were on its trend path'.[5] Normal output is defined as its trend path, and this is derived by regressing the logarithm of seasonally adjusted real output on time,

$$\ln X_t = \alpha_0 + \alpha_1 t + u_t \tag{1}$$

in which X_t is real output at time t, t is time, and u_t is an n.i.d. random variable. The predicted value of the dependent variable within the sample period is the logarithm of normal output, ln XN:

$$\ln XN_t \equiv \hat{\alpha}_0 + \hat{\alpha}_1 t \qquad (2)[6]$$

It is then hypothesised that actual hours, earnings and employment are determined as, among other things, some function of output. By estimating such models and setting actual output equal to normal output it is possible to generate within-sample predictions of hours, earnings and employment conditional upon output being on its trend path, i.e. normal values of those variables. Given these normalised variables, normal unit labour costs can be calculated. This approach is, however, potentially deficient in that it attributes to manufacturers the benefit of foresight not available currently.

2.2. *Hours*

Godley and Nordhaus hypothesise that the important proximate determinants of desired average hours worked per week are deviations of real output from its trend and standard, nationally negotiated, hours, although long-run trends may also be relevant.

$$H_t^* = \beta_0 + \beta_1 HS_t + \beta_2 \ln\left(\frac{X}{XN}\right)_t + \beta_3 t \qquad (3)$$

$$H_t - H_{t-1} = \gamma\,(H_t^* - H_{t-1}) + u_t \qquad (4)$$

hence

$$H_t^* = \beta_0\gamma + \beta_1\gamma\,HS_t + \beta_2\gamma \ln\left(\frac{X}{XN}\right)_t + \beta_3\gamma t + (1-\gamma)\,H_{t-1} + u_t \,(5)$$

in which H_t^* is desired average hours worked per week; HS_t is standard, nationally negotiated, hours worked per week; $\ln(X/XN)_t$ is the residuals from estimating equation 1;[7] t is time; H_t is actual average hours worked per week; and u_t is an n.i.d. random variable.

The model is theoretically weak in that it is not based on hypothesised maximising behaviour of households and firms. It is not clear, for example, whether the relationship refers to the demand side or to the supply side of the labour market; it is not obvious by whom the hours are 'desired'. The inclusion of ln $(X/$

$XN)_t$, however, suggests a demand-side interpretation. Moreover the price content of this model is nil; desired hours are not dependent on the price of labour services.

Using this model, customary hours, HC, defined as desired hours at a normal level of output, would be given by

$$HC \equiv \hat{\beta}_0 + \hat{\beta}_1 HS + \hat{\beta}_3 t \qquad (6)$$

Godley and Nordhaus estimated separate hours equations for men and women, in both levels and first differences, investigated the lag structures on standard hours and excess demand, $\ln (X/XN)$, and found the coefficient on the lagged dependent variable to be insignificantly different from zero and negatively signed. A problem which arises in estimating separate models for men and women is that the data do not distinguish between output produced by men and by women. It is necessary, therefore, to use total output of manufacturing excluding food, drink and tobacco in the disaggregated equations. It is thus assumed that the relative proportions of total output produced by men and by women remain constant over the cycle.

Pesaran's work differs in that he abandoned the sex disaggregation and his data on hours, which are base-weighted, cover manufacturing excluding food, drink and tobacco whereas the Godley–Nordhaus hours data are for total manufacturing and have current weights. Pesaran does not report testing for the adjustment of actual to desired hours. Previous preferred estimates of these hours equations are:

Godley–Nordhaus

Men: $H_t = 20 \cdot 1 + 0 \cdot 636\, HS_t + 12 \cdot 51 \ln (X/XN)_t$
       $[25 \cdot 7]\,[35 \cdot 33][1 \cdot 27]$

   $R^2 = 0 \cdot 974, \mathrm{DW} = 1 \cdot 59 [t]$

Women: $H_t = 17 \cdot 0 + 0 \cdot 537\, HS_t + 7 \cdot 69 \ln (X/XN)_t$
         $[8 \cdot 3][11 \cdot 2][4 \cdot 7]$

   $- 4 \cdot 93 \ln (X/XN)_{t-1} - 1 \cdot 78 \ln (X/XN)_{t-2} - 0 \cdot 042\, t$
   $[2 \cdot 2][1 \cdot 16][5 \cdot 25]$

   $\bar{R}^2 = 0 \cdot 991, \mathrm{DW} = 1 \cdot 814$

Pesaran

Men + women: $H_t = 16 \cdot 54 + 0 \cdot 69790 \, HS_t + 12 \cdot 33 \ln (X/XN)_t$
$\qquad \qquad \quad [21 \cdot 30] \quad [38 \cdot 09] \qquad \qquad [11 \cdot 34]$

$$\bar{R}^2 = 0 \cdot 9789, \, \text{DW} = 1 \cdot 65$$

In the present study the structural parameters of the model with adjustment of actual to desired hours were estimated by maximum likelihood for the period April 1953 to October 1969, thirty-four observations on biannual data, using the methods described in Dhrymes (1971).[8] Furthermore, since the Durbin–Watson statistic is biased towards its mean when one of the regressors is a lagged dependent variable, and since Durbin's (1970) h statistic may be biased in small samples in that it may tend to reject the null hypothesis of zero first-order autocorrelation when in fact that hypothesis is true (B. G. Spencer, 1975) and thus result in a type one error, the possibility of first-order autocorrelation was allowed for in the estimation by assuming that the error in equation 5 followed a first-order auto-regressive scheme,

$$u_t = \rho u_{t-1} + v_t, \, |\rho| < 1 \text{ and } v_t \text{ is n.i.d.}$$

For both men and women the first-order auto-regressive parameter was insignificantly different from zero. It was assumed that the error u_t was n.i.d. and the hours equations re-estimated, giving, in structural form:[9]

Men:[10]
$H_t^* = 21 \cdot 0847 + 0 \cdot 6110 \, HS_t + 12 \cdot 2187 \ln (X/XN)_t$
$\qquad \quad [24 \cdot 324] \quad [29 \cdot 904] \qquad [10 \cdot 151]$

$(H_t - H_{t-2}) = 0 \cdot 8825 \, (H_t^* - H_{t-2}) \qquad \qquad R^2 = 0 \cdot 9756$
$\qquad \qquad \quad [10 \cdot 848]$

Women:
$H_t^* = 17 \cdot 1598 + 0 \cdot 5518 \, HS_t + 7 \cdot 6363 \ln (X/XN)_t$
$\qquad \quad [7 \cdot 459] \quad [11 \cdot 036] \qquad [4 \cdot 954]$

$\qquad + 2 \cdot 7941 \ln (X/XN)_{t-1} - 8 \cdot 2990 \ln (X/XN)_{t-2} - 0 \cdot 0202 \, t$
$\qquad \quad [1 \cdot 086] \qquad \qquad \quad [3 \cdot 629] \qquad \qquad \quad [4 \cdot 560]$

$(H_t - H_{t-2}) = 0 \cdot 8953 \, (H_t^* - H_{t-2}) \qquad \qquad R^2 = 0 \cdot 9922$
$\qquad \qquad \quad [6 \cdot 668]$

In these models the point estimates of the partial adjustment parameter are both less than unity, although not significantly so.[11] However, there appears no justification for constraining that parameter to be unity, indicating complete adjustment over two quarters, as both Godley and Nordhaus and Pesaran have done. Moreover, if the adjustment parameter is included, the coefficient on the second lagged demand variable in the hours equation for women, which Godley and Nordhaus believe should be included on plausibility grounds even though they found it to be insignificantly different from zero, becomes significant.

2.3. *Earnings*

Godley and Nordhaus postulate the major observable determinants of average weekly earnings to be basic hourly rates, the number of hours worked and the size of the overtime premium. Earnings drift is allowed for with an exponential time trend:

$$AWE = e^{\partial_0 + \partial_1 t} . \, BHR^{\,\partial_2} \, [HS + \partial_4 (H - HS)]^{\partial_3} . \, e^{u_t} \, , \, \partial_2 = \partial_3 = 1 \quad (7)$$

in which AWE is average weekly earnings; BHR is basic hourly rates; HS is standard hours; H is actual hours worked; $(H-HS)$ is overtime hours, i.e. hours worked in excess of standard hours; δ_4 is the overtime premium: so $[HS + \delta_4 (H-HS)]$ is actual hours in standard-hour-equivalent units; δ_2 is the proportional impact of basic hourly rates on average weekly earnings; and δ_3 is the proportional impact of actual hours measured in standard-hour-equivalent units on average weekly earnings. This model is purely statistical; its price-theoretic content is nil. The justification for using such a model is that the aim is to generate within-sample predictions of the dependent variable, and so it is appropriate to use a model which predicts accurately.

From equation 7,

$$\ln AWE = \partial_0 + \partial_1 t + \partial_2 \ln BHR + \partial_3 \ln[HS + \partial_4 (H - HS)] + u_t \quad (8)$$

which is non-linear in the parameters to be estimated. Now,

$$[HS + \partial_4 (H - HS)] = \left[HS \left\{ 1 + \partial_4 \left(\frac{H - HS}{HS} \right) \right\} \right] \quad (9)$$

and after taking logarithms the right-hand side of equation 9 may be written as

$$\partial_3 \ln HS + \partial_3 \ln \left\{ 1 + \partial_4 \left(\frac{H-HS}{HS} \right) \right\}$$

Since

$$\partial_4 \left[\frac{H-HS}{HS} \right] > -1$$

and small in absolute value, then, neglecting squared and higher terms of the Taylor expansion, equation 8 may be written as

$$\ln AWE = \partial_0 + \partial_1 t + \partial_2 \ln BHR + \partial_3 \ln HS + \partial_3 \partial_4 \left(\frac{H-HS}{HS} \right) + u_t \,(10)$$

The logarithm of normal earnings is given by

$$\ln AWEN \equiv \hat{\partial}_0 + \hat{\partial}_1 t + \hat{\partial}_2 \ln BHR + \hat{\partial}_3 \ln [HS + \hat{\partial}_4 (HC - HS)] \,(11)$$

or, using the Taylor approximation, by

$$\ln AWEN \equiv \hat{\partial}_0 + \hat{\partial}_1 t + \hat{\partial}_2 \ln BHR + \hat{\partial}_3 \ln HS + \hat{\partial}_3 \hat{\partial}_4 \left(\frac{HC-HS}{HS} \right) \,(12)$$

Godley and Nordhaus estimated equation 10 in first differences by OLS for men and women, whilst Pesaran estimated equation 8 using data aggregated over sex by ML with alternative specifications of the error process. Their preferred estimates are:

Godley and Nordhaus

Men:

$$\Delta \ln AWE = \underset{[4 \cdot 73]}{0 \cdot 0107} + \underset{[9 \cdot 43]}{0 \cdot 7592} \Delta \ln BHR + \underset{[2 \cdot 71]}{0 \cdot 6032} \Delta \ln HS$$

$$+ \underset{[7 \cdot 45]}{1 \cdot 102} \Delta \left(\frac{H-HS}{HS} \right)$$

$$\bar{R}^2 = 0 \cdot 795, \text{DW} = 1 \cdot 59$$

Women:

$$\Delta \ln AWE = 0{\cdot}0122 + 0{\cdot}6122 \, \Delta \ln BHR + 0{\cdot}5079 \, \Delta \ln HS$$
$$\quad\quad\quad\quad [4{\cdot}88] \quad [6{\cdot}15] \quad\quad\quad\quad [2{\cdot}11]$$

$$+ \, 0{\cdot}8427 \, \Delta\!\left(\frac{H-HS}{HS}\right)$$
$$\quad [3{\cdot}70]$$

$$\bar{R}^2 = 0{\cdot}566, \, \mathrm{DW} = 1{\cdot}52$$

Pesaran[12]

Men + women:

$$\ln AWE = \; -2{\cdot}62465 + 0{\cdot}02203t + 0{\cdot}77037 \ln BHR$$
$$\quad\quad\quad\quad [4{\cdot}36] \quad\quad [6{\cdot}11] \quad\quad [9{\cdot}88]$$

$$+ \, 0{\cdot}94531 \ln [HS + 1{\cdot}5(H - HS)] + \hat{u}_t$$
$$\quad [8{\cdot}40]$$

$$\hat{u}_t = 0{\cdot}5437 \, \hat{u}_{t-1} + \hat{v}_t, \, \bar{R}^2 = 0{\cdot}9995$$
$$\quad [3{\cdot}47]$$

The estimated coefficients on basic hourly rates in all the above models and standard hours in the Godley–Nordhaus model are significantly less than their expected values on the basis of t tests at the 5 per cent significance level:

	BHR	*HS*
	$H_N\!: \hat{\partial}_2 = 1{\cdot}0$	$H_N\!: \hat{\partial}_3 = 1{\cdot}0$
	$H_A\!: \hat{\partial}_2 < 1{\cdot}0$	$H_A\!: \hat{\partial}_3 < 1{\cdot}0$
G–N: men	$-2{\cdot}99$	$-1{\cdot}78$
G–N: women	$-3{\cdot}90$	$-2{\cdot}04$
P: men + women	$-2{\cdot}95$	$-0{\cdot}49$

The Godley–Nordhaus earnings equations were re-estimated by OLS, April 1953 to October 1969 (thirty-four biannual observations), and the residuals in the earnings equation for women were found to be heteroscedastic. Theil's BLUS test against heteroscedasticity was used, and the F statistic to test the null hypothesis of homoscedastic residuals was $F_{(15,15)} = 3{\cdot}59$, which exceeds the critical value at the 5 per cent level of $2{\cdot}4$, rejecting that hypothesis.[13] The restriction that the coefficients on basic hourly rates and standard hours were simultaneously unity was imposed and the Godley–Nordhaus earnings equations re-estimated. This resulted in the residuals of both equations becoming heteroscedastic, in which case an F test to test the null hypothesis that $\partial_2 = \partial_3 = 1$ is invalid. That some of the estimated coefficients are significantly different from their expected values and that the residuals are heteroscedastic when the constraints are imposed suggests some specification error.[14]

The proxying of earnings drift by an exponential time trend appears to be inadequate. The basic model is one which directly considers those operatives paid according to time, yet in 1961 about 40 per cent of male and 50 per cent of female operatives in manufacturing were paid according to results, and in firms employing both those paid by results and those paid by time the earnings of the latter are related to those of the former. Because of data constraints it is not possible to estimate a separate model for those paid by results; however, since such forms of payment result in drift, it is crucial that drift be modelled adequately. Other factors which contribute to drift are the payment of time rates above the national minimum bonuses, merit payments and the structure of employment.[15]

A labour market demand variable may well be a suitable variable with which to pick up the effects of drift. However, it must be remembered that the objective is to calculate normal average weekly earnings, and if, for example, percentage unemployment were used, then it would be necessary to find values of that variable when output was on its trend path.

Following Lydall (1958) and Turner (1960), it is hypothesised that drift is a function of productivity. Furthermore, drift lags behind productivity. In firms with a high proportion of piece workers an increase in their output leads to an increase in their earnings and hence drift. In such firms the earnings of time workers are tied to those of piece workers and so time workers' earnings rise, but after a lag. In firms with a much smaller proportion of piece workers earnings move in line with earnings in other firms, but this lag will be longer than the first. Since the proportion of male employees paid by results is less than that of female employees,[16] the lag of time workers' earnings behind productivity is expected to be greater in models estimated for men than in those estimated for women. Some contributory factors to drift, particularly some types of bonus and the structure of employment, may not be directly related to productivity. Since there are no suitable data on such factors, their influence is assumed constant over the estimation period.

If drift is predominantly a function of lagged output per operative hour, then the basic model becomes:

$$AWE = e^{\partial_0}\left(\frac{X}{L.H}\right)_{t-i}^{\partial_1} \cdot BHR^{\partial_2} \cdot [HS + \partial_4(H - HS)]^{\partial_3} \cdot e^{u_t} \tag{13}$$

in which L is operatives' employment and the other variables are as defined above. Hence

$$\ln AWE = \partial_0 + \partial_1\ln\left(\frac{X}{L.H}\right)_{t-i} + \partial_2 \ln BHR$$

$$+ \partial_3 \ln [HS + \partial_4(H - HS)] + u_t \tag{14}$$

from which

$$\ln AWEN \equiv \hat{\partial}_0 + \hat{\partial}_1\ln\left(\frac{XN}{LN.HC}\right)_{t-i} + \hat{\partial}_2 \ln BHR$$

$$+ \hat{\partial}_3 \ln [HS + \hat{\partial}_4(HC - HS)] \tag{15}$$

It was assumed that the error in equation 14 followed a first-order auto-regressive scheme, separate dummies, 68_A, 68_O and 69_A, were added for April 1968, October 1968 and April 1969, to pick up the effects of negative wage drift which occurred in those periods as a result of important settlements in engineering, and the model estimated by ML simultaneously searching for ρ and δ_4, the overtime premium, over the grids $|\rho| < 1$ and $1 \cdot 0 < \delta_4 < 2 \cdot 5$. [17]

The maximum likelihood estimates are:

Men:

$$\ln AWE = \underset{[0 \cdot 841]}{-0 \cdot 9582} + \underset{[1 \cdot 009]}{0 \cdot 0864} \ln \frac{X}{L.H_{t-1}} - \underset{[0 \cdot 1326]}{0 \cdot 0141} \ln \frac{X}{L.H_{t-2}}$$

$$+ \underset{[2 \cdot 889]}{0 \cdot 1577} \ln \frac{X}{L.H_{t-3}} + \underset{[18 \cdot 726]}{1 \cdot 0241} \ln BHR + \underset{[3 \cdot 626]}{0 \cdot 6623} \ln [HS$$

$$+ \underset{[3 \cdot 120]}{2 \cdot 1} (H - HS)] - \underset{[4 \cdot 784]}{0 \cdot 0262} \, 68_A - \underset{[2 \cdot 896]}{0 \cdot 0180} \, 68_O - \underset{[3 \cdot 999]}{0 \cdot 0208} \, 69_A + \hat{u}_t$$

$$u_t = \underset{[8 \cdot 39]}{0 \cdot 825} \, \hat{u}_{t-1} + \hat{v}_t \qquad R^2 = 0 \cdot 9986$$

Women:

$$\ln AWE = \underset{[2\cdot688]}{-2\cdot1697} + \underset{[0\cdot4005]}{0\cdot0168} \ln \frac{X}{L.H_t} + \underset{[2\cdot507]}{0\cdot1410} \ln \frac{X}{L.H_{t-1}}.$$

$$+ \underset{[19\cdot940]}{0\cdot9770} \ln BHR + \underset{[6\cdot751]}{0\cdot9129} \ln \underset{[6\cdot611]}{[HS + 1\cdot3(H - HS)]}$$

$$- \underset{[6\cdot569]}{0\cdot032768}_A - \underset{[4\cdot939]}{0\cdot027968}_O - \underset{[2\cdot385]}{0\cdot011369}_A + \hat{u}_t$$

$$\hat{u}_t = \underset{[3\cdot147]}{0\cdot475} \, \hat{u}_{t-1} + \hat{v}_t, \qquad R^2 = 0\cdot9996$$

The productivity variables perform well, although some are apparently insignificant as a result of multicollinearity. The t statistics to test the null hypothesis that the estimated coefficients on $\ln BHR$, ∂_2, and $\ln[HS + \partial_4(H - HS)]$, ∂_3, are individually unity are given below:

	$H_N:\partial_2 = 1$	$H_N: \partial_3 = 1$
	$H_A: \partial_2 < 1$	$H_A: \partial_3 < 1$
Men:	$0\cdot441$	$-1\cdot849$
Women:	$-0\cdot469$	$-0\cdot644$

The restriction $\partial_2 = \partial_3 = 1$ was imposed and the models were re-estimated. For men the calculated F statistic, $F_{(2,24)}$, was $1\cdot55$, which is less than the critical value of $3\cdot40$ at the 5 per cent level, and for women $F_{(2,26)}$ is $0\cdot18$, less than its critical value at the 5 per cent level of $3\cdot37$. The null hypothesis is not rejected in either model. The point estimate of the overtime premium in the earnings equation for men is $2\cdot1$, which, although the same as that found by Pesaran as the ML estimate, appears high. However, the t statistic to test the null hypothesis that it is equal to its usually assumed value of $1\cdot5$ (on which the work of Neild and Rushdy and Lund is based) is $0\cdot891$, which does not reject that hypothesis. When the constraint that $\partial_2 = \partial_3 = 1$ was imposed the point estimate of the overtime premium in the earnings equation for men was $1\cdot4$. The point estimate of the overtime premium in the earnings equation for women is $1\cdot3$, which is plausible and, being smaller in magnitude than that for men, consistent with there being fewer women working less overtime than men.

2.4. *Employment–output*

Little *a priori* reasoning is presented for the employment–output relation that desired employment is a multiplicative function of output and customary hours,

$$L_t^* = e^{\epsilon_0 + \epsilon_1 t + \epsilon_2 t^2} \cdot X_{t-i}^{\epsilon_3} \cdot HC_{t-j}^{\epsilon_4} \qquad (16)$$

Adding the appropriate form of the partial adjustment mechanism,

$$\left[\frac{L_t}{L_{t-1}} \right] = \left[\frac{L_t^*}{L_{t-1}} \right]^\theta \cdot e^{u_t} \qquad (17)$$

then

$$\ln L_t = \epsilon_0 \theta + \epsilon_1 \theta t + \epsilon_2 \theta t^2 + \epsilon_3 \theta \ln X_{t-i} + \epsilon_4 \theta \ln HC_{t-j}$$
$$+ (1 - \theta) L_{t-1} + u_t \qquad (18)$$

in which L_t^* is desired employment, X is real output, HC is customary hours, and L_t is actual employment. Normal employment, LN_t, is defined as:

$$\ln LN_t \equiv \hat{\epsilon}_0 + \hat{\epsilon}_1 t + \hat{\epsilon}_2 t^2 + \hat{\epsilon}_3 \ln XN_{t-i} + \hat{\epsilon}_4 \ln HC_{t-j} \qquad (19)$$

In estimating employment–output relationships Godley and Nordhaus abandoned their disaggregation by sex in favour of a split between operatives and administrative, technical and clerical staff. For both these groups, indices of male-equivalent employment were constructed by weighting female employees by the ratio of male to female earnings. Godley and Nordhaus found a lagged dependent variable '... useless in view of the high serial correlation of the employment series...'.[18] Their preferred relationships estimated for the period 1954.I–1969.IV are:

Operatives: $\Delta \ln L_{op.} = -0.00433 - 0.000012t + 0.486 \, \Delta \ln X'$
$\qquad\qquad\qquad\quad$ [5·42]$\qquad$ [3·00]$\qquad$ [12·15]

$$-0.770 \, \Delta \ln HC'$$
$$[2\cdot98]$$

$$\bar{R}^2 = 0.747, \, DW = 1.05$$

ATC staff: $\Delta \ln L_{ATC} = 0 \cdot 00749 - 0 \cdot 000085t + 0 \cdot 229 \, \Delta \ln X''$
$$\quad\quad [3 \cdot 71] \quad\quad [2 \cdot 02] \quad\quad |1 \cdot 99]$$
$$\bar{R}^2 = 0 \cdot 100, \, DW = 2 \cdot 20$$

in which
$$\ln X' = \sum_{i=0}^{n-1} \frac{2(n-i)}{n(n+1)} \ln X_{-i} \text{ for } n = 6$$

$$\ln HC' = \sum_{i=0}^{n-1} \frac{2(n-i)}{n(n+1)} \ln HC_{-i} \text{ for } n = 4$$

$$\ln X'' = \sum_{i=0}^{n-1} \frac{2(n-i)}{n(n+1)} \ln X_{-i} \text{ for } n = 8$$

'Notice that it was necessary to impose the lags on output and customary hours. The Durbin–Watson statistic indicates significant positive serial correlation in the residuals of the operatives' employment equation. In the model of employment of administrative, technical and clerical staff the explanatory power is low, which is potentially serious, since the model is used to generate within-sample conditional predictions.

Following Godley and Nordhaus, Pesaran estimated separate employment–output relationships for operatives and administrative, technical and clerical employees but, rather than use first differences because of autocorrelation in levels, used the levels formulation with alternative specifications of the error process. He does not report testing for an adjustment mechanism. Pesaran's preferred estimates are:

Operatives: $\ln L_{op.} = 7 \cdot 30 - 0 \cdot 00147t - 0 \cdot 0004t^2 - 0 \cdot 00502S_1$
$$\quad\quad\quad [8 \cdot 49] \; [2 \cdot 16] \quad\quad [6 \cdot 99] \quad\quad [8 \cdot 24]$$

$$- 0 \cdot 0073S_2 - 0 \cdot 0050S_3 + 0 \cdot 07672 \ln X_t$$
$$\quad [9 \cdot 78] \quad\quad [8 \cdot 40] \quad\quad [2 \cdot 72]$$

$$+ 0 \cdot 12328 \ln X_{t-1} + 0 \cdot 14299 \ln X_{t-2}$$
$$\quad [4 \cdot 44] \quad\quad\quad\quad [5 \cdot 17]$$

$$+ 0 \cdot 07778 \ln X_{t-3} + 0 \cdot 04054 \ln X_{t-4}$$
$$\quad [2 \cdot 83] \quad\quad\quad\quad [1 \cdot 60]$$

$$- 0 \cdot 26685 \ln HC_t + \hat{u}_t$$
$$\quad [1 \cdot 31]$$

$$\hat{u}_t = 1 \cdot 2514 \, \hat{u}_{t-1} - 0 \cdot 3907 \, \hat{u}_{t-2} + \hat{v}_t \quad \bar{R}^2 = 0 \cdot 9835$$
$$\quad [9 \cdot 50] \quad\quad\quad [3 \cdot 13]$$

ATC staff: $\ln L_{ATC} = 4 \cdot 92 + 0 \cdot 00597t - 0 \cdot 00004t^2 - 0 \cdot 00129 S_1$
                          $[5 \cdot 06]$ $[1 \cdot 77]$ $[2 \cdot 53]$ $[1 \cdot 08]$

   $- 0 \cdot 00257 S_2 - 0 \cdot 00211 S_3 + 0 \cdot 04253 \sum_{i=0}^{\infty} 0 \cdot 9^i \ln X_{t-i} + \hat{u}_t$
   $[1 \cdot 89]$ $[1 \cdot 80]$ $[2 \cdot 31]$ $[12 \cdot 76]$

          $\hat{u}_t = 0 \cdot 7993 \, \hat{u}_{t-1} + \hat{v}_t,$ $\bar{R}^2 = 0 \cdot 9987$
          $[7 \cdot 76]$

The source of these estimates is Pesaran (1972a), in which it is
stated that 'We also found *no* significant effect of *lagged* customary
hours (*HC*) on operatives' employment'.[19] In the published version
of the paper (Pesaran, 1972b) the same equation, but with the
t statistic on customary hours omitted, is reported, and on that
equation Pesaran comments, 'We also found a *significant* effect of
lagged customary hours (*HC*) on operatives' employment.'[20] His
discussion of his results appears inconsistent. It seems, however,
that he found the coefficient on current customary hours to be
insignificantly different from zero.

Pesaran did not specify the range of the grid over which he
searched for the distributed lag parameter, λ, in the ATC
employment model. It was found that the value he reported for that
coefficient was on the boundary in a search over the range $0 \cdot 1 < \lambda$
$< 0 \cdot 9$. On re-estimation, searching over the grids $0 \cdot 1 < \lambda < 0 \cdot 996$
and $- 0 \cdot 95 < \rho < 0 \cdot 95$, we found

ATC staff:[21] $\ln L_{ATC} = - 35 \cdot 84 - 0 \cdot 0870t - 0 \cdot 0001t^2 - 0 \cdot 0012 S_2$
                            $[7539 \cdot 9]$ $[1 \cdot 63]$ $[1 \cdot 02]$ $[1 \cdot 46]$

  $- 0 \cdot 0008 S_3 + 0 \cdot 0013 S_4 + 0 \cdot 0627 \sum_{i=0}^{\infty} 0 \cdot 996^i \ln X_{t-i} + \hat{u}_t$
  $[0 \cdot 84]$ $[1 \cdot 55]$ $[5 \cdot 06]$ $[868 \cdot 4]$

        $\hat{u}_t = 0 \cdot 71 \, \hat{u}_{t-1} + \hat{v}_t,$ $R^2 = 0 \cdot 996,$ $\Gamma = 42 \cdot 8662$
        $[8 \cdot 31]$

The estimated value of the distributed lag parameter in the
re-estimated model (in which that estimated parameter is also on
the boundary) implies an average lag of employment of
male-equivalent ATC staff behind output of 249 quarters! Clearly,
the model is misspecified.

The employment equations estimated for this paper are based on
equations 16 and 17 above but with a distributed lag on output, the

lag distribution having geometrically declining weights summing to unity. Seasonal dummy variables were added. This gives an estimating equation of the form:

$$\ln L_t = \epsilon_0\theta + \epsilon_1\theta t + \epsilon_2\theta t^2 + \epsilon_3\theta(1-\lambda) \sum_{i=0}^{\infty} \lambda^i \ln X_{t-i} + \epsilon_4\theta \ln HC_{t-j}$$

$$+ \epsilon_5\theta S_2 + \epsilon_6\theta S_3 + \epsilon_7\theta S_4 + (1-\theta) \ln L_{t-1} + u_t \qquad (20)^{22}$$

A first-order auto-regressive scheme was included to test for the presence of first-order serial correlation in the residuals. The disaggregation is by sex and by type of employment. The preferred estimates of the structural parameters for male and female operatives and female administrative, technical and clerical staff are shown in table 11.1. Simple lags were tried on customary hours in the models of operatives, but that variable was always insignificant; it performed least badly with a lag of one quarter, and that variable was included on *a priori* grounds. The customary hours variable was not included in the female ATC equation because administrative, technical and clerical *staff* are not usually employed on an hourly basis. For female ATC staff the first-order auto-regressive parameter was insignificantly different from zero, and so the error in equation 20 was assumed n.i.d. and the model re-estimated. The second-order polynomial in time in the model for female ATC staff was insignificantly different from zero and resulted in heteroscedastic residuals. It was omitted from the model, with little effect on the estimated coefficients of the remaining explanatory variables. The average lags of *desired* employment behind output are:

Quarters[23]

Male operatives	1·86
Female operatives	0·52
Female ATC staff	1·76

Pesaran found an average lag of 1·75 quarters of *actual* employment of operatives as a whole behind real output. The proportion by which *actual* employment is adjusted to desired employment, θ, is almost the same for male and female operatives but lower for female ATC staff. This parameter reflects the costs of adjustment of actual to desired employment and possible uncertainty about the

Table 11.1

$$\ln L = \epsilon_0\theta + \epsilon_1\theta t + \epsilon_2\theta t^2 + \epsilon_3\theta(1-\lambda)\sum_{i=0}^{\infty}\lambda^i \ln X_{t-i} + \epsilon_4\theta \ln HC_{t-1} + \epsilon_5\theta S_2 + \epsilon_6\theta S_3 + \epsilon_7\theta S_4 + (1-\theta)\ln \dot L_{t-1} + u_t$$

$$u_t = \rho u_{t-1} + v_t$$

	ϵ_0	ϵ_1	ϵ_2	ϵ_3	ϵ_4	ϵ_5	ϵ_6	ϵ_7	λ	θ	ρ	Γ	R^2
Male operatives	3·1394 [1·640]	−0·00078 [1·038]	−0·00007 [9·921]	0·8316 [8·230]	0·4330 [1·056]	−0·0032 [1·491]	0·0075 [2·527]	0·0121 [4·131]	0·650 [243·7]	0·3913 [8·137]	0·360 [2·805]	1·4228	0·9733
Female operatives	6·3566 [2·212]	−0·0059 [5·948]	−0·0001 [10·00]	0·8655 [7·096]	−0·6333 [1·238]	0·0248 [2·678]	0·0326 [3·305]	0·0597 [4·763]	0·340 [25·22]	0·3834 [6·967]		1·4681	0·9767
Female ATC staff	4·3537 [21·23]			0·4746 [10·69]		−0·0061 [1·046]	0·0053 [0·773]	0·0312 [4·318]	0·638 [47·35]	0·3599 [9·723]	0·538 [4·772]	0·6967	0·9885

Note. For male operatives: $HC = 21\cdot0847 + 0\cdot6110\ HS$. For female operatives: $HC = 17\cdot1598 + 0\cdot5518\ HS$.

permanence of a new level of desired employment. To the extent that the uncertainty is the same irrespective of the type of labour services, then the cost of hiring or firing male and female operatives is almost equal, but it is greater for female ATC staff.

Whilst the above three employment–output relations are well characterised by a single model, this was not the case for male ATC staff. Indeed, after extensive empirical investigation no satisfactory relationship was found for this type of labour. Employment of male ATC staff is independent of output and hence invariant with respect to the trend path of output, normal output. This result is not unexpected. The literature on short-term employment functions makes a distinction between 'direct' labour, which contributes directly to output, and 'overhead' labour, which is independent of the flow of output (Ball and St Cyr, 1966). Male and female ATC staff are two different types of labour. The former constitutes a large proportion of overhead labour, being predominantly higher administrative and technical staff employed on long contracts or for life. The latter includes many secretarial and clerical staff whose employment changes as output rises and falls.

2.5. *Calculation of normal historical current average cost*

Since the normal value of a variable is defined as that value it takes when output is on its trend path, i.e. when $X \equiv XN$, the normalised variables can be calculated by substituting XN for X (and HC for H) in our estimated relationships and so current normal unit labour cost, $ULCN$, derived:

$$ULCN \equiv W_1 \frac{AWEN_{M}.LN_{M.OP}}{XN} + W_2 \frac{AWEN_{F}.LN_{F.OP}}{XN}$$

$$+ W_3 \frac{S(LN_{M.ATC} + W_f LN_{F.ATC})}{XN} + W_4 \frac{EC}{XN} \qquad (21)[24]$$

where S is average salaries (of male ATC staff) per head; W_i, $i=1$ to 4, are weights of the proportion of total unit labour costs attributed to male operatives' earnings, female operatives' earnings, salaries, and employers' contributions;[25] W_f is the ratio of earnings of female ATC staff to earnings of male ATC staff;[26] and EC is employers' contributions.

For this study, two alternative normal historical cost variables were generated — one under the extreme assumption of historical cost pricing[27] and the other a more flexible distributed lag. Godley and Nordhaus showed that their assumption of historical cost pricing determines the lag of price behind cost.[28] The basic procedure is first to calculate the average length of time between purchasing factors and the sale of final products, which Godley and Nordhaus show can be calculated from data on stocks, sales, the share of materials in sales, and an assumption about the proportion of materials entering the production process at the beginning. These 'production periods' are calculated for five sectors of manufacturing. Allowance is then made for inter-industry flows by the construction of a simple input–output model of the five sectors. An input flow is then traced through the input–output model until it leaves in the form of sales outside manufacturing. For a given change in cost the change in the price of output occurs when output is sold outside manufacturing. The distributed lag of price behind cost is determined on the basis of the proportion of each input that remains within aggregate manufacturing during each quarter after its entry.

The assumption of the proportion of materials entering the production process at the beginning is arbitrary.[29] Godley and Nordhaus assumed it to be two-thirds, whilst Pesaran used maximum likelihood to estimate the parameter and found the ML estimate to be zero. However, in testing the normal cost hypothesis Pesaran obtains identical results irrespective of whether the proportion of materials entering the production process at the beginning is two-thirds or zero.[30] Because of this, and since it is useful to be able to compare the results obtained here with those of Pesaran and Godley and Nordhaus, the distributed lag imposed on the cost variables here is that calculated by Pesaran in which the proportion of materials entering at the beginning is two-thirds.[31] Pesaran's lag weights are preferred to those of Godley and Nordhaus because the former were calculated iteratively by computer whereas the latter were calculated by hand and in the process arbitrary assumptions were made to reduce the amount of calculation.[32]

The cost data used in the present study are those used by Godley and Nordhaus, together with the unit labour cost variables of the present section. Two advantages of using these data are that they readily facilitate comparison of the results obtained here with other work and that they do consist of one of the most comprehensive cost bases ever constructed for a study of the price equation. However, some of the quarterly cost series (services and indirect taxes paid by manufacturers for the whole time period and materials and fuel after 1961) were constructed by interpolation. Moreover capital costs and taxes on profits are omitted.

Given the assumption of historical cost pricing, historical current values of the individual unit-cost components ($ULCN$, and the unit prices of materials, fuel, services and indirect taxes paid by manufacturing) were calculated by imposing on those variables the lag distribution weights. That is, the historical current value of a variable is merely its distributed lag value. Individual historical current average cost components were then added together using input–output weights to give a historical unit-cost variable.[33] Using normal unit labour costs together with materials, fuel, services and indirect taxes gives a normal historical current average-cost variable. The predicted price variable, $NP1$, is then the 1963 mark-up, a constant, multiplied by normal historical current average costs.[34]

A second predicted price variable was derived. The assumption of historical cost pricing, with its implied distributed lag of price behind cost, was relaxed. A current cost variable was calculated by adding current costs using the same 1963 input–output weights as before. With this variable the distributed lag was determined empirically, within the price equation, but with the restriction that the lag distribution had geometrically declining weights summing to unity. With this variable, time lags other than those which arise merely through historical cost pricing are permitted to enter the cost–price relationship. Such other time lags could occur as a result of output produced to contract at a fixed price, the existence of stocks of output produced at the old cost of factor inputs, and the time taken for the management to respond to a cost stimulus to change price and the setting of the new price.

3.   Tests of the normal cost hypothesis

The simple mark-up model is usually portrayed as one in which the firm sets the price level as a mark-up over costs, i.e.

$$P_t = \alpha_0 M_t^{\alpha_1} . NP_t^{\alpha_2} , \alpha_0 = \alpha_1 = \alpha_2 = 1 \qquad (22)$$

where P_t is the output price level, NP_t is the predicted normal price, and M_t is the multiplicative mark-up.[35] De Menil (1974) and others have shown that the mark-up of price over marginal cost depends on the elasticity of demand facing the representative firm. Over the cycle there are two opposing forces on the elasticity of demand. Harrod (1936) argued that during a recession the demand curve facing the firm becomes more elastic because consumers are more aware of price differentials and shop around. However, Heflebower (1941) believed that during a slump, in aggregate, the demand curve is less elastic because a greater proportion of goods consumed have inelastic demand curves than at other times. De Menil rejected this, since recent recessions have been mild. Given Harrod's hypothesis, there is a positive relationship between the mark-up and the level of demand.

$$\Delta \ln M_t = \beta_1 \Delta \ln \left(\frac{X}{XN} \right)_{t-i} \tag{23}$$

Taking logarithmic first differences of equation 22 and substituting equation 23 gives:

$$\Delta \ln P = \Delta \ln \alpha_0 + \alpha_1 \beta_1 \Delta \ln \left(\frac{X}{XN} \right)_{t-i} + \alpha_2 \Delta \ln NP_t \tag{24}[36]$$

Since the historical current average cost (and hence predicted price) variables are constructed by imposing a moving average on the components of current average cost, it is expected that the estimated residuals of this model would be autocorrelated. It was assumed that the error in equation 24 followed a linear first-order auto-regressive scheme. Two alternative predicted normal price variables were used; $NP1$ was generated using Pesaran's lag distribution weights, which assume that the proportion of materials entering at the beginning of the production process is two-thirds; $NP2$ was formed as a distributed lag of normal current average cost, the lag distribution having geometrically declining weights summing to unity and being estimated by maximum likelihood.[37] The models were estimated for the period 1957.I–1969.IV, with lags of up to three quarters on the demand variables. The most appropriate lags on the demand variables were found to be one quarter.

$$\Delta \ln P_t = 0 \cdot 004 + 0 \cdot 593 \, \Delta \ln NP1_t + 0 \cdot 0072 \, \Delta \ln \left(\frac{X}{XN} \right)_{t-1} + \hat{u}_t$$
$$[1 \cdot 49] \quad [17 \cdot 8] \quad\quad\quad [2 \cdot 45]$$

$$\hat{u}_t = 0 \cdot 61 \, \hat{u}_{t-1} + \hat{v}_t, \quad R^2 = 0 \cdot 9931$$
$$[5 \cdot 52]$$

$$\Delta \ln P_t = 0 \cdot 019 + 0 \cdot 678 \, \Delta \ln NP2_t + 0 \cdot 0063 \, \Delta \ln \left(\frac{X}{XN} \right)_{t-1} + \hat{u}_t$$
$$[1 \cdot 57] \quad [22 \cdot 8] \quad\quad\quad [2 \cdot 39]$$

$$\hat{u}_t = 0 \cdot 54 \, \hat{u}_{t-1} + \hat{v}_t, \quad R^2 = 0 \cdot 9978$$
$$[4 \cdot 73]$$

In both models the coefficients on the predicted normal price variables are significantly less than their expected values at the 5 per cent level: the t statistic for the test of the null hypothesis that the coefficient on $NP1$ is unity is $-12 \cdot 2$ and that for the test that the coefficient on $NP2$ is unity is $-10 \cdot 8$, which appears to be sufficient to refute the strict form of both hypotheses. Coutts *et al.*, however, argue that because '... predicted and actual prices are known to contain sizeable errors in measurement and specification', and because omitted variables may affect the mark-up,[38] one would not expect a unit coefficient on predicted price. Measurement errors and omitted explanatory variables would result in estimated coefficients which are biased and inconsistent. However, Coutts *et al.* appear to want things both ways: 'Our view remains that lagged normal cost traces out the quarterly pattern of observed prices sufficiently well for analysis of the relationship between the two series to reveal whether or not fluctuations in demand alter prices other than in factor markets.'[39] It is usually assumed as part of the null hypothesis that there are no measurement errors. Consider firms making a pricing decision. Do firms have complete knowledge of their historical unit costs? If in setting prices firms themselves incorrectly measure historical average costs and base their pricing decision on these variables which are measured with error, then the errors of measurement argument is irrelevant.[40]

Consider the Godley–Nordhaus statement of their hypothesis, 'the mark-up ... is independent of the conditions of demand...',[41] together with their comment on their results: 'The most important fact is that the coefficient on the demand variable is insignificant...'.[42] It seems that, according to Godley and Nordhaus, in so far as the normal cost hypothesis is concerned a necessary and sufficient condition for its refutation is that the demand variable(s) be significant. In our tests of that hypothesis the demand variables have their expected signs and are significantly different from zero at the 5 per cent level on a two-tailed test; the normal cost hypothesis is refuted.

4. Conclusion

Some of the previous work on the normal cost hypothesis for aggregate manufacturing industry in the United Kingdom has been examined. It was found to be potentially inadequate in that the models used to generate normal costs appear misspecified, with the result that previous predicted normal price variables are of doubtful use in testing the normal cost hypothesis. When the underlying relationships used to generate the normalised unit labour cost variable have improved statistical credentials, the normal cost hypothesis is refuted.

Often, in the context of policy, attention centres on two issues associated with the demand variable in the price equation: the magnitude of its coefficient and whether or not it is significantly different from zero. In the context of the normal cost hypothesis the magnitude of the coefficient on demand is not of great importance. Monetary expansion results in excess demand for products which is eliminated by prices rising. Moreover, even if the demand variable were insignificantly different from zero, care must be exercised in making policy prescriptions. In this case the implication is not that demand does not affect prices. Sargan (1980b) notes, 'The final form ... explaining prices can be obtained by substituting these subsidiary equations explaining costs into their equation explaining manufacturer's price...'[43] Since demand variables enter these auxiliary equations, demand affects prices. Policies based on the assumption that it does not would be inappropriate.[44]

Notes

1   This is a slightly revised version of a paper written in 1975 and never submitted for publication. I am indebted to David Laidler, Richard Morley, Michael Parkin and Michael Sumner for helpful comments on the earlier draft. I am also grateful to W. A. H. Godley for making his data available to me, and to him and K. J. Coutts for discussions on the normal price hypothesis. The responsibility for any errors is mine.

2 Results reported for manufacturing excluding food, drink and tobacco reported in Coutts *et al.* should be corrected as follows. The coefficients α_1 (table 2.1, p. 25) and b_3 (table 2.2, p. 28) are 12·33 and 0·94531 respectively. The natural logarithm of customary hours is omitted as a regressor in table 2.3, p. 31; its estimated coefficient is $-0·26685$ and t statistic is [1·31].

3 Coutts *et al.* (1978), pp. 32–3.

4 *Ibid.*, fig. 1.1–7, pp. 13–8.

5 Godley and Nordhaus (1972), p. 854.

6 This model assumes the proportional rate of growth of seasonally adjusted real output to be constant.

7 This is an excess demand variable generated such that the level of excess demand is, on average, zero over the estimation period of equation 1.

8 The regressions estimated for this paper were run on the CDC 7600 computer of the University of Manchester Regional Computer Centre. The maximum likelihood programs were written by Linda Ward and the OLS package, REGRESS, by Ericq J. R. Horler.

9 This results in more efficient estimates of the structural parameters and is consistent with Theil's simplicity criteria for econometric models (Theil, 1970, p. 205).

10 Throughout this paper time subscripts refer to quarters. These models were estimated on biannual data, hence the adjustment is over two quarters, but as equation 3 was estimated on quarterly data it was possible to include quarterly lags on demand.

11 The t statistics to test the null hypothesis that $\gamma = 1$ are 1·444 for men and 0·780 for women.

12 The maximum likelihood estimate of the overtime premium was 2·1. Pesaran, however, used the often assumed value of 1·5 on the grounds that this was not significantly different from the estimated value (1972b, p. 99).

13 The algorithm for BLUS residuals was written by R. W. Farebrother.

14 The heteroscedasticity may arise as a result of using the Taylor approximation and consequent omission of quadratic and higher terms from the model. I am indebted to Richard Morley for this point.

15 Office of Manpower Economics (1973)

16 Department of Employment (1971), table 80, p. 157.

17 I am indebted to M. R. Gray, who produced the theory to calculate the asymptotic standard errors in these models, and to E. J. R. Horler, who wrote the program to implement that theory.

18 Godley and Nordhaus (1972), p. 860.

19 Pesaran (1972a), p. 12; emphasis added.

20 Pesaran (1972b), p. 103; emphasis added.

21 Γ is the truncation remainder (Dhrymes, 1971, p. 98).

22

$$(1-\lambda) \sum_{i=0}^{\infty} \lambda^i \ln X_{t-i} = (1-\lambda) \sum_{i=0}^{t-1} \lambda^i \ln X_{t-i} + \Gamma \lambda^t$$

23   Average lag $= \lambda/(1-\lambda)$.

24   Since $L_{\text{M. ATC}}$ is independent of X, and hence XN, we use $LN_{\text{M. ATC}}= L_{\text{M. ATC}}$.

25   Calculated from Department of Employment (1971), table 40, pp. 102–3, and Central Statistical Office (1970). table 16, p. 22.

26   Department of Employment (1971), table 53, pp. 122–3.

27   An assumption which appears reasonable if the rate of inflation is close to zero. When the rate of inflation is high firms may base prices on the replacement cost of factor inputs.

28   Only a brief outline is given here. The reader is referred to Godley and Nordhaus (1972), pp. 862–5 and 879–82, and Pesaran (1972b), pp. 104–11, where the method is presented in great detail.

29   Godley and Nordhaus (1972), p. 865.

30   Pesaran (1972b), p. 114.

31   *Ibid.*, p. 112.

32   Godley and Nordhaus (1972), p. 882.

33   The weights were taken from Central Statistical Office (1970), table 1, pp. 6–7.

34   When such variables are used in regression analysis there results a problem with degrees of freedom; the number of degrees of freedom 'used up' by such a variable is not explicit.

35   The multiplicative mark-up appears appropriate when the price level is trended. An additive mark-up seems plausible only when the price of output is a stationary series.

36   Problems can arise if first differences are used, rather than proportional rates of change. Differentiating equation 22 with respect to time gives:

$$\frac{dP}{dt} = M \ \frac{dNP}{dt} + NP \frac{dM}{dt}$$

If the mark-up is constant, $dM/dt = 0$, then the coefficient on the change in predicted normal price, M, is constant. However, suppose the mark-up is not constant. The coefficients on the change in predicted normal price and the change in the mark-up will be variable. If, however, both sides of the present equation are divided by P (with appropriate simplification), then the variables become proportional rates of change and coefficients would be constant. If a price change equation is to be estimated, then it is preferable to use proportional rates of change, in which case the coefficients would be constant.

37   $NP2$ was estimated as $(1-0\cdot577) \ \Sigma 0\cdot577^i \ NUC_{t-i}$

$$[22\cdot8]$$

where NUC is normal current average cost.

38   Coutts *et al.* (1978), p. 62.

39   *Ibid.*, p. 63.

40   There is, however, an aggregation problem with the dependent variable. Theil (1954) shows that if the aggregate variables are defined such that their logarithms are linear combinations of the

logarithms of the corresponding micro variables, and if the two sets of variables are connected by a relationship having a constant elasticity, then the aggregation conditions are identical with those of linear relationships. In which case unique and linear aggregate coefficients are obtained if the weights used in the construction of the aggregate indices are identical for dependent and explanatory variables and if the micro coefficients are linear and identical, or if they are linear and the micro explanatory variables all change in a parallel fashion. However, on aggregating over firms the dependent variable becomes the arithmetic average of the logarithm of individual firms' output prices. This implies that the aggregate price level is a geometric average of individual firms' prices. However, the Department of Industry's index of the price of output of manufacturing, which is to be the dependent variable, is an aggregate Laspeyres index in which the weights are output or sales in the base year; that is, the data are not in the form of geometric averages. This aggregation problem cannot be overcome.

41   Godley and Nordhaus (1972), p. 869.
42   *Ibid.*, p. 870.
43   Sargan (1980b), p. 121.
44   It is possible that in this case 'world' excess demand may be a potentially important explanatory variable. The excess demand for internationally tradable manufactured goods in the UK readily spills over into the balance of payments and puts little pressure on UK prices, given fixed exchange rates.

Industrial structure and the inflationary process

1.   Introduction

The last twenty years have seen a significant change in the structure of British manufacturing industry. The change has manifested itself in a marked increase of industrial concentration in a large number of sectors, a trend which has been viewed with some concern by many economists. Yet it has been assisted at various times by the industrial policies which have been pursued by the government.

Against this background there has also been a reduction in the size of the manufacturing sector as a whole in terms of employment, and a rise in the level of competitive imports. This latter phenomenon may be important in the context of rising concentration in domestic industries, since it could well mitigate the potential market power effects which derive from a high level of concentration. Nevertheless the structural changes which have taken place in British industry continue to attract much critical comment.

In this chapter[1] we examine the influence of industrial structure, specifically industrial concentration, on the inflationary mechanism. We also consider whether industrial policies which have promoted this change are compatible with policies aimed at bringing the rate of inflation under control. In section 2 we take a look at concentration in the manufacturing sector and the impact of import penetration. In section 3 we discuss briefly the main determinants of the structural change which has taken place in recent years. In section 4 we analyse the influence of industrial structure on the inflationary process, and finally in section 5 we conclude by uncovering some of the potential conflicts between industrial and prices policies.

Table 12.1   *Industrial concentration in the UK*

	Hannah and Kay (1977)		Prais (1976)		Aaronovitch and Sawyer (1974)	
Year	1957	1969	1963	1968	1958	1968
Mean concentration ratios	64·7	77·2	62	66	58.7	69·0
Change of concentration (%)	19·3		6·5		17.5	
Definition of concentration ratios	(a)		(b)		(b)	

Notes

(a)   Share of assets of the ten largest firms in SIC-order industry groups.
(b)   Share of sales of the five largest firms in sub-MLH industry groups.

For the classification of industry groups, including Minimum List Headings (MLH), see *Standard Industrial Classification* (HMSO, 1968).

Sources. Hannah and Kay (1977, pp. 89–91), Prais (1976, p. 20), Aaronovitch and Sawyer (1974, p. 15).

2.   Concentration in UK manufacturing

That industrial concentration has been rising over the last fifteen or twenty years has been established beyond reasonable doubt by several recently published studies. The only discrepancies between them concern the extent to which it has increased. These discrepancies, however, are due largely to variations in the time periods studied and, more important, to differences in the measure of industrial concentration, i.e. the concentration ratio used which defines the proportion of output, employment or assets accounted for by the largest (usually four or five) firms in the industry.[2] Measured in either of these alternative ways, the concentration ratio gives a useful indication of the degree to which a handful of large firms dominate an individual industry.

Table 12.1 summarises the results of three studies which have examined the evolution of industrial concentration in the UK. For all three cases the figures reported relate to unweighted means of industry concentration ratios, but the level of aggregation at which these are defined is not the same across the three studies. Note that weighting the concentration ratios by industry size makes no significant difference to the results. Each of the studies records an increase in concentration, and the two which cover approximately the same period show remarkably similar increases even though the level of aggregation at which concentration is measured differs between the two. All three imply an annual increase of concentration for the period from 1957 to 1969 of over 1 per cent per annum. They also indicate a high average *level* of concentration in the late 1960s, at around 70 per cent.

However, as mentioned earlier, a major weakness of the concentration ratio as an indicator of market power is that it is measured by reference to domestic production only. To the extent that imports are a substantial proportion of total home sales, the concentration ratio will overestimate the percentage accounted for by the four or five largest firms and thus their effective dominance of the market. This problem needs to be considered carefully because the degree of competitive import penetration in the UK has risen appreciably in recent years. For example, in 1960 the proportion of imports in home sales of manufactured goods was 5·4 per cent. By 1975 the figure had risen to 13·3 per cent. However, as will be argued below, increasing import penetration need not necessarily lead to a reduction of market power in domestic industries.

There are many problems in trying to adjust the industry concentration ratios by taking account of competitive imports. Besides the data problems regarding the classification of imports to SIC-industry categories, and the identification of re-exports, the main difficulty in such adjustment concerns the assumption that manufactured imports are actually competitive imports. Many UK companies import goods and then resell them as their own products. Ford UK, which imports the Granada model, is a prime example. In many other cases UK companies are granted franchises by the overseas importers. Such imports clearly do not compete with domestic output and do not reduce the market power of local firms. However, it is impossible to distinguish such imports in the official statistics, and any indiscriminate adjustments in the domestic concentration ratio could err in the downward direction. Similar problems arise when unfinished goods and components to be used in UK manufacturing are classified as manufactured imports, thus overstating further the degree of competitive import penetration.

Some sectors have, however, been clearly affected by such imports, a notable example being the motor vehicle manufacturing industry. But as a recent study has shown,[3] attempts to make precise adjustments to concentration ratios using import data are fraught with difficulties and the results must inevitably be treated with great care. Hence, whilst keeping the potential influence of competitive imports firmly in mind, there remains little doubt that the degree of industrial concentration in manufacturing has increased substantially and is now at significantly higher levels than in the early 1960s.

3. The determinants of concentration in UK manufacturing

The rise in levels of industrial concentration has led many commentators to try and identify its causes. Researchers now agree that a most important contributing factor during this period has been the high incidence of merger activity. Hannah and Kay (1977) estimated that mergers contributed 116 per cent to the rise in concentration; that is, in the absence of mergers concentration would actually have fallen. Less dramatic but nonetheless important contributions by mergers have been estimated by Prais (1976) at 50 per cent (for 1958–70) and by Aaronovitch and Sawyer (1975) at 62 per cent (for 1958–68). Clearly there is a consensus that the merger boom was a major determinant of the rise in concentration.

It is important to stress that the merger boom and hence the trend towards higher concentration received official blessing from the government and was indeed assisted by industrial policy during the 1960s. For example, speaking in 1969, the President of the Board of Trade clearly affirmed his faith in the merger movement: '...I believe that in Britain at this moment in time, the trend to mergers has been on balance beneficial. A number of our industries are too fragmented to achieve the economies of scale needed to compete effectively in international markets.'[4] The statement also makes clear the rationale of promoting mergers, namely the search for efficiency gains through scale and other economies associated with large size. Whether such economies would generally be forthcoming are questions which have only recently been asked.

Economists have traditionally viewed high concentration with concern on account of the adverse market power effects that are

associated with it. These derive from the static welfare losses which
result from positive deviations of prices from marginal costs under
monopoly and oligopoly.[5] Such effects could be mitigated,
however, or even offset if substantial economies were gained
through larger firm size, which implies, *ceteris paribus*, a higher
level of concentration. There is clearly a trade-off involved here,
and careful assessment is required in order to evaluate the net
effects of mergers. This is precisely what the study by Cowling *et al*.
(1980) attempted to do. Its findings, which are confirmed by other
less wide-ranging investigations (e.g. Meeks, 1977), indicate that
whilst the market-power effects are considerable, the efficiency
gains have been negligible in most cases. The merger boom appears
to have yielded little of its original promise.

Another aspect of industrial concentration which has not
hitherto attracted as much attention in the UK is its influence on the
process of inflation. It is to this issue that we now turn.

4.   Concentration and the dynamics of inflation

The influence of market structure on inflation has traditionally
been a controversial subject. However, in an orthodox theoretical
framework it can be shown that industry price–cost margins and
hence the price level are positively related to seller concentration.[6]
This implies that only *continual* increases in concentration will lead
to an upward trend in prices and thus to inflationary pressures.
Moreover the empirical evidence suggests that the contribution of
changing market structure to rising prices is quantitatively small in
relation to other proximate causes, and that it is largely a long-run
effect not perceptible over short periods of time.[7] This dynamic
aspect of market power is to be distinguished from the welfare
effects discussed above. Thus, while *changes* in price–cost margins
may be small, their *level*, and consequently the deadweight welfare
losses, may be substantial.

However, all this ignores the fact that concentration can
influence the transmission if not the underlying causes of
inflationary pressures working their way through the economy. For
market structure determines not only the level or prices above cost
but also the speed with which prices rise in response to cost
increases. If, as will be argued below, the speed of price adjustment
is positively related to concentration, then the latter will have

important implications for the inflationary process which are wholly independent of the static links outlined above.

The basic hypothesis which underpins the relationship between concentration and the rate of adjustment and which will be sketched only briefly here is that in concentrated industries, where the costs of search and collusion among sellers are low, firms can effectively co-ordinate their price adjustments and thus restore equilibrium more rapidly than those in more fragmented sectors. This implies faster price increases in response to upward movements in costs, i.e. a positive relationship between concentration and the speed of price adjustment. A more formal statement of this suggested link will be found in Cowling *et al.* (1980, chapter 13). Here we shall concentrate on the empirical findings and their implications.

Before going on to give a precise quantitative definition of the rate of price adjustment we shall briefly discuss its other major determinant, namely the technology of production. This essentially defines the actual length of the production process, i.e. the time taken between the purchase of inputs and their transformation into finished goods. This in turn influences the length of time after which cost increases are translated into price increases. Consider a simple example, the chemical processing and the mechanical engineering sectors. Since we know that the former will typically have a far shorter production period than the latter,[8] we would expect a faster price increase in the chemical sector following an increase in raw material prices because its output will embody the higher priced raw material earlier than in the engineering sector. A technical analysis of the influence of the length of production on the lag of price adjustment has recently been conducted by Coutts, Godley and Nordhaus (1978, chapter 3), to which the interested reader is referred. The above discussion should make it sufficiently clear, however, that market structure is only a partial determinant of the speed of adjustment.

We can now give a precise definition to the rate of adjustment by using the familiar partial adjustment model:

$$(P_t - P_{t-1}) = \lambda(P_t^* - P_{t-1}), 0 < \lambda \leqslant 1 \tag{1}$$

where P_t^* is the industry equilibrium price in period t and λ is the price adjustment coefficient. It defines the proportion of the long-run adjustment which is actually carried out in the current period. It is easily shown that this adjustment process implies a geometrically distributed lag structure of prices. Equation 1 can be rearranged to give:

$$P_t = \lambda P_t^* + (1 - \lambda) P_{t-1} \tag{2}$$

Substituting P_t^* by a linear combination of current cost variables results in an equation which can be estimated empirically for different industries:

$$P_t = \lambda \beta_1 C_{1t} + \lambda \beta_2 C_{2t} + (1 - \lambda)P_{t-1} + u_t \tag{3}$$

where C_1 and C_2 are indicators of material and unit labour costs respectively and u_t is a disturbance term.[9] The next step in the analysis is to relate the estimates of λ derived from a set of equations such as 3 above to market structure variables. The problem in estimating a cross-section relationship of this kind is that data on the length of the production period, which, as suggested above, is another important influence on λ, are not available at an individual industry level of aggregation. However, since extraneous information suggests that engineering industries typically have a far longer gestation period of output than others, it can be accommodated in an estimating equation by using a dummy variable as follows:

$$\hat{\lambda}_i = b_0 + b_1 CR_i + b_2 ED_i + v_i \qquad i = 1, \dots 21 \tag{4}$$

where CR_i = concentration ratio of industry i, ED_i = dummy variable taking the value of 1 for an engineering industry and 0 otherwise. v_i = disturbance term. Equation 4 implies a common slope coefficient for all industries (we expect $b_1 > 0$) but, on average, a different rate of adjustment (we expect $b_2 < 0$) for engineering industries.

This two-stage empirical analysis was recently carried out by Domberger (1979) for a sample of twenty-one British manufacturing industries, in which information concerning estimation methods, functional forms and full findings can be found. Here we shall report a single regression estimate of equation 4 which represents the salient feature of the results. These

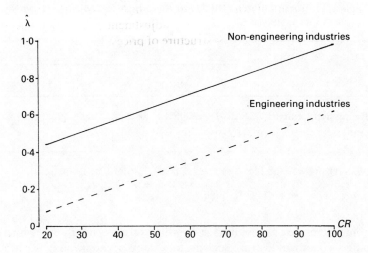

Fig. 12.1 Price adjustment and industrial structures: estimated relationship. $\hat{\lambda}$, estimated price adjustment coefficient; *CR*, five-firm (1971) concentration ratio.

estimates indicate that λ rises steadily with the level of concentration but is lower at every level for the engineering sectors. The estimated relationship is depicted graphically in fig. 12.1.

The relationship implies that input price increases will be passed on more rapidly in concentrated industries. An initial shock such as, for example, a rise in the price of oil, will lead to larger price rises in these sectors in the short run, with correspondingly smaller increases in unconcentrated industries. The implied pattern of adjustment is independent of the ultimate size of the price increase and relates solely to its distribution through time.

This immediately raises the question: what do faster adjustments in individual sectors imply for inflationary price dynamics which follow from exogenous cost increases? In an economy as highly industrialised as the UK the degree of interdependence between sectors is such that the adjustment behaviour of any one sector will influence the others through the intermediate chain of production. Thus price adjustments in one sector will have ripple effects through the entire industrial system. As an example consider the case of the mineral oil refining industry raising its prices following an increase in the price of crude oil. The speed at which the

Table 12.2 *Price adjustment and industrial structure. Dependent variable:*
λ. *Linear specification*

	Coefficient					
	$\hat{b}_0$	$\hat{b}_1$	$\hat{b}_2$	R^2	F	N
Regression estimate	0·3141	0·0066	−0·3549	0·44	6·96	21
t ratios	(2·3464)	(2·6734)	(−3·2526)			

Note. Using weighted least squares makes no difference to the results.

Source. Domberger (1979), table 3.

domestic price of refined oil rises will determine the rate at which oil-consuming industries, such as, for example, chemicals, will raise their prices in turn, and so on through the rest of the economy.

These dynamic interactions can be explored only in a model which takes explicit account of industrial interdependence, i.e. in a general equilibrium framework of analysis. Domberger (1980) developed such a model, which represents a generalised form of the price equation where a system of equations, one for each industry, replaces equation 3 above. The structural (β) coefficients for such a large economic system could not be estimated empirically and were derived instead from the input–output tables for the UK. The price adjustment coefficients, which are not available from any other source, were obtained from the cross-section relationship reported in table 12.2. It should be clear that such a system can accommodate any number of interconnected sectors provided the input–output data are available.

Thus, using input–output coefficients as weights, a linear combination of intermediate and primary input prices is substituted for P_t^*; incorporating the further restriction of constant base-period profit margins in the long run, and finally writing the resulting system in first differences for convenience, we get:

$$[\Delta P_t] = [\hat{\lambda} A'] [\Delta P_t] + [\hat{\lambda} B'] [\Delta V_t] + [\hat{\lambda} \hat{\gamma}] [\Delta P_t] + [I - \hat{\lambda}] [\Delta P_{t-1}] \quad (5)$$

where $[A] = n \times n$ matrix of input–output coefficients, $[B] = n \times m$ matrix of primary input coefficients, including imports, $[\hat{\lambda}] = n \times n$

diagonal matrix of price adjustment coefficients, $[\hat{\gamma}] = n \times n$ diagonal matrix of base-period profit margins, $[\Delta P_t] = n \times 1$ vector of output price changes in period t, $[\Delta V_t] = m \times 1$ vector of primary input price changes in period t. Note that there are n endogenous (interdependent) sectors in this system and m exogenous sectors. Each of the former has its own rate of adjustment, given by a single non-zero element in $[\hat{\lambda}]$.

Solving equation 4 for $[\Delta P_t]$, we get:

$$[\Delta P_t] = \left[I - \hat{\lambda}\,[A' + \hat{\gamma}]\right]^{-1}\left[[\hat{\lambda}B']\,[\Delta V_t] + [I - \hat{\lambda}]\,[\Delta P_{t-1}]\right] \quad (6)$$

Thus changes in final output prices are given as a weighted sum of current primary input price changes and intermediate price changes in the previous period, all pre-multiplied by: $[I - \hat{\lambda}\,(A' + \hat{\gamma})]^{-1}$. This matrix is a modified Leontief inverse which captures the direct and indirect effects of price changes in the *current period*.[10] The matrix can thus distribute the n price adjustments over time following an exogenous shock, and the system as a whole incorporates the dynamic as well as the cross-section interactions between industrial prices.

The dynamic input–output model outlined above can be used to examine the impact of concentration on the dynamics of the price level. The effect of a fourfold (300 per cent) increase in the price of oil on industrial prices was therefore simulated under two different adjustment regimes. In the first the $[\hat{\lambda}]$ matrix was essentially based on 1971 levels of concentration, and in the second the coefficients of $[\hat{\lambda}]$ had been reduced to reflect the levels of concentration of the early 1960s.[11] The adjustment coefficients for each sector under the two regimes are reported in the appendix.

The working model was based on the 1971 input–output tables for the UK with thirty-six endogenous and sixty-eight exogenous or primary sectors. Since the simulation produces thirty-six individual price changes in each quarterly period, an aggregate wholesale price index (WPI) was constructed as a weighted average similar to the one published by the Department of Industry. Sympathetic wage responses were assumed to take place following changes in WPI.[12]

The results of the simulation are reported in table 12.3 for both WPI and the general chemicals industry. This sector was selected out of the thirty-six because of its clear dependence on oil as an

Table 12.3   *The impact of concentration on the inflationary process: the oil price rise under different adjustment regimes*

| | Industry | | | | | |
| | General Chemicals | | | Aggregate WPI | | |
Quarter	1 Original $[\lambda]$	2 Reduced $[\lambda]$	3 1−2	4 Original $[\lambda]$	5 Reduced $[\lambda]$	6 4−5
0	100	100	0	100	100	0
1	102·5	101·9	0·6	102·7	102·4	0·3
2	109·4	107·6	1·8	109·3	108·3	1·0
3	114·7	112·5	2·2	112·3	111·4	0·9
4	118·2	116·1	2·1	114·3	113·4	0·9
5	120·5	118·7	1·8	115·7	114·9	0·8
6	121·9	120·5	1·6	116·8	116·0	0·8
7	123·0	121·8	1·2	117·7	117·0	0·7
8	123·7	122·8	0·9	118·5	117·8	0·7

Notes
The price of oil doubles successively in quarters 1 and 2.
WPI: wholesale price index.

essential raw material. It can be seen that the rate of increase in the price level following the oil price rise is reduced appreciably under the alternative $[\hat{\lambda}]$. The difference in the price index is particularly significant in the early periods of the simulation, and tapers off only slowly thereafter. It stands at a maximum of 2·2 index number points for the chemical industry in the third quarter, but is still 0·9 in the eighth quarter of the simulation. For WPI the absolute difference is less marked, with a maximum of one index number point in the second quarter, but it falls off even more slowly in each successive quarter. Thus the influence of a reduction in $[\hat{\lambda}]$ persists through time largely because of the myriad indirect effects among industrial prices and between prices and wages.

Table 12.4   *The rate of inflation under different adjustment regimes**

Period (quarters)	Industry			
	General Chemicals		Aggregate WPI	
	Original $[\hat{\lambda}]$	Reduced $[\hat{\lambda}]$	Original $[\hat{\lambda}]$	Reduced $[\hat{\lambda}]$
0–2	18·8	15·2	18·6	16·6
1–3	23·8	20·8	18·7	17·6
2–4	16·1	15·8	9·1	9·4
3–5	10·1	11·0	6·1	6·3
4–6	6·3	7·6	4·4	4·6
5–7	4·1	5·2	3·5	3·7
6–8	3·0	3·8	2·9	3·1

* The rate of inflation is defined as the annual percentage change in the price index calculated from table 12.3 by applying the formula:

$$\left[\frac{WPI_2 - WPI_0}{WPI_0} \right] \times 200$$

The influence of concentration on the dynamics of price adjustment is thus clearly demonstrated by these results, but we also need to consider the implications for the rate of inflation as conventionally defined. For this purpose we used the simulation results reported above to derive the rate of inflation in terms of the *proportionate* change in the price level. The rate of inflation thus defined was 'annualised' from six-monthly changes in the price index, and the results are reported in table 12.4. It can be seen that the impact of concentration is to shift the time distribution of inflation towards the present. Furthermore, under the original $[\hat{\lambda}]$ the rate of inflation which follows from the oil price rise has a significantly higher peak than under the reduced $[\hat{\lambda}]$ regime. For the general chemicals industry inflation is 3·6 percentage points higher in the first six months of the simulation, and for the industrial sector as a whole there is a difference of two percentage points. After approximately four quarters the difference in the rates of inflation under the two adjustment regimes is reversed, but it is important to notice that the difference now becomes small in absolute terms, far smaller than in the early phase of the simulation. Moreover this difference occurs at a point in time when the rate of inflation itself has fallen by half from its peak of the first two quarters. This reversal reflects the catching-up effect of the price index under the reduced $[\hat{\lambda}]$ in the later period of the simulation, for it is clear from the model that the long-run equilibrium price level is the same irrespective of $[\hat{\lambda}]$. Thus the impact of concentration through faster price adjustments is to heighten an inflationary shock in the short run, i.e. to raise the rate of inflation to a peak where it would otherwise be spread more evenly over time.

The significance of this impact stems from the following additional considerations. First there is the well known feedback from prices to wages. The sequential relationship between wages and prices has been firmly established by empirical research. Henry, Sawyer and Smith (1976) found that the regression coefficient on the proportional price change in their wage equation became highly significant when the estimation period included data for the inflationary 1970s. Their results suggest that wages are responsive to a high absolute rate of inflation, even if it is of short duration, whereas they do not respond to a prolonged but 'creeping' inflation. The existence of such threshold effects was confirmed independently by Hamermesh (1970), using US data. Both pieces of evidence indicate that spreading inflation over a longer period of time following an exogenous shock could actually make a difference to the long-run rate of price change by dampening feedback effects from wages. The short-run peak in inflation associated with higher concentration is likely to sensitise inflationary expectations throughout the economy, and it is in this context that the influence of concentration gains special significance.

Another reason why faster short-run adjustments could imply a higher rate of inflation in the long run has to do with the industrial sector itself. The dynamic input–output model implies that the ultimate, long-run, increase in prices is independent of the rate of adjustment. However, in practice this need not be so. In industries where firms are constrained in the rate at which they can pass on cost increases the threat of liquidation will impose greater pressures on them to absorb such increases either through productivity gains or through input substitutions. This factor was considered of prime importance by the Monopolies Commission (1973) when it examined the influence of parallel pricing behaviour on the inflationary process.[13] For it is clear that from the firm's viewpoint a delay in price adjustment may have the same consequences as no adjustment at all. Thus industrial concentration, by allowing firms with market power to resist temporary reduction in their price–cost margins, can contribute to the long-run upward drift in the price level.

Finally we need to consider the assumptions upon which the simulation, and thus the reported inflationary impact, is based. The use of a 15 per cent change in industry concentration ratios to derive the reduced [$\hat{\lambda}$] would seem a most conservative estimate. Taking a longer view of changes in industrial structure would suggest that far greater reductions in the concentration ratios would represent an equally plausible assumption. Furthermore, applying uniform changes in every industrial sector may by itself attenuate the impact of market structure on inflation. It is obvious that certain sectors, by virtue of their position in the intermediate chain of production, are of greater importance than others. The mineral oil refining industry is, once again, an appropriate example in the context of the oil price rise. Hence changes in concentration in key sectors of industry are potentially far more significant for the inflationary process than the results reported above would indicate.

To sum up, our analysis suggests that industrial market structure has an important influence on the inflationary process. The main impact of concentration is to raise the short-run rate of inflation which follows from an exogenous shock to peaks which would otherwise not be attained. Considered against the background of the present UK inflationary experience, such an influence is of considerable significance.

5. Conclusions and implications for policy

We began this chapter by drawing attention to the role of government policy in hastening the move towards greater concentration. The most aggressive pro-merger policy was launched in 1966 with the creation of the Industrial Reorganisation Corporation. Among many others, two of the largest amalgamations ever to take place in the UK were sponsored by the

IRC, namely the GEC–AEI and the Leyland mergers. This instrument of policy came into conflict with another whose purpose was to uncover anti-competitive behaviour, i.e. the Monopolies and Mergers Commission. This divergence of policy must now seem even more striking in light of the disappointing results from mergers.

However, we argued in this chapter that the trend to concentration has important implications for the inflationary mechanism. That is not the same as saying that concentration actually causes inflation. What we have shown is that a high level of concentration will give added added impetus to inflationary pressures which are working their way through the economy. More significantly, by the time concentration had risen to its highest ever levels in the early 1970s, world-wide inflationary pressures began to follow one another in quick succession. The wage explosion, the commodity price boom and the OPEC oil price rise following the Yom Kippur war all conspired to raise the rate of inflation in the UK to unprecedented heights. In this context the transmission process of price increases, and hence the role of market structure, becomes a critical factor.

These conclusions are highlighted by the government's current reliance on competitive forces in the industrial sectors to contain rising prices. But while a statutory prices policy has been abandoned in favour of competition policy as a major instrument in the fight against inflation, no one appears to have seriously considered the question whether effective price competition is the order of the day in British manufacturing. The analysis presented in this chapter casts some doubt on the notion and suggests that if competition policy is going to be used as a tool for the management of inflation, then the relationship between industrial structure and the process of inflation needs to be looked at much more closely.

Notes

1   Without implicating them, I wish to thank the co-authors of this book for their helpful comments, Phil Murphy for technical assistance and the Nuffield Foundation for financial support.
2   Pressure of space does not allow us a fuller discussion of the merits of various concentration indices, but details can be found in Hannah and Kay (1977), chapter 4.
3   See UK Government (1978), pp. 57–9.

4　　See *ibid.*, p. 154.

5　　For a comprehensive review of the welfare effects of monopoly and oligopoly see Scherer (1980), chapter 17.

6　　See Hannah and Kay (1977), chapter 3.

7　　See Cowling and Waterson (1976).

8　　Details are given in Coutts, Godley and Nordhaus (1978), table 3.1.

9　　Note the close resemblance of this specification to that of equation 9 in chapter 10.

10　Note that $[\Delta P_t]$ is fed back to determine $[\Delta P_{t+1}]$, then $[\Delta P_{t+1}]$ to determine $[\Delta P_{t+2}]$, and so on in successive loops.

11　The estimates of equation 4 reported in table 12.2 were used to reduce $[\hat{\lambda}]$ by applying a uniform 15 per cent decrease in the concentration ratios.

12　The dyamic input–output model was 'closed' by means of a wage equation based on Henry, Sawyer and Smith (1976). Only the more important features of the model and of the simulation are reported in this chapter. For further results see Domberger (1980).

13　See Monopolies Commission (1973), p. 30.

Appendix

Price adjustment coefficients: original and reduced

Industry title	Original λ	λ based on 15% reduction in CR_{71}
1. Mineral Oil Refining	0·80	0·73
2. General Chemicals	0·48	0·41
3. Synthetic Resins	0·62	0·57
4. Pharmaceutical Chemicals	0·62	0·57
5. Other Chemicals	0·39	0·32
6. Iron Castings	0·38	0·34
7. Iron and Steel	0·59	0·51
8. Aluminium	0·64	0·59
9. Non-ferrous Metals	0·72	0·66
10. Industrial Plant	0·74	0·72
11. Office Machinery	0·22	0·18
12. Mechanical Handling Equipment	0·27	0·24
13. Other Mechanical Engineering	0·31	0·23
14. Instrument Engineering	0·19	0·16
15. Electronics and Telecommunications	0·54	0·46
16. Domestic Electrical Appliances	0·36	0·30
17. Electrical Machinery	0·38	0·32
18. Shipbuilding	0·28	0·23
19. Wheeled Tractors	0·57	0·48
20. Motor Vehicles	0·42	0·35
21. Other Vehicles	0·53	0·44
22. Engineers' Small Tools	0·09	0·07
23. Wire Manufacture	0·63	0·59
24. Other Metal goods	0·50	0·47
25. Man-made Fibres	1·00	0·90
26. Other Textiles	0·64	0·61
27. Leather	0·47	0·45
28. Clothing	0·47	0·45
29. Footwear	0·52	0·49
30. Building Materials	0·66	0·61
31. Timber and Furniture	0·40	0·39
32. Paper and Board	0·79	0·75
33. Paper Products	0·53	0·50
34. Rubber	0·68	0·62
35. Plastics	0·42	0·40
36. Other Manufactures	0·54	0·50

Source. Domberger (1980)

13   Graham W. Smith

Inflation expectations: direct observations and their determinants

1.   Introduction

Over the last decade increasing importance has been attached to the role of inflation expectations in macroeconomics. In theoretical models explicit attention has been given to the inclusion and modelling of these expectations, particularly in so far as they determine the time path of real output and inflation. In empirical work there has been a trend away from the use of simple proxies for inflation expectations in favour of using more direct measures. These are said to avoid the problem of joint hypothesis testing, that is, testing a hypothesis conditional on the assumption that an auxiliary hypothesis is true. Moreover they provide the opportunity to test alternative hypotheses of expectations formation. Direct measures are derived from survey data, of which two types have been used. The Livingston surveys for the United States ask for the exact figure expected for the value of a specific price index at some future point in time. Such data can readily be transformed to expected inflation. The CBI and Gallup surveys for Great Britain ask respondents to indicate only the direction of change. Carlson and Parkin (1975) have shown how the Gallup data could be transformed to give a measure of inflation expectations, and derived a time series. The purpose of this chapter[1] is to revise and extend the Carlson–Parkin (1975) time series of consumers' inflation expectations and to investigate the determinants of those expectations. In the next section the derivation of the expectations series is discussed. In section 3 some models of expectations formation are examined, and in section 4 some tentative results are presented. Section 5 has concluding comments.

2. The survey data and their transformation

Social Surveys (Gallup Poll) Ltd has carried out monthly surveys of
a stratified sample of approximately 1,000 consumers in Great
Britain since 1961. Many questions are asked in the survey, the
answers to which are of potential interest to economists. The one
relevant here is 'Do you expect that prices will go up, decrease, or
remain the same during the next six months?' Over the period
1961–77 at least fifty per cent of respondents every month replied
'Go up.' On nine occasions less than 0·5 per cent of those sampled
replied, 'Decrease.' In all surveys some consumers have answered,
'Remain the same.' In general the proportion answering 'Go up'
has tended to rise over the period, whereas those answering
'Decrease' or 'Remain the same' has fallen. The proportion
replying 'Don't know' has fallen, especially since 1974.

The basic theory for deriving a time series expectational variable
from sample survey responses of direction of change was
formulated by Theil (1952). A similar approach was developed
independently by Carlson and Parkin, to which the reader is
referred for a discussion of the theory. In particular, Carlson and
Parkin show that:

$$\Delta P_t^e = -\delta_t\left(\frac{a_t + b_t}{a_t - b_t}\right) \tag{1}$$

and

$$\sigma_t = 2\delta_t\left(\frac{1}{a_t - b_t}\right) \tag{2}$$

where ΔP_t^e is the expectation formed in period t of inflation in
period $t+1$, σ_t is the standard deviation of inflation expectations, δ_t
is the scaling factor, and a_t, b_t are the abscissae of a cumulative
standard distribution corresponding to the proportions of
respondents expecting prices not to rise, and expecting prices to
fall, respectively. In computing the expected inflation series it then
becomes necessary to (i) interpret the 'Don't know' responses, (ii)
make an assumption about the distribution of inflation
expectations, and (iii) determine the value of δ_t. These
requirements are discussed in turn.

Carlson and Parkin argued that a constant proportion of
interviewees, α, are incapable of forming inflation expectations.

Those capable of forming expectations who answer 'Don't know' rather than 'Remain the same' do so because their subjective distributions have different dispersions. Consequently

$$(D_t - \alpha) = \beta C_t + u_t \tag{3}$$

where D_t and C_t are the percentages replying 'Don't know' and 'Remain the same' and u_t is sampling noise. After rearranging equation 3, they estimated the relationship by ordinary least squares and then, detecting significant positive first-order serial correlation in the residuals, re-estimated the parameters, assuming the error followed a first-order autoregressive scheme. They found:

$$D_t = 2 \cdot 539 + 0 \cdot 201 \, C_t + \hat{u}_t$$
$$[3 \cdot 18] \quad [6 \cdot 70]$$

$$\hat{u}_t = 0 \cdot 494 \, \hat{u}_{t-1} + \hat{v}_t \qquad \bar{R}^2 = 0 \cdot 61$$
$$[12 \cdot 05]$$

where figures in parentheses are ratios of the estimated coefficients to their asymptotic standard errors. However, on re-estimating the model it was found that the original estimates were for the period 1961–71, not 1961–73 — the time span over which ΔP_t^e was computed. Using the program RALS from the Autoreg library, the model was re-estimated over the period 1961–71 with a linear twelfth-order autoregressive scheme, since the data are monthly. The relationship seemed best characterised as:

$$D_t = 2 \cdot 884 + 0 \cdot 179 \, C_t + \hat{u}_t$$
$$[6 \cdot 12] \quad [6 \cdot 82]$$

$$\hat{u}_t = 0 \cdot 255 \, \hat{u}_{t-1} + 0 \cdot 357 \, \hat{u}_{t-2} + 0 \cdot 006 \, \hat{u}_{t-3} + 0 \cdot 003 \, \hat{u}_{t-4}$$
$$[2 \cdot 74] \qquad [3 \cdot 80] \qquad [0 \cdot 06] \qquad [0 \cdot 03]$$

$$- 0 \cdot 194 \, \hat{u}_{t-5} + 0 \cdot 184 \, \hat{u}_{t-6} + \hat{v}_t \qquad \hat{\sigma} = 1 \cdot 27$$
$$[2 \cdot 04] \qquad [1 \cdot 97]$$

The χ^2 statistic for the test of the null hypothesis that the autoregressive restrictions are valid is 8·05, which is less than the 5 per cent critical value of $\chi^2_{(6)}$ of 12·59; the restrictions are not rejected. The Pierce (1971) residual correlogram statistic is 5·48, which is less than the 5 per cent criticial value of $\chi^2_{(20)}$ of 31·41, indicating serially independent residuals. Moreover a test of parameter stability for the period 1972–73 finds $\chi^2_{(24)} = 4·12$, which is less than the 5 per cent critical value of 36·41, not rejecting parameter stability. Consequently the model was estimated over the period 1961–73, 1974–77 being used for the test of parameter stability. $\chi^2_{(48)}$ was found to be 72·46, which is greater than the 5 per cent critical value of 65·16, rejecting the null hypothesis and indicating an incorrectly specified model and a change in the stochastic properties of the variables in the true data generation process of D_t. Although Carlson and Parkin used a relationship estimated over the period 1961–71 to generate data for the period 1961–73, this has not resulted in an internally inconsistent ΔP_t^e for the period 1961–73, for two reasons: first, their value of α of 2·5 is not significantly different from the value estimated above on the basis of a t test; second, the hypothesis of parameter stability over the period 1972–73 is not rejected. However, the relationship cannot be used in transforming the sample survey data to 1977. Between 1961 and 1971 D_t was less than 2·5 on eight occasions but from 1972 until 1977 D_t was less than 2·5 in thirty-four surveys. This is too large a frequency to have occurred by chance. Under the Carlson–Parkin hypothesis it implies that on those occasions a greater proportion of respondents formed inflation expectations than were actually capable of so doing. The hypothesis was rejected. Moreover, after considerable experimentation, it was not possible to find a stable relationship for the whole period. The absence of such a relationship is consistent with findings by Smith (1978) in work on the UK which used the CBI *Industrial Trends* survey and Danes (1975), which used data from the *Survey of Industrial Trends* of the Australian Chamber of Manufacturers and Bank of New South Wales. As an alternative hypothesis, those who replied 'Don't know' were interpreted as not being interested in the question. Assuming such responses are distributed independently of the other responses (that is, independently of inflation expectations) in the population, they can be considered purely random. This is equivalent to assuming $D_t = \alpha$. The data were transformed so that:

$$A_t^* = \frac{A_t}{1 - \dfrac{D_t}{100}}, \qquad B_t^* = \frac{B_t}{1 - \dfrac{D_t}{100}} \text{ and } C_t^* = \frac{C_t}{1 - \dfrac{D_t}{100}}$$

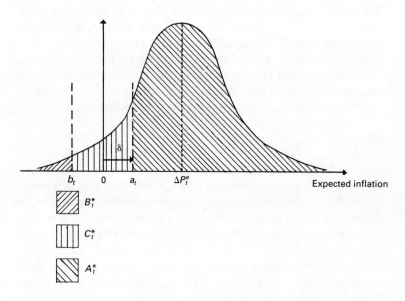

Fig. 13.1 Subjective probability density function of expected inflation

where A_t, B_t, C_t and D_t are the percentages of respondents answering 'Go up', 'Decrease', 'Remain the same' and 'Don't know' respectively and where:

$$A_t^* + B_t^* + C_t^* = 100$$

The second question which arises in transforming the survey data is the form of the distribution of inflation expectations. Carlson and Parkin, and others, have assumed that at a point in time expected inflation is normally distributed across the population. Such a distribution is illustrated in fig. 13.1. The sample survey responses do not provide sufficient information to test this assumption for the Gallup data. However, necessary conditions for a symmetrical unimodal distribution are not rejected (Smith, 1980). In the absence of further information on which to choose between alternative symmetrical unimodal distributions, and following many other researchers in this area, normality is assumed. In certain circumstances this can result in problems. Specifically, in nine surveys $B_t = 0$; that is, less than 0·5 per cent answered,

'Decrease', and with rounded data this is reported as zero. Assuming a normal distribution of expected inflation, then the probability that $B_t = 0$ is itself zero and, as $B_t \to 0$, $b_t \to -\infty$. Equation 1 cannot be used to calculate expected inflation in such circumstances, and in previous work the problem has been dealt with in two ways. Theil replaced zero values by 0·25 per cent.[3] Carlson and Parkin, however, used the relationship:

$$\Delta P_t^e = \delta - a_t \sigma_t$$

instead of equation 1, the value of σ_t being the larger of the two on either side of the observation for which $B_t = 0$. In the present study, where $B_t < 0·5$, the actual unrounded values of the aggregate survey results have been calculated from data disaggregated by sex, age, class and region. On no occasion was the value of B_t calculated as zero.

The third issue which merits attention is the determination of the value of the scaling factor, δ_t. This has been approached in three ways. In some studies a constant value has been imposed; for example, Knöbl (1974) took $\hat{\delta} = 2·00$, whereas Juster (1975) used $\hat{\delta} = 1·25$. De Menil (1974) and Danes (1975) estimated the scaling factor. Their survey data had a question about actual price changes over the previous period as well as expected price changes in the future. By calculating a time series of actual inflation a scaling factor was found between that series and a corresponding measure calculated from published government statistics. This value was then used in constructing the expectational variable. Carlson and Parkin did not have survey data on actual price changes. They scaled their measure so that the average values of expected and actual inflation are equal over the sample period, that is,

$$\delta = \sum_{t-1}^{T} \Delta P_t \left/ \sum_{t-1}^{T} - \left(\frac{a_t + b_t}{a_t - b_t} \right) \right.$$

where

$$\Delta P_t = \frac{P_t - P_{t-12}}{P_{t-12}} \cdot 100$$

and P_t is the general index of retail prices (all items) at time t. A similar method is used here. The particular specification of Δp_t

which Carlson and Parkin used in calculating $\hat{\delta}$ and in their empirical work on the proximate determinants of ΔP_t^e suffers from a potential weakness. Prices could stop rising or even be falling for a few months, and yet their series could have $\Delta P_t > 0$. Although there is no theoretical basis for choosing the period over which to take differences in calculating actual inflation, for consistency a six-month logarithmic change is used, since expectations are reported for a six-month horizon. Hence in this study,

$$\Delta P_t = \left(\ln \frac{P_t}{P_{t-6}} \right) . 200 \approx \frac{P_t - P_{t-6}}{P_{t-3}} \quad 200$$

If actual inflation is approximately constant over the six-month period, then this measure approximates the inflation rate in the middle of the period. The more inflation increases over the period, the closer the measure approximates the inflation rate at the end of the six months. On six occasions in the early part of the period, ΔP_t was negative and so the expectational variable was scaled so that its mean equalled the mean of the modulus of the actual rate of inflation over the period 1961–77; $\hat{\delta} = 2 \cdot 1386$.

The time series of consumers' inflation expectations is tabulated in the appendix and plotted in fig. 13.2 together with, for the purpose of simple comparison, actual inflation calculated as described above. The graphs are aligned so that at time t actual inflation is compared with its expectation formed six months earlier. Comparing the measure presented here with that of Carlson and Parkin, the two, of course, move together, although the former series generally takes values greater than the latter and has greater variation. Both these characteristics arise as a result of the different procedures used in handling the 'Don't know' responses and in calculating the scaling factor. So far as the occasions when $B = 0$ are concerned, in three cases the value of ΔP_t^e calculated here exceeds that of Carlson and Parkin, whereas in two the reverse is true. The mean absolute difference expressed as a percentage of the average value of the Carlson–Parkin measure in the periods when $B_t = 0$ is 12·5. Their method of dealing with such cases appears to have produced plausible results. In comparing the expected and actual inflation series in fig. 13.2, the former appears noisier than the latter. However, the degree of noise in the actual inflation series would increase as the time span over which the price

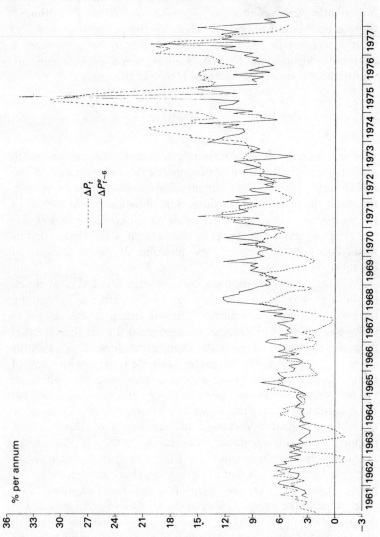

Fig. 13.2 Expected and actual inflation, 1961–77

level is differenced is reduced. In the period to 1967 the expected inflation rate precedes the actual inflation rate with a cycle that has a smaller amplitude. The former fluctuates about a higher mean, hence expected inflation exceeds actual inflation at peaks and troughs. For the rest of the period, however, cycles in expected and actual inflation have similar amplitudes. In the next section alternative hypotheses of expectations formation are discussed before being tested with these data.

3. Expectations formation hypotheses

The hypotheses to be examined can usefully be classified into two basic groups: error-learning and extrapolative models. First the error-learning models will be presented, then the extrapolative models, and finally a general model, which includes the two basic groups as special cases, will be outlined.

First-order error-learning, or adaptive expectations, postulates that expectations are revised by a constant proportion of the most recent error:

$$\Delta P_t^e - \Delta P_{t-1}^e = \lambda(\Delta P_t - \Delta P_{t-1}^e) \qquad 0 < \lambda \le 1 \qquad (6)$$

where ΔP_t^e is the subjective anticipation formed at time t of inflation at time $t+1$, and ΔP_t is the actual rate of inflation at time t. Muth (1960) and Theil and Wage (1964) have shown that adaptive expectations are an optimal linear predictor in the sense of producing minimum mean square error forecasts if the series being predicted is generated by an autoregressive moving average process. Rose (1972) has shown, however, that if the time path of the variable to be forecast evolves according to an ARIMA (autoregressive integrated moving average) process, then for error-learning to be optimal, in yielding minimum mean-square error forecasts, all previous errors must be considered. Carlson and Parkin presented and tested a second-order error-learning model:

$$\Delta P_t^e - \Delta P_{t-1}^e = \lambda_1 (\Delta P_t - \Delta P_{t-1}^e) + \lambda_2(\Delta P_{t-1} - \Delta P_{t-2}^e) \qquad (7)[4]$$

which may be expressed more generally as:

$$\Delta P_t^e - \Delta P_{t-1}^e = \sum_{i=0}^{\infty} \lambda_i(\Delta P_{t-i} - \Delta P_{t-i-1}^e) \qquad (8)$$

Flemming (1976) examines the adaptive expectations hypothesis within the framework of rational expectations, which '... postulates that on average, and in the long run, people's expectations will be fulfilled' (p. 58). He distinguishes what he calls stronger and weaker forms of the rational expectations hypothesis. The former argues that the assumption of rationality implies that expectations are generated by the theory believed, by the theorist, to be supported by the empirical evidence. The latter, however, is based on the premise that, because of costs and difficulties in theorising, economic agents rationally form expectations on the basis of rules of thumb. 'Their "rationality" only implies that a rule of thumb will be abandoned if it is shown to be consistently wrong' (p. 59). Flemming discusses a multi-geared first-order error-learning hypothesis. Adaptive expectations produce consistently inaccurate forecasts if the variable being predicted is trended.[5] It seems reasonable, therefore, to postulate that economic agents use the adaptive expectations mechanical rule on the lowest-order difference of the inflation process to have shown no trend. With Flemming's hypothesis, upward changes of gear occur when agents *perceive* that the variable to which they have been applying adaptive expectations is trended. A downward change of gear occurs when the economic agent perceives that the next variable down is not trended.

Frenkel (1975) outlines an error-learning expectations-formation scheme based on the distinction between long-term and short-term expectations. Long-term expectations are related to actual inflation by a first-order error-learning process:

$$\Delta P_t^{le} - \Delta P_{t-1}^{le} = \lambda_1 (\Delta P_t - \Delta P_{t-1}^{le}) \tag{9}$$

where Δp_t^{le} is the 'long term' expectation formed at time t. Short-term expectations are revised by constant proportions of the most recent error in short-term expectations and the difference between the long-term expectation and the actual rate of inflation:

$$\Delta P_t^e - \Delta P_{t-1}^e = \lambda_2 (\Delta P_t^e - \Delta P_{t-1}^e) + \lambda_3 (\Delta P_t^{le} - \Delta P_t) \tag{10}$$

From equation 9, expressing long-term expectations as an infinite distributed lag of past actual inflation rates before substituting for ΔP_t^{le} in equation 10 and simplifying gives:

$$\Delta P_t^e - \Delta P_{t-1}^e = (\lambda_2 - \lambda_3)(\Delta P_t - \Delta P_{t-1}) + \lambda_1 \lambda_2 (\Delta P_{t-1} - \Delta P_{t-2}^e)$$
$$+ (1 - \lambda_1 - \lambda_2)(\Delta P_{t-1}^e - \Delta P_{t-2}^e) \tag{11}$$

If a random error having the usual classical properties was included in equation 10, then equation 11 would have a first-order moving average error.

The basic model of extrapolative expectations hypothesises that the most recent actual rate of inflation is adjusted by a constant proportion of the recent change in the inflation rate, to give expected inflation:

$$\Delta P_t^e = \Delta P_t + \theta(\Delta P_t - \Delta P_{t-1}) \tag{12}$$

Second-order extrapolative expectations may be characterised as:

$$\Delta P_t^e = \Delta P_t + \theta_1(\Delta P_t - \Delta P_{t-1}) + \theta_2(\Delta P_{t-1} - \Delta P_{t-2}) \tag{13}$$

More generally, extrapolative expectations may be written as:

$$\Delta P_t^e = \theta_0 + \sum_{i=1}^{\infty} \theta_i \Delta P_{t-i+1} \tag{14}$$

With the possible exception of Flemming's hypothesis, the models reviewed can be encompassed within a more general formulation. Consider the model:

$$\Delta P_t^e = \mu_1 \Delta P_t + \mu_2 \Delta P_{t-1} + \ldots + \mu_{(n+1)} \Delta P_{t-n}$$
$$+ v_1 \Delta P_{t-1}^e + v_2 \Delta P_{t-2}^e + \ldots + v_m \Delta P_{t-m}^e \tag{15}$$

where expected inflation is a distributed lag of actual inflation and of previous expectations of inflation. Now, for example, if $m = n+1 = 2$, $\mu_1 = 1 - v_1 = \lambda_1$ and $\mu_2 = -v_2 = \lambda_3$, we have second-order error-learning. If $m = n+1 = 1$ and $\mu_1 = 1 - v_1 = \lambda_1$, then the general model reduces to adaptive expectations. If all v_i are zero we have the general extrapolative model, and if in addition $\mu_1 - 1 = -\mu_2 = \theta$ the extrapolative model of equation 12 is derived. If all μ_i are zero, then expectations formation is characterised as autoregressive. Having outlined some basic models of expectations formation and a general formulation, tests of alternative hypotheses are described in the next section.

4.   Empirical results

The empirical estimation was primarily centred on the general model, equation 15. A constant term was included in that model and an error term added. However, because of well known and potentially serious econometric problems which can arise in estimating such models, a linear autoregressive error structure was hypothesised.[6] The choice of estimation period was determined by two main criteria: the results of previous empirical work, and econometric requirements specific to this study. Previous work by Carlson and Parkin found that expectations formation depended, to some extent, on whether inflation was 'high' or 'low'.[7] Any such distinction is somewhat arbitrary, but after inspection of fig. 13.2 three sub-periods were chosen: May 1961–June 1967, June 1967–December 1972 and January 1973–December 1977. As a check for model adequacy, the last six observations in each sub-period were not used for estimation but were retained for a test of parameter stability. The strategy adopted was to estimate a general model and to impose successively more restrictive constraints. In presenting results it seems useful first to discuss the main positive results and then describe some of the negative ones which emerged in investigating many models. To help focus attention, a generalised second-order error-learning model is presented for each sub-period; the results are presented in table 13.1. For the first estimation sub-period, May 1961–December 1966, the coefficients on ΔP_t and ΔP_{t-1} are individually insignificantly different from zero on the basis of t tests at the 5 per cent level. The null hypothesis that ΔP_t and ΔP_{t-1} have no influence on the mean of ΔP_t^e was accepted on the basis of an F test at the 5 per cent level.[8] Equation 2 of table 13.1 is the model with this restriction imposed; for this sub-period inflation expectations appear to be autoregressive.[9] Equation 3 in table 13.1 is a generalised second-order error-learning model augmented by a dummy variable for the sterling devaluation of November 1967 and estimated over the period June 1967–June 1972. The null hypothesis that the coefficients on ΔP_{t-1}^e and ΔP_{t-2}^e are simultaneously zero is not rejected on the basis of an F test at the 5 per cent level. Neither is the null hypothesis that the coefficients on ΔP_{t-1}^e, ΔP_{t-2}^e and D, the devaluation dummy variable, are simultaneously zero.[10] The models having these restrictions

Table 13.1 *The dependent variable is ΔP_t^e*

Time period	Constant	ΔP_t	ΔP_{t-1}^e	ΔP_{t-1}	ΔP_{t-2}^e	D	ρ	σ	DW	Z_1	Z_2
1. May 1961–Dec. 1966	1·575 [2·571]	0·052 [0·562]	0·404 [3·100]	−0·070 [0·767]	0·278 [2·090]		0·311 [2·154]	0·949		9·09	8·28
2. May 1961–Dec. 1966	1·489 [2·542]		0·400 [3·127]		0·285 [2·248]		0·275 [2·025]	0·937		8·70	8·39
3. June 1967–June 1972	5·632 [3·635]	0·380 [1·508]	0·176 [1·266]	−0·322 [1·378]	0·161 [1·110]	1·937 [1·033]	−0·340 [2·330]	1·764		11·61	5·16
4. June 1967–June 1972	8·266 [13·331]	0·551 [2·316]		−0·428 [1·857]		1·545 [0·827]	−0·336 [2·362]	1·791		10·17	11·70
5. June 1967–June 1972	8·410 [14·237]	0·582 [2·489]		−0·478 [2·167]			−0·348 [2·514]	1·785		10·23	13·52
6. Jan. 1973–June 1977	9·999 [4·178]	0·556 [1·846]	0·072 [0·505]	−0·571 [1·991]	0·057 [0·393]			4·070		4·77	5·33
7. Jan. 1973–June 1977	11·141 [6·813]	0·638 [2·364]		−0·636 [2·390]				4·006	1·79	5·56	6·60

Note. Figures in parentheses are absolute values of ratios of estimated coefficients to standard errors. D is a dummy variable for November 1967. ρ is a seventh-order autoregressive parameter in equations 1 and 2 and fifth-order in equations 3–5. σ is the residual error standard deviation, and DW is the Durbin–Watson statistic. Z_1 is a tests statistic for parameter stability using the actual values of the regressors for the six months after the estimation period. Z_2 is the Pierce (1971) residual correlogram statistic based on the sum of squares of the first twelve autocorrelations of residuals.

imposed are presented in table 13.1, equations 4 and 5. The results indicate that over this period consumers' inflation expectations depend on recent actual inflation rates. Contrary to the findings of Carlson and Parkin, devaluation apears to have no proximate direct effect on inflation expectations other than through its influence on actual inflation. There are two possible reasons for the difference in results: the alternative formulation of actual inflation used in this study, and the fact that November 1967 was one of the observations for which Carlson and Parkin had to derive ΔP_t^e from an alternative to equation 1, since B was reported as zero in that month. Broadly similar results were found for the estimation period January 1973 to June 1977, although for this period no autoregressive scheme was found necessary. In particular the inclusion of ΔP_{t-1}^e and ΔP_{t-2}^e as regressors was rejected on the basis of an F test; for this period, expected inflation appears to depend on recent actual rates of inflation.[11]

Some of the principal negative results may be of interest. First, tests of the multi-geared adaptive expectations hypothesis proved difficult to implement. Although it is possible to find when, for example, the inflation rate is trended, difficulties arise in attempting to identify when economic agents perceive that the variable is trended and consequently change up a gear. The absence, therefore, of empirical evidence for the hypothesis should not be taken as evidence refuting it. Following Carlson and Parkin, dummy variables were included in an attempt to pick up any effects of economic policy variables and political considerations on inflation expectations. Their broad findings were confirmed, although whereas they found an almost significant effect for the Confederation of British Industry's voluntary price restraint of July 1971 in a model estimated to the end of 1971, no similar effect was found in this study. In an unpublished study Smith (1975) found that there was an impact effect on inflation expectations of a reduction of almost five percentage points associated with the election result of March 1974; that result is not confirmed. Moreover, although dummy variables for phases 2 and 3 of the 1972–74 anti-inflation policy were negatively signed, they were insignificantly different from zero on the basis of t tests at the 5 per cent level.

The question arises as to whether the inflation expectations used in this study are rational in the sense that they fully incorporate all information present, directly or indirectly, in actual inflation. Mullineaux (1978), following Pesando (1975), shows that this imposes two requirements, efficiency and consistency. The former requires efficient utilisation of information present in actual inflation to generate one-period predictions. The latter requires that the information be used consistently in the generation of multi-span forecasts. More formally, consider the following three equations:

$$\Delta P_t = \alpha_1 \Delta P_{t-1} + \alpha_2 \Delta P_{t-2} + \dots + \alpha_n \Delta P_{t-n} + u_{1t} \tag{16}$$

$$_t\Delta P^e_{t-1} = \beta_1 \Delta P_{t-1} + \beta_2 \Delta P_{t-2} + \dots + \beta_n \Delta P_{t-n} + u_{2t} \tag{17}$$

$$_t\Delta P^e_{t-2} = \gamma_1(_{t-1}\Delta P^e_{t-2}) + \gamma_2 \Delta P_{t-2} + \dots + \gamma_n \Delta P_{t-n} + u_{3t} \tag{18}$$

where $_t\Delta P^e_{t-1}$ is the expectation formed in $t-1$ of actual inflation in time t and $_t\Delta P^e_{t-2}$ is the expectation formed in period $t-2$ of actual inflation in t. The null hypothesis of rationality requires efficiency, that is, $\alpha_i = \beta_i$ for all $i = 1 \dots n$, and consistency, that is, $\beta_i = \gamma_i$ for all $i = 1 \dots n$. Clearly, since for this study data of multi-span forecasts are not available, only the hypothesis that $\alpha_i = \beta_i$ for all $i = 1 \dots n$ can be tested. A necessary condition for rationality is potentially testable, but this condition is not sufficient. Hence on the basis of the results it is not possible to say that the expectations are rational. The test for efficiency proposed by Mullineaux is found by subtracting equation 17 from equation 16:

$$\Delta P_t - {_t\Delta P^e_{t-1}} = (\alpha_1 - \beta_1) \Delta P_{t-1} + (\alpha_2 - \beta_2) \Delta P_{t-2} + \dots$$
$$+ (\alpha_n - \beta_n) \Delta P_{t-n} + u_{1t} - u_{2t} \tag{19}$$

The test involves adding an intercept to equation 19 and assuming the error follows an autoregressive process. Efficiency requires that all the estimated coefficients are simultaneously insignificantly different from zero and that the residuals are serially independent. The model was estimated for $n = 3$ and assuming a twelfth-order autoregressive process.[12] The model was estimated for the whole data period and for the three sub-periods used earlier in this chapter. The result for the first period is similar to those for the second and whole periods, whereas the result for the third is atypical. Consequently only the results for the first and third periods are reported.

May 1961 to December 1966

$$\Delta P_t - \Delta P^e_{t-1} = -3{\cdot}480 + 1{\cdot}063\,\Delta P_{t-1} - 0{\cdot}091\,\Delta P_{t-2} - 0{\cdot}368\,\Delta P_{t-3} + \hat{u}_t$$
$$\qquad\qquad\quad [5{\cdot}641]\quad [4{\cdot}079]\qquad\quad [0{\cdot}227]\qquad\quad [1{\cdot}446]$$

$$\hat{u}_t = 0{\cdot}083\,\hat{u}_{t-1} - 0{\cdot}021\,\hat{u}_{t-2} + 0{\cdot}289\,\hat{u}_{t-3} + 0{\cdot}268\,\hat{u}_{t-4}$$
$$\qquad [0{\cdot}488]\qquad [0{\cdot}127]\qquad [1{\cdot}929]\qquad [1{\cdot}748]$$

$$\qquad + 0{\cdot}218\,\hat{u}_{t-5} - 0{\cdot}472\,\hat{u}_{t-6} + 0{\cdot}103\,\hat{u}_{t-7} - 0{\cdot}007\,\hat{u}_{t-8}$$
$$\qquad\quad [1{\cdot}368]\qquad [3{\cdot}075]\qquad [0{\cdot}607]\qquad [0{\cdot}047]$$

$$\qquad - 0{\cdot}040\,\hat{u}_{t-9} + 0{\cdot}134\,\hat{u}_{t-10} + 0{\cdot}025\,\hat{u}_{t-11} + 0{\cdot}025\,\hat{u}_{t-12}$$
$$\qquad\quad [0{\cdot}268]\qquad [0{\cdot}933]\qquad [0{\cdot}170]\qquad [0{\cdot}172]$$

January 1973 to June 1977

$$\Delta P_t - \Delta P^e_{t-1} = -7{\cdot}553 + 0{\cdot}398\,\Delta P_{t-1} + 0{\cdot}186\,\Delta P_{t-2} + 0{\cdot}203\,\Delta P_{t-3} + \hat{u}_t$$
$$\qquad\qquad\quad [5{\cdot}189]\quad [0{\cdot}884]\qquad\quad [0{\cdot}238]\qquad\quad [0{\cdot}454]$$

$$\hat{u}_t = -0{\cdot}030\,\hat{u}_{t-1} - 0{\cdot}074\,\hat{u}_{t-2} - 0{\cdot}172\,\hat{u}_{t-3} - 0{\cdot}095\,\hat{u}_{t-4}$$
$$\qquad\quad [0{\cdot}167]\qquad [0{\cdot}393]\qquad [0{\cdot}969]\qquad [0{\cdot}521]$$

$$\qquad - 0{\cdot}190\,\hat{u}_{t-5} - 0{\cdot}288\,\hat{u}_{t-6} + 0{\cdot}090\,\hat{u}_{t-7} - 0{\cdot}091\,\hat{u}_{t-8}$$
$$\qquad\quad [1{\cdot}071]\qquad [1{\cdot}532]\qquad [0{\cdot}467]\qquad [1{\cdot}039]$$

$$\qquad - 0{\cdot}118\,\hat{u}_{t-9} + 0{\cdot}156\,\hat{u}_{t-10} + 0{\cdot}067\,\hat{u}_{t-11} - 0{\cdot}100\,\hat{u}_{t-12}$$
$$\qquad\quad [0{\cdot}641]\qquad [0{\cdot}864]\qquad [0{\cdot}369]\qquad [0{\cdot}537]$$

For both periods the hypothesis that the lagged inflation variables have no influence on the error in expectations formation is rejected on the basis of an *F* test. For the period January 1973 to June 1977 this is the case even though individual lagged inflation variables are apparently insignificantly different from zero on the basis of individual *t* tests; there is considerable multicollinearity among the regressors.[13] For the earlier period the hypothesis that all the autoregressive parameters are zero is rejected, although it is accepted for the more recent period.[14] On the basis of this test, therefore, the efficiency hypothesis, and hence rationality, are rejected.

5.   Conclusion

The main findings of this chapter might usefully be summarised. In attempting to extend the Carlson–Parkin inflation expectations series over the period 1974–77 a statistical relationship upon which their series was based was found not to hold and was consequently rejected. An alternative hypothesis was maintained and an expectations series which has broadly similar properties to the earlier one was derived. An econometric investigation of the proximate determinants of expected inflation found that in the early 1960s it was autoregressive, but in more recent periods actual inflation was a significant determinant. The hypothesis of rationality was rejected.

Notes

1   The work reported in this paper was supported by a grant from the Social Science Research Council.

2   Such a scheme was chosen on simplicity criteria.

3   Theil (1952) p. 115, n. 2.

4   Rose (1972, p. 19) shows that $0 < \lambda_1 < 2$.

5   For example, if ΔP_t is trended ΔP_t^e can be trended only if $\Delta P_t^e < \Delta P_t$.

6   All regressions were run on the CDC 7600 computer at the University of Manchester Regional Computer Centre, using the Autoreg package.

7   This suggests that some of the estimated parameters may not be constant over the period. In empirical studies it is usually assumed that all the regressors influence the regressand with constant effect throughout the period. Because this may not be the case in studies of expectations formation, the findings of such studies should be regarded as tentative.

8   The calculated F statistic was $0\cdot29$, which is less than the 5 per cent critical value, $F_{(2,56)} = 3\cdot17$.

9   In table 13.1 the null hypothesis of parameter stability is accepted in all models, since Z_1 is less than the 5 per cent critical value of $\chi^2_{(6)} = 12\cdot59$. Similarly the null hypothesis of a random residual correlogram is accepted for all models; Z_2 is less than 5 per cent critical value of $\chi^2_{(12)} = 21\cdot03$.

10   Calculated F statistics are $1\cdot81$ and $1\cdot44$, which are less than the 5 per cent critical values of $F_{(2,50)} = 3\cdot18$ and $F_{(3,50)} = 2\cdot79$ respectively.

11    $F_{(2,48)} = 0\cdot22$, which is less than the 5 per cent critical value of $3\cdot19$.

12   It would, perhaps, have been desirable to have included further lagged inflation variables, but, given the twelfth-order autoregressive scheme chosen because the observations are monthly, program limitations restricted n to 3.

13   The F statistics for the vector of explanatory variables for the two periods are $42\cdot46$ and $27\cdot48$, both of which exceed the 5 per cent critical values of $F_{(3,58)} = 2\cdot78$ and $F_{(3,44)} = 2\cdot82$ respectively.

14   For the earlier period $\chi^2_{(12)} = 31\cdot00$ and for the later period $\chi^2_{(12)} = 6\cdot55$; the 5 per cent critical value is $21\cdot03$.

Data appendix

Inflation expectations, ΔP_t^e

	1961	1962	1963	1964	1965	1966	1967	1968
Jan.	3·0834	4·8123	3·9363	3·6846	8·2154	4·5417	5·1579	12·4150
Feb.	3·7094	6·7176	3·5313	3·4243	5·9733	6·2075	6·3841	10·6776
Mar.	3·1810	5·1151	3·3824	4·3743	5·4248	5·5974	4·7252	10·6776
Apr.	3·4547	5·5974	2·8172	4·0159	5·9733	5·6416	4·3856	9·4823
May	3·9476	3·9243	2·7573	3·5313	6·2392	6·0001	6·7693	8·5933
June	4·6718	5·0619	3·3016	3·9970	4·6716	7·6002	5·7287	7·2443
July	6·2706	3·7070	4·0032	4·1142	4·4532	7·1081	8·3431	7·2118
Aug.	5·9733	4·7391	2·9429	4·1583	5·3694	4·0259	5·3732	7·7774
Sept.	4·1932	4·0120	3·8414	3·4010	4·0939	6·0783	6·6838	6·4092
Oct.	3·9624	3·6799	3·8893	4·1251	3·6224	4·9748	9·3491	7·6513
Nov.	3·8893	4·9654	3·4010	4·8869	4·1758	5·1872	11·7206	7·8149
Dec.	5·0764	3·4515	3·6816	5·6626	6·6254	4·9444	12·3519	9·3951

1969	1970	1971	1972	1973	1974	1975	1976	1977
8·5129	9·3951	9·7884	6·7764	7·8912	10·5807	34·2505	8·4763	12·4150
9·3031	12·2632	10·6224	9·9870	9·3951	15·0331	10·7195	6·8437	11·3397
8·4083	8·9105	10·6224	5·1269	8·3775	6·4147	12·3727	7·3174	12·4150
12·2632	7·7774	8·3431	6·6782	9·0362	8·3431	15·0994	9·1030	10·6776
8·8018	7·7774	12·3325	10·0268	11·1812	8·3431	15·0331	8·4763	12·9415
7·8149	5·6008	9·4312	9·9870	14·9790	11·2360	8·5495	10·0268	15·0331
8·5129	8·2976	11·0493	8·3914	12·8027	9·0884	8·5933	8·9133	10·0268
8·4250	11·1812	7·1098	9·0362	12·3325	12·8577	9·1423	11·3036	6·5232
7·0922	11·1812	9·0362	10·5807	10·6224	12·8577	7·8166	12·4150	7·8119
7·7774	8·4152	9·4312	11·2360	10·0268	11·1812	11·1665	10·9312	4·9098
10·5807	15·0331	6·7764	6·7693	10·0268	10·6224	7·2511	20·1405	5·4151
7·7774	10·6224	7·8499	4·6230	12·3727	14·3429	9·4823	7·9851	6·0918

References

Aaronovitch, S., and M.L. Sawyer (1974), 'The concentration of British manufacturing', *Lloyds Bank Review*, 114, October, pp. 14–23

Abbot, M., and O. Ashenfelter (1976), 'Labour supply, commodity demand and the allocation of time', *Review of Economic Studies*, XLIII (3), No. 135, pp. 389–411

Addison, J.T. (1981), 'Incomes policy: the recent European experience', in J.L. Fallick and R.F. Elliott (eds.), *Incomes Policies, Inflation and Relative Pay*, London, Allen & Unwin

— and W. Siebert (1979), *The Market for Labour: an analytical treatment*, Santa Monica, Cal., Goodyear Publishing Co., pp. 465–88

Apps, R.J. (1977), 'The relationship between unemployment and vacancies; further considerations' (mimeo), University of Manchester

Artis, M.J. (1972), 'Fiscal policy for stabilisation', in W. Beckerman (ed.), *The Labour Government's Economic Record, 1964–1970*, London, Duckworth

— (1976), 'Is there a wage equation?' (mimeo), University of Manchester

— (1979), 'Recent developments in the theory of fiscal policy: a survey', in S. Cook and P.M. Jackson (eds.), *Current Issues in Fiscal Policy*, London, Martin Robertson

— (1981), 'Incomes policies: some rationales', in J.L. Fallick and R.F. Elliott (eds.), *Incomes Policies, Inflation and Relative Pay*, London, Allen & Unwin

— and D.A. Currie (1981), 'Monetary targets and the exchange rate: a case for conditional targets,' *Oxford Economic Papers*, 33, July, pp. 176–200

— and M.H. Miller (1979), 'Inflation, real wages and the terms of trade', in J.K. Bowers (ed.), *Inflation, Development and Integration*, Leeds University Press

Ashenfelter, O., and J. Heckman (1974), 'The estimation of income and substitution effects in a model of family labour supply', *Econometrica*, 42, January, pp. 73–85

Bacon, R., and W. Eltis (1976), *Britain's Economic Problem: Two Few Producers,* London, Macmillan

Ball, R.J., and E.B.A. St Cyr (1966), 'Short-term employment functions in British manufacturing industry', *Review of Economic Studies*, XXXIII (3), No. 95, pp. 179–207

Barker, T.S. (1976), *Economic Structure and Policy,* London, Chapman & Hall

Barro, R.J., and H. Grossman (1976), *Money, Employment and Inflation,* Cambridge University Press

Becker, G. (1965), 'A theory of the allocation of time', *Economic Journal,* LXXV, September, pp. 493–517

— and N. Tames (1976), 'Child endowments and the quantity and quality of children', *Journal of Political Economy,* 84, August, pp. 5143–78

Beenstock, M., and S. Bell (1979), 'A quarterly econometric model of the capital account in the UK balance of payments', *Manchester School,* March, pp. 33–62

Behrend, H. (1973), *Incomes Policy, Equity and Pay Increase Differentials,* Edinburgh, Scottish Academic Press

Bilson, J.F.O. (1979), 'Recent developments in monetary models of exchange rate determination', *IMF Staff Papers,* 25, June, pp. 201–23

Blackaby, D., and D. Leslie (1980), 'The school-leaving decision: a cross-section study for 1971' (mimeo), University of Manchester

Blackaby, F.T. (1978),'Incomes policy', in F.T. Blackaby (ed.), *British Economic Policy, 1960–74,* Cambridge University Press

Blaug, M. (1970), *An Introduction to the Economics of Education,* Penguin Modern Economic Texts

Blinder, A.S., and S.M. Goldfeld (1976), 'New measures of fiscal and monetary policy, 1958–73', *American Economic Review,* 66, December, pp. 780–96

— and R.M. Solow (1974), 'Analytical foundations of fiscal policy', in *Economics of Public Finance,* Washington D.C., Brookings Institute

Blundell, R., and I. Walker (1980), 'Demand for leisure and goods with female labour supply and rationing: testing for separability', University of Manchester Discussion Paper Series, No. 12

Bowers, J. (1975), 'British activity rates: a survey of research', *Scottish Journal of Political Economy,* 22, February, pp. 57–90

Bristow, J.A. (1968), 'Taxation and income stabilization', *Economic Journal,* LXXVIII, June, pp. 299–311

Brown, C.V., *et al.* (1976), 'Estimates of labour hours supplied by married male workers in Great Britain', *Scottish Journal of Political Economy,* 23, November, pp. 261–77

Brown, R.N., C.A. Enoch and P.D. Mortimer-Lee (1980), 'The interrelationships between costs and prices in the United Kingdom', *Bank of England Discussion Paper,* No. 8, March

Buiter, W.H. (1980), 'The macroeconomics of Dr Pangloss: a critical survey of the new macroeconomics', *Economic Journal,* 90, March, pp. 34–50

Burrows, P., and T. Hitiris (1972), 'Estimating the impact of incomes policy', in M. Parkin, and M.T. Sumner (eds.), *Incomes Policy and Inflation,* Manchester University Press

Carlson, J.A. (1975), 'Are price expectations normally distributed?', *Journal of the American Statistical Association,* 70, December, pp. 749–54

— and M. Parkin (1975), 'Inflation expectations', *Economica*, 42, May, pp. 123–38

Carlson, K.M., and R.W. Spencer (1975), 'Crowding-out and its critics', *Federal Reserve Bank of St Louis Review*, LVII, December, pp. 2–17

Central Statistical Office (1970), *Input–Output Tables for the United Kingdom, 1963*, London, HMSO

Corrigan, E. (1970), 'The measurement and importance of fiscal policy changes', *Monthly Review of the Federal Reserve Bank of New York*, 52, June, pp. 133–45

Corry, B.A., and J.A. Roberts (1970), 'Activity rates and unemployment: the experience of the UK, 1951–66'. *Applied Economics*, 2, September, pp. 179–201

— (1974), 'Activity rates and unemployment: the UK experience — some further results', *Applied Economics*, 6, March, pp. 1–22

Coutts, K., W. Godley and W. Nordhaus (1978), *Industrial Pricing in the United Kingdom*, London, Cambridge University Press

Cowling, K., and M. Waterson (1976), 'Price–cost margins and market structure', *Economica*, 43, August, pp. 267–74

— *et al.* (1980),*Mergers and Economic Performance*, London, Cambridge University Press

Cripps, F., W. Godley and M. Fetherstone (1974), 'Public expenditure and the management of the economy', *Minutes of Evidence taken before the Expenditure Committee (General Sub-committee, Session, 1974, 30 July 1974)*, HC 328, London, HMSO

Cubbin, J.S., and K. Foley (1977), 'The extent of benefit-induced unemployment in Great Britain — some new evidence', *Oxford Economic Papers*, 29 (1), March, pp. 128–40

Currie, D.A. (1978), 'Macroeconomic policy and government financing: a survey of recent development', in M.J. Artis and A.R. Nobay (eds.), *Studies in Contemporary Economic Analysis*, I, London, Croom Helm

— (1981), 'Monetary and fiscal policy and the crowding-out issue', in M.J. Artis and M.H. Miller (eds.), *Essays in Fiscal and Monetary Policy*, London, Oxford University Press

Dalton, J.A. (1973), 'Administered inflation and business pricing: another look', *Review of Economics and Statistics*, 40, December, pp. 516–19

Danes, M. (1975), 'The measurement and explanation of inflationary expectations in Australia', *Australian Economic Papers*, 19, June, pp. 75–87

Davidson, J.E.H., D.F. Hendry, F. Srba and S. Yeo (1978), 'Econometric modelling of the aggregate time-series relationship between consumers' expenditure and income in the United Kingdom', *Economic Journal*, 88, December, pp. 661–92

Davies, R.J. (1979), 'Economic activity, incomes policy and strikes — a quantitative analysis', *British Journal of Industrial Relations*, XVII, July, pp. 205–23

Dean, A.J.H. (1981), 'Public and private sector pay and the economy', in J.L. Fallick and R.F. Elliott (eds.), *Incomes Policies, Inflation and Relative Pay*, London, Allen & Unwin

Department of Employment (1971), *British Labour Statistics Historical Abstract, 1886–1968*, London, HMSO
— (1976), 'Final report of the working party on the changed relationship between unemployment and vacancies' (mimeo), July, London
Dhrymes, P.J. (1971), *Distributed Lags,* San Francisco, Cal., Holden-Day
Dixit, A.R. (1976), 'Public finance in a Keynesian temporary equilibrium', *Journal of Economic Theory,* 12, April, pp. 242–58
Doherty, N.A. (1979), 'National Insurance and absence from work', *Economic Journal,* 89, March, pp. 50–65
Domberger, S. (1979), 'Price adjustment and market structure', *Economic Journal,* 89, March, pp. 96–108
— (1980), 'Price dynamics and industrial structure in the UK: an input–output analysis', *Manchester School,* 48, September, pp. 284–306
Dornbusch, R. (1976), 'Expectations and exchange rate dynamics', *Journal of Political Economy,* 84, December, pp. 1161–76
Durbin, J. (1970), 'Testing for serial correlation in least squares regression when some of the regressors are lagged dependent variables', *Econometrica,* 38, May, pp. 410–21
Ehrenberg, R.G. (1970), 'Absenteeism and the overtime decision', *American Economic Review,* LX, June, pp. 352–7
Elias, P. (1980), 'A time series analysis of the labour force participation of married women in the UK, 1968–1975', University of Warwick, *Manpower Research Group Discussion Paper*
Elliott, R.F. (1976), 'The national wage round in the UK: a sceptical view', *Bulletin of the Oxford University Institute of Economics and Statistics,* XXXVIII, August, pp. 179–202
— and J.L. Fallick (1979), 'Pay differentials in perspective: a note on manual and non-manual pay over the period 1951–75', *Economic Journal,* 89, June, pp. 377–84
Farebrother, R.W. (1976), 'BLUS residuals', *Applied Statistics,* 25, No. 3, pp. 317–22
Fetherston, M.J. (1977), *Technical Manual of the CEPG Model,* Cambridge Economic Policy Group, second edition (mimeo), May
Fisher, D.H. (1970), 'The instrument of monetary policy and the generalised trade-off function for Britain, 1955–68', *Manchester School,* XXXVIII, September, pp. 209–22
Fleming, J. (1962), 'Domestic financial policies under fixed and under floating exchange rates', *IMF Staff Papers,* IX, No. 3, pp. 369–80
Flemming, J.S. (1976), *Inflation,* London, Oxford University Press
Frenkel, J.A. (1975), 'Inflation and the formation of expectations', *Journal of Monetary Economics,* I, pp. 403–21
— and C.A. Rodriguez (1975), 'Portfolio equilibrium and the balance of payments: a monetary approach', *American Economic Review,* 65, September, pp. 674–88
Friedman, M. (1968), 'The role of monetary policy', *American Economic Review,* 58, March, pp. 1–17
— (1975), *Inflation vs. Unemployment,* Occasional Paper 44, London, Institute of Economic Affairs

Fromm, G., and L.R. Klein (1973), 'A comparison of eleven econometric models of the United States', *American Economic Review, Papers and Proceedings,* 63, May, pp. 385–93

Garrison, K., and P. Muchinsky (1977), 'Evaluating the concept of absentee-proneness with two measures of absence', *Personnel Psychology,* 24, autumn, pp. 389–93

Gillion, C. (1968),'Wage rates, earnings and wage-drift', *National Institute Economic Review,* No. 68, November, pp. 52–67

Godfrey, L.G. (1971), 'The Phillips curve: incomes policy and trade union effects', in H.G. Johnson and A.R. Nobay (eds.), *The Current Inflation;* abridged and amended version in M. Parkin and M.T. Sumner (eds.), *Incomes Policy and Inflation,* Manchester University Press

Godley, W.A.H., and W.D. Nordhaus (1972), 'Pricing in the trade cycle', *Economic Journal,* 82, September, pp. 853–82

Greenhalgh, C. (1977), 'A labour supply function for married women in Great Britain', *Economica,* 44, August, pp. 249–66

— (1979), 'Male labour force participation in Great Britain', *Scottish Journal of Political Economy,* 26, November, pp. 275–86

— (1980), 'Participation and hours of work for married women in Great Britain', *Oxford Economic Papers,* 32, July, pp. 263–83

— and K. Mayhew (1979), 'Labour supply in Great Britain: theory and evidence' (mimeo), University of Oxford

Griliches, Z. (1967), 'Distributed lags: a survey', *Econometrica,* 35, January, pp. 16–49

Gronau, R. (1973), 'The intra-family allocation of time: the value of the housewife's time', *American Economic Review,* 63, September, pp. 634–51

Grossman, H.I. (1972), 'Was Keynes a "Keynesian"?', *Journal of Economic Literature,* X, March, pp. 26–30

Hahn, F.H. (1980),'Monetarism and economic theory', *Economica,* 47, February, pp. 1–17

Hamermesh, D.S. (1970), 'Wage bargains, threshold effects, and the Phillips curve', *Quarterly Journal of Economics,* 84, September, pp. 501–17

Handy, L.J. (1968), 'Absenteeism and attendance in the British coal-mining industry: an examination of post-war trends', *British Journal of Industrial Relations,* IV, March, pp. 27–50

Hannah, L., and J.A. Kay (1977), *Concentration in Modern Industry,* London, Macmillan

Harkness, R., and B. Krupinski (1977), 'A survey of absence rates', *Work and People,* 3, winter, pp. 3–9

Harrod, R.F. (1936), 'Imperfect competition and the trade cycle', *Review of Economics and Statistics,* 18, May, pp. 84–8

Hart, P.E., and R. Clark (1980), *Concentration in British Industry, 1935–75,* London, Cambridge University Press

Hartley, N., and C. Bean (1978), 'The standardized budget balance', *Government Economic Service Working Paper,* No. 1

Hays, S., *et al.* (1971), 'Notes on statistics of manpower costs and unemployment in major industrial countries', *National Institute Economic Review*, vol. 58, May, pp. 64–9

Heflebower, R. (1941), 'The effects of dynamic forces on the elasticity of revenue curves', *Quarterly Journal of Economics*, 56, February, pp. 653–66

Hendershott, P.H. (1968), *The Neutralized Money Stock: an unbiased Measure of Federal Reserve Policy Actions*, Purdue University Monograph Series No. 5

Hendry, D.F., and F. Srba (1980), 'Autoreg: a computer program library for dynamic econometric models with autoregressive errors', *Journal of Econometrics*, 12, pp. 85–102

Henry, S.G.B. (1981), 'Incomes policy and aggregate pay', in J.L. Fallick and R.F. Elliott (eds.), *Incomes Policy, Inflation and Relative Pay*, London, Allen & Unwin

— and P.A. Ormerod (1978), 'Incomes policies and wage inflation: empirical evidence for the UK, 1961–1977', *National Institute Economic Review*, No. 85, August, pp. 60–71

— M.C. Sawyer and P. Smith (1976). 'Models of inflation in the United Kingdom: an evaluation', *National Institute Economic Review*, No. 77, August, pp. 60–71

Hicks, J.R. (1974), *The Crisis in Keynesian Economics*, Oxford, Basil Blackwell

— (1975), 'What is wrong with monetarism?', *Lloyds Bank Review*, No. 118, October, pp. 1–13

HM Treasury (1977), Treasury Macroeconomic Model Technical Manual

— (1979), Treasury Macroeconomic Model, Public Version, February

Hopkin, W.A.B., and W.A.H. Godley (1965), 'An analysis of tax changes', *National Institute Economic Review*, No. 32, May, pp. 33–42

House of Commons Select Committee (on the Treasury and Civil Service) (1980), *Memoranda on Monetary Policy*, Session 1979–80

Hyman, R. (1972), *Strikes*, London, Fontana/Collins

Jackson, D., H.A. Turner and F. Wilkinson (1972), 'Do trade unions cause inflation?', University of Cambridge Department of applied Economics Occasional Paper No. 36, Cambridge University Press

Johnson, H.G. (1971), 'Introduction' to H.G. Johnson and A.R. Nobay, *The Current Inflation*, London, Macmillan

Johnston, J. (1967), 'The price level under full employment in the UK', in D.C. Hague (ed.), *Price Formation in Various Economies*, London, Macmillan

— and M. Timbrell (1973), 'Empirical tests of a bargaining theory of wage rate determination', *Manchester School*, XLI, No. 2, June, pp. 141–67

Jones, R.M. (1971), *Absenteeism*, Department of Employment Manpower Paper No. 4, London, HMSO

Juster, F.T. (1975), 'Uncertainty, price expectations and the personal saving rate', in Burkhard Strumpel *et al.* (eds.), *Surveys of Consumers, 1972–3*, University of Michigan, Institute of Social Research

Kalecki, M. (1944), 'Three ways to full employment', in Oxford University Institute of Statistics, *The Economics of Full Employment*, Oxford, Basil Blackwell

Keynes, J.M. (1936), *The General Theory of Employment, Interest and Money*, London, Macmillan

— (1940), *How to Pay for the War*: a Radical Plan for the Chancellor of the Exchequer, London, Macmillan

Kmenta, J. (1971), *Elements of Econometrics*, London, Macmillan

Knöbl, A. (1974), 'Price expectations and actual price behaviour in Germany', *International Monetary Fund Staff Papers*, 21, January, pp. 83–100

Laidler, D.E.W. (1971), 'The influence of money on economic activity: a survey of some current problems', in G. Clayton, J. Gilbert and R. Sedgwick (eds.), *Monetary Theory and Monetary Policy in the 1970s*, London, Oxford University Press

— (1973), 'Expectations, adjustment and the dynamic response of income to policy changes', *Journal of Money, Credit and Banking* , V, February, pp. 157–72

— and M. Parkin (1975), 'Inflation: a survey', *Economic Journal*, 85, December, pp. 741–809

Laury, J.S.E., G.R. Lewis and P.A. Ormerod (1978), 'Properties of macroeconomic models of the UK economy: a comparative study', *National Institute Economic Review*, No. 83, February, pp. 52–72

Layard, R., *et al.* (1980), 'Married women's participation and hours in Great Britain', *Economica*, 47, February, pp. 51–72

— and S. Nickell (1980), 'The case for subsidising extra jobs', *Economic Journal*, 90, March, pp. 51–73

Leslie, D. (1980), 'A supply and demand analysis of hours of work', in D. Currie and W. Peters (eds.), *Contemporary Economic Analysis*, 2, pp. 131–69

Lipsey, R.G., and M. Parkin (1970), 'Incomes policy: a reappraisal', *Economica*, 37, February, pp. 115–38; reprinted in M. Parkin and M.T. Sumner (eds.), *Incomes Policy and Inflation*, Manchester University Press

Lomax, R., and M. Denham (1978), 'The model of external capital flows', *Government Economic Service Working Paper No. 17* (Treasury Working Paper No. 8), December

London Business School (1977), *The London Business School Quarterly Econometric Model of the United Kingdom Economy: a description of the Basic Model as at September 1977*

Lustgarten, S. (1975), 'Administered inflation: a reappraisal', *Economic Inquiry*, 13, pp. 191–206

Lucas, R.B. (1976), 'Econometric policy evaluation: a critique', in K. Brunner and A.N. Meltzer (eds.), *The Phillips curve and Labour Markets*, Amsterdam: North-Holland

Lydall, H. (1958), 'Inflation and the earnings gap', *Bulletin of the Oxford University Institute of Economics and Statistics*, 20, August, pp. 285–304

McCallum, B.T. (1970), 'The effect of demand on prices in British manufacturing: another view', *Review of Economic Studies*, 37, pp. 147–55

— (1975), 'Rational expectations and the natural rate hypothesis: some evidence for the United Kingdom', *Manchester School*, 43, March, pp. 56–67

McKinnon, R.A. (1969), 'Portfolio and balance of payments adjustments', in R.A. Mundell and A. Swoboda (eds.), *Monetary Problems of the International Economy*, University of Chicago Press

— (1976), 'The limited role of fiscal policy in an open economy', *Quarterly Review of the Banca Nazionale del Lavoro*, September, pp. 95–117

— and W.E. Oates (1966), 'The implications of international economic integration for monetary, fiscal and exchange rate policy', *Princeton Studies in International Finance*, No. 16, March

McNabb, R. (1977), 'The labour force participation of married women', *Manchester School*, 45, September, pp. 221–35

McKay, D.I., *et al.* (1971), *Labour Markets under Different Employment Conditions*, London, Macmillan

Maki, D., and Z.A. Spindler (1975), 'The effect of unemployment compensation on the rate of unemployment in Great Britain', *Oxford Economic Papers*, 27, November, pp. 440–55

Malinvaud, E. (1977), *The Theory of Unemployment Reconsidered*, Oxford, Basil Blackwell

— (1980), *Profitability and Unemployment*, Cambridge University Press

—Meade, J.E. (1951), *The Theory of International Economic Policy*, I, *The Balance of Payments*, London, Oxford University Press

Means, G.C. (1935), *Industrial Prices and their Relative Inflexibility*, US Senate Document 13, 74th Congress, 1st Session, Washington D.C.

— (1959), *Administration Inflation and Public Policy*, Washington D.C., Anderson Kramer

— (1972), 'The administered-price thesis reconfirmed', *American Economic Review*, 62, June, pp. 292–306

— (1975), 'Simultaneous inflation and unemployment', in J.M. Blair (ed.), *The Roots of Inflation*, London, Wilton House

Meeks, G. (1977), *Disappointing Marriage: a Study of the Gains from Mergers*, London, Cambridge University Press

de Menil, G. (1974), 'Aggregate price dynamics', *Review of Economics and Statistics*, 56, May, pp. 129–40

— (1974), 'The rationality of popular price expectations' (mimeo), Princeton University

Metcalf, D., *et al.* (1976), 'The structure of hours and earnings in British Manufacturing industries', *Oxford Economic Papers*, 38, July, pp. 284–303

Monopolies Commission (1973), *Parallel Pricing — a Report on the General Effect on the Public Interest of the Practice of Parallel Pricing*, Cmnd 5330, London, HMSO

Moses, L.N. (1962), 'Income, leisure and wages pressures', *Economic Journal*, LXXII, June, pp. 320–44

Muellbauer, J., and R. Portes (1978), 'Macroeconomic models with quantity rationing', *Economic Journal*, December, pp. 788–821

Mullineaux, D.J. (1978), 'On testing for rationality: another look at the Livingston price expectations data', *Journal of Political Economy*, 86, April, pp. 329–36

Mundell, R.A. (1962), 'The appropriate use of monetary and fiscal policy for internal and external stability', *IMF Staff Papers*, 9, No. 1, March, pp. 70–7

— (1963), 'Capital mobility and stabilisation policy under fixed and flexible exchange rates', *Canadian Journal of Economics and Political Science*, XXIX, November, pp. 475–85

Musgrave, R.A. (1964), 'On measuring fiscal performance', *Review of Economics and Statistics*, XLVI, May, pp. 213–20

Muth, J.F. (1961), 'Rational expectations and the theory of price movements', *Econometrica*, 29, July, pp. 315–35

— (1960), 'Optimal properties of exponentially weighted forecasts', *Journal of the American Statistical Association*, 55, June, pp. 299–306

National Board for Prices and Incomes (1970), *Hours of Work, Overtime and Shift Working Report and Supplement*, Report No. 161, London, HMSO

National Institute of Economic and Social Research (1977), *Listing of the National Institute Model III*, NIESR Discussion Paper No. 7

Neild, R.R. (1963), *Pricing and Employment in the Trade Cycle*, Occasional Paper XXI, National Institute of Economic and Social Research, Cambridge University Press

Nicholson, N., *et al.* (1977), 'The probability of absence and propensity to leave from employees' job satisfaction and attitudes towards influence in decision-making', *Human Relations*, 30, June, pp. 499–514

Nickell, S.J. (1979), 'The effect of unemployment and related benefits on the duration of unemployment', *Economic Journal*, 89, March, pp. 34–49

Nordhaus, W.D. (1972), 'Recent developments in price dynamics', in O. Eckstein (ed.), *The Econometrics of Price Determination Conference*, Washington D.C., Board of Governors of the Federal Reserve System

Office of Manpower Economics (1973), *Wage Drift*, London, HMSO

Ott, D.J., and A.F. Ott (1965), 'Budget balance and equilibrium income', *Journal of Finance*, 20, January, pp. 71–7

Parkin, M. (1970), 'Incomes policy: some further remarks on the rate of change of money wages', *Economica*, 37, November, pp. 386–401

— (1978), 'Alternative explanations of United Kingdom inflation', in M. Parkin and M. .Sumner (eds.), *Inflation in the United Kingdom*, Manchester University Press, pp. 11–51

— M.T. Sumner and R.A. Jones (1972), 'A survey of the econometric effects of incomes policy on the rate of inflation', in M. Parkin and M.T. Sumner (eds.), *Incomes Policy and Inflation*, Manchester University Press

— M.T. Sumner, and R. Ward (1976), 'The effects of excess demand, generalized expectations and wage–price controls on wage inflation in the UK', in K. Brunner and A. Meltzer (eds.), *The Economics of Wage and Price Controls*, New York, Brookings Institute

Pearce, I.F., R.K. Trivedi, C.T. Stromback and G. Anderson (1976), *A Model of Output, Employment, Wages and Prices in the UK*, Cambridge University Press

Pesando, J. E. (1975), 'A note on the rationality of the Livingston price expectations', *Journal of Political Economy*, 83, August, pp. 849–58

Pesaran, H. (1972a), 'A dynamic inter-industry model of price determination — a test of the normal price hypothesis' (mimeo), Department of Applied Economics, University of Cambridge

— (1972b), 'A dynamic inter–industry model of price determination — a test of the normal price hypothesis', *Quarterly Journal of Economic Research of the Institute for Economic Research*, University of Teheran, pp. 88–123

Phelps, E.S. (1970), 'Money wage dynamics and labour market equilibrium', in E.S. Phelps (ed.), *Microeconomic Foundations of Employment and Inflation Theory*, New York, Norton

Phillips, A.W. (1958), 'The relation between unemployment and the rate of change of money wage rates in the United Kingdom, 1861–1957', *Economica*, November, pp. 283–99

Phlips, L. (1971), *Effects of Industrial Concentration*, Amsterdam, North-Holland

Pierce, D.A. (1971), 'Distribution of residual autocorrelations in the regression model with autoregressive moving average errors', *Journal of the Royal Statistical Society* (series B), 33, No. 1, pp. 140–6

Poole, W. (1970), 'Optimal choice of monetary policy instruments in a simple stochastic macro model', *Quarterly Journal of Economics*, 84, June, pp. 197–216

Prais, S.J. (1976), *The Evolution of Giant Firms in Britain*, London, Cambridge University Press

Price, R.W.R. (1978), 'Public expenditure', in F. T. Blackaby (ed.), *British Economic Policy, 1960–74*, Cambridge University Press

Reddaway, R.B. (1970), *Effects of the Selective Employment Tax. First Report. The Distributive Trades*, London, HMSO

Rees, A. (1966), 'Information networks in labour markets', *American Economic Review*, LVI, May, pp. 559–66

— (1970), 'The Phillips curve as a menu for policy choice', *Economica*, XXXVII, No. 147, pp. 227–38

Robinson, J. (1937), *Essays in the Theory of Employment*, London, Macmillan

Rose, D.E. (1972), 'A general error-learning model of expectations formation' (mimeo), University of Manchester

Rushdy, F., and P.J. Lund (1967), 'The effect of demand on prices in British manufacturing industry', *Review of Economic Studies*, 34, pp. 361–71

Sargan, J.D. (1964), 'Wages and prices in the United Kingdom: a study in econometric methodology', in P.E. Hart, G. Mills and J.K. Whitaker (eds.), *Econometric Analysis for National Economic Planning*, London, Butterworth

— (1971), 'A study of wages and prices in the United Kingdom, 1949–68', in H.G. Johnson and A.R. Nobay (eds.), *The Current Inflation*, London, Macmillan

— (1980a), 'À model of wage–price inflation', *Review of Economic Studies*, 47, pp. 97–112

— (1980b), 'The consumer price equation in the post-war British economy: an exercise in equation specification testing', *Review of Economic Studies*, 47, pp. 113–35

Sargent, T.J., and N. Wallace (1976), 'Rational expectations and the theory of economic policy', *Journal of Monetary Economics*, 2, pp. 169–83

Scherer, F.M. (1980), *Industrial Market Structure and Economic Performance*, Chicago, Rand McNally

Shepherd, J.R., and M.J.C. Surrey (1968), 'The short-term effect of tax changes', *National Institute Economic Review*, No. 46, November, pp. 36–41

Shorey, J. (1975), 'The size of the work unit and strike incidence', *Journal of Industrial Economics*, XXIII, March, pp. 175–88

Sleeper, R.D. (1970), 'Manpower redeployment and the selective employment tax', *Bulletin of the Oxford University Institute of Economics and Statistics*, 32 (4), November, pp. 273–90

Smith G.W. (1975), 'The determinants of UK price expectations' (mimeo), University of Manchester

— (1978a), 'Producers' price and cost expectations', in M. Parkin and M.T. Sumner (eds.), *Inflation in the United Kingdom*, Manchester University Press

— (1978b), 'Price determination', in M. Parkin and M.T. Sumner (eds.), *Inflation in the United Kingdom*, Manchester University Press

— (1980), 'Inflation expectations: a critique of Foster and Gregory' (mimeo), University of Manchester

Spence, M. (1973), 'Job market signalling', *Quarterly Journal of Economics*, LXXXVII, August, pp. 355–74

Spencer, B.G. (1975), 'The small sample bias of Durbin's tests for serial correlation when one of the regressors is a lagged dependent variable and the null hypothesis is true', *Journal of Econometrics*, 3, pp. 249–54

Spencer P., and C. Mowl (1978), 'The model of the domestic monetary system', *Government Economic Service Working Paper No. 17* (Treasury Working Paper No. 8), December

Solow, R.M. (1969), *Price Expectations and the Behaviour of the Price Level*, Manchester University Press

Stoneman, P. (1979), 'A simple diagrammatic apparatus for the investigation of a macro-economic model of temporary equilibria', *Economica*, 46, February, pp. 61–6

Sumner, M.T. (1978), 'Wage determination', in M. Parkin and M.T. Sumner (eds.), *Inflation in the United Kingdom*, Manchester University Press, pp. 75–92

Swan, T.W. (1955), 'Longer-run problems of the balance of payments', paper presented to the Congress of the Australian and New Zealand Association for the Advancement of Science, Melbourne, reprinted in H.W. Arndt and W.N. Corden (eds.), *The Australian Economy: a Book of Readings*, Melbourne, F.W. Cheshire, 1963

Tarling, R., and F. Wilkinson (1977), 'The social contract: post–war incomes policies and their inflationary impact', *Cambridge Journal of Economics*, I, December, pp. 395–414

Taylor, J. (1972), 'Incomes policy, the structure of unemployment and the Phillips curve: the United Kingdom experience, 1953–70', in M. Parkin and M.T. Sumner (eds.), *Incomes Policy and Inflation*, Manchester University Press

— (1974), *Unemployment and Wage Inflation*, London, Longman

— (1977), 'A note on the comparative behaviour of male and female unemployment rates in the UK, 1951–76' (mimeo), University of Lancaster

Theil, H. (1952), 'On the time shape of economic microvariables and the Munich business test', *Review of the International Statistical Institute*, 20, pp. 105–20

— (1954), *Linear Aggregation of Economic Relations*, Amsterdam, North-Holland

— (1958), *Economic Forecasts and Policy*, Amsterdam, North-Holland

— (1970), *Economic Forecasts and Policy*, second edition, Amsterdam, North-Holland

— and S. Wage (1964), 'Some observations on adaptive forecasting', *Management Science*, 10, January, pp. 198–206

Tinbergen, J. (1952), *On the Theory of Economic Policy*, Amsterdam, North-Holland

— (1956), *Economic Policy: Principles and Design*, Amsterdam, North-Holland

Tobin, J., and W. Buiter (1976), 'Long-run effects of fiscal and monetary policy on aggregate demand', in J. L. Stein (ed.), *Monetarism*, Amsterdam, North-Holland

Trades Union Congress (1978), *Economic Review*, London Congress House, February

Turner, H.A. (1960), 'Wages, productivity and the level of unemployment: more wage drift', *Manchester School*, 28, January, 84–123

UK Government (1966), *The Selective Employment Tax*, Cmnd 2891, May, London, HMSO

— (1978), *A Review of Monopolies and Mergers Policy: a Consultative Document*, Cmnd 7198, London, HMSO

Vaubel, R. (1980), 'International shifts in the demand for money, their effects on exchange rates and price levels and their implications for the pre–announcement of monetary expansion', *Weltwirtschaftliches Archiv*, I, pp. 1–44

Worswick, G.D.N. (1944), 'The stability and flexibility of full employment', in Oxford University Institute of Statistics, *The Economics of Full Employment*, Oxford, Basil Blackwell

Waiss, L.W. (1966), 'Business pricing policies and inflation reconsidered', *Journal of Political Economy*, 74, February, pp. 177–87

Ward, T., and R.R. Neild (1978), *The Measurement and Performance of Budgetary Policy*, London, Heinemann

Yolles, S.F., *et al.* (1977), *Absenteeism in Industry*, Springfield, Ill.

Ziderman, A. (1978), *Manpower Training: Theory and Policy*, London, Macmillan

Name index

Aaronovitch, S., 241
Abbot, M., 81
Apps, R. J., 112
Addison, J. T., 134, 162
Artis, M. J., 28n, 46n, 54, 153, 159, 160
Ashenfelter, O., 80, 81

Bacon, R., 145
Ball, R. J., 229
Barker, T. S., 69n
Barro, R. J., 21
Barton, A., 90
Becker, G., 78, 80
Beenstock, M., 53
Behrend, H., 162
Bell, S., 53
Bilson, J. F., 69n
Blackaby, D. A., 90
Blackaby, F., 153
Blaug, M., 77
Blinder, A. S., 28n, 30, 31, 32, 61
Blundell, R., 81
Bowers, J., 78
Bristow, J. A., 46n
Brown, C. V., 54
Buiter, W., 28n

Carlson, J. A., 147, 256, 258, 259, 260, 261, 266, 268, 271
Carlson, K. M., 27n, 57, 59
Clarke, R., 212

Corrigan, E., 32
Corry, B. A., 87, 88
Coutts, K. W., 213, 235, 253
Cowling, K., 194, 201, 211, 253
Cripps, E., 28
Cubbin, G. S., 118
Currie, D. A., 28, 54

Dalton, J. A., 200
Danes, M., 258, 260
Davidson, J. E. H., 189
Davies, R. J., 158
De Menil, R., 232, 260
Dean, A. S. H., 166
Denham, M., 69n
Dhrymes, P. J., 217
Dixit, A., 28n
Doherty, N. A., 97
Domberger, S., 244, 246
Dornbusch, R., 8, 50

Ehrenberg, R. G., 102, 103
Elias, P., 90
Elliott, R. F., 164, 169n
Eltis, W., 145
Enoch, C. A., 54

Fallick, J. L., 164, 169n
Fetherston, M. J., 10, 28
Fleming, J. M., 50, 52–55
Flemming, J. S., 264
Foley, K., 118

Frenkel, J. A., 69n
Friedman, M., 19, 72
Fromm, G., 57

Garrison, K., 107
Gillion, C., 188
Greenhalgh, C., 88, 89
Godfrey, C. G., 147
Godley, W. A. H., 28, 31, 46n, 207, 208, 212n, 213, 216, 218, 219, 220, 224, 225, 230, 233, 235n, 236n, 237n
Gronau, R., 78, 81
Grossman, H. I., 21, 28n

Hahn, F. H., 28n
Handy, L. J., 104
Hamermesh, D., 250
Hannah, L., 194, 211n, 252, 253n
Harkness, R., 107
Harrod, R., 232
Hart, P. E., 212
Hays, S., 79
Heflebower, R., 232
Heckman, J., 80
Hendershott, P. H., 47n
Henry, S. G. B., 147, 152n, 157, 166, 173, 176, 250
Hicks, J. R., 27n, 73, 168n, 170
Hopkin, W. A. B., 30, 46n
Horler, E. J., 189n, 236
Hyman, R., 106

Jackson, D., 145, 170, 175
Johnson, H. G., 170
Johnston, J., 145
Jones, R. A., 207
Jones, R. M., 99
Juster, F. T., 260

Kalecki, M., 3, 28n
Kay, J. A., 194, 211n, 252n, 253n
Keynes, J. M., 1, 28n
Klein, L., 57
Kmenta, J., 86
Knobl, A., 260
Krujinski, B., 107

Laidler, D., 27n, 28n, 69n
Laury, S. S. E., 57, 59
Layard, R., 74, 90, 93
Leslie, D., 90, 93, 107
Lewis, G. R., 57, 59
Lomax, R., 69n
Lucas, R. B., 20
Lund, P. J., 204, 205, 206, 212n, 223
Lustgarten, S., 198, 199, 200, 211n
Lydall, H., 221

MacKay, D. I., 165
MacKinnon, R. I., 28n
McCallum, B. T., 147, 149, 209, 210
McNabb, R., 119
Maki, D., 118
Malinvaud, E., 21, 23, 28n
Mayhew, K., 87
Miller, M., 28n, 160
Meade, J. E., 3
Means, G. C., 192, 193, 198
Meeks, G., 242
Metcalf, D., 93, 94, 107
Mortimer-Lee, P. D., 54
Moses, L. N., 100
Mowl, C., 70n
Muchinsky, 104
Muellbauer, J., 28n
Mullineaux, D. J., 269
Mundell, R. A., 3, 27n
Musgrave, R., 46n
Muth, J. F., 263

Neild, R. R., 46n, 202–207, 212n, 213, 223
Nickell, S. J., 74, 127
Nordhaus, W. D., 207, 208, 211n, 213, 214, 216, 218, 220, 224, 225, 230, 235n, 236n, 237n, 253

Oates, W. E., 28n
Ormerod, P., 57, 59, 157, 166, 173, 176
Ott, A. F., 28n
Ott, D. J., 28n

Paish, F., 209
Parkin, M., 134, 147, 207, 210, 256, 258, 259, 260, 261, 266, 268, 271
Pesando, J. E., 269
Pesaran, H., 208, 213, 225, 226, 230, 235n
Phelps, E. S., 72
Phillips, A. W., 16
Phlips, C., 199
Pierce, D. A., 257
Poole, W., 28n
Portes, R., 28n
Prais, S. J., 241
Price, R. W. R., 46n

Reddaway, R. D., 114
Roberts, J. A., 87, 88
Robinson, J., 3, 28n
Rodriguez, C. A., 69n
Rose, D. E., 263
Rushdy, F., 204, 205, 206, 212n, 213

Sargan, J. D., 146, 150, 170, 234, 237n
Sawyer, M. C., 150, 152n, 168n, 173, 241, 250, 253n
Scherer, F. M., 253n
Shepherd, J. R., 46n
Siebert, W., 134
Shorey, J., 107
Sleeper, L. D., 115, 116
Smith, G. W., 147, 152n, 173
Solow, R. M., 28n, 30, 31, 32, 174, 209, 210

Spence, M., 77
Spencer, P., 57
Spencer, R. W., 27n, 57, 59, 217
Spindler, D., 118
St Cyr, E. B. A., 229
Stoneman, P., 28
Sumner, M. T., 111, 114, 118, 129n, 147, 148, 207, 210
Surrey, M. J. C., 46n
Swan, T. W., 3

Tarling, R., 156, 158, 162, 164, 176
Taylor, J., 118, 145
Theil, H., 3, 235n, 257
Timbrell, M., 145, 173
Tinbergen, J., 3, 154
Tomes, N., 78
Turner, H. A., 145, 170, 175, 221

Vaubel, R., 29n

Waiss, L. W., 200
Walker, I., 81
Ward, R., 147, 210
Ward, T., 46n
Waterson, M., 194, 201, 211n, 253
Wilkinson, F., 145, 156, 158, 162, 164, 169n, 175, 176
Williamson, J., 207
Wilson, H., 169n
Worswick, G. D. N., 28

Yolles, S. F., 104

Zabalza, A., 90
Ziderman, A., 77

Subject index

Absenteeism in UK labour market
  Coal industry and, 104–8
  Data sources of, 97–8
  Definition of, 99
  'Income preferrers' and 'leisure preferrers', 100–1
  Overtime and, 102–4
Activity rate
  Arbitrary convention and, 78
  Custom and social convention, 79–80
  Definition of, 77
  Economic circumstances and, 77
  General health and, 79
  Government legislation and, 78
  Personal characteristics, 77–8
Added worker effect, 87, 89
Administered inflation hypothesis, 192–4
ARIMA (Autoregressive Intergrated Moving Average) process, 263
Assignment problem, 7–8, 154
Autoregressive scheme, 257

Balance of payments, 33, 40, 42, 50
  Wealth effects and, 13
Benefit–earnings ratio
  Data, 117,
  Department of Health and Social Security ratio, 118–19
  Unemployment and, 113–14
  See also Unemployment, adjusted series

Bond coupon effect, 59, 60
  Comparative dynamic simulations on the Treasury model and, 64–6
Bretton Woods, 3
Budget constraint
  Government, 12
  Household, 82
Budget surplus
  Actual, 32
  Full employment, 27n, 30, 32
  Weighted standardised, 32, 34

Cambridge Economic Policy Group, 146
Capital mobility, 3, 7, 10, 53; see also IS–LM analysis
Catch-up pay settlements, 166, 176, 193; see also Incomes policy
CBI
  Inflation survey, 255
  Industrial trend survey, 258
Classical economics, 3
Coal industry, absenteeism in, 104–8
Cobb–Douglas production function, 197
Consumption function, in macro-econometric models, 56–7, 61
Correlogram, 257
Cost–benefit analysis, 25
Counter–cyclical policy, 20
Cournot–Nash solution to oligopoly, 194, 211n

Crowding–out
  Due to inappropriate financial policies, 5–6
  Econometric models and, 48–70
  IS–LM framework, 13–15
  Laury, Lewis and Ormerod (1978) and, 59–64
  Malinvaud's model and, 23
  Negative, 59
  Wealth effects and, 13–15
Customary hours, 216

Deflation, 145, 159
Demand management
  Conventional wisdom on, 5–13
  Rationed equilibrium and, 21–5
  Rules *v.* discretion and, 25–7
  Supply constraints and, 15–21
  Wealth effects, 13–15
Department of Employment, 172, 235, 236
Department of Health and Social Security
  Benefit–earnings ratio, 118
  Retention ratio and, 173
Dicks Mireaux–Dow index, 204
Discouraged worker effect, 87, 93
Disequilibrium macroeconomics, 3
Distributed lag function, 203, 204, 205, 206
Distributed lag parameter, 226
Durbin–Watson statistic, 217
Dynamic multiplier, 57

Earnings drift, 218–23
Efficiency, 269
Elasticity
  Of expenditure function and the effectiveness of monetary/fiscal policy, 49
  Of money demand and the effectiveness of monetary–fiscal policy, 49
  Of demand, 232
  See also IS–LM analysis
Empirical studies on labour supply
  Activity rates and, 87–91
  Hours of work studies, 93–6

Equilibrium prices, 196
Exchange rate
  Changes and the real wage, 16–17
  Determination of, 4, 56
  Expectations in Fleming–Mundell model, 69n
  Floating, 9–10
  Transmission mechanism and, 26
  See also Expectations
Expectations
  Adaptive, 136, 172, 176, 209
  Error–learning and extrapolation models, 263–5
  Inflation and, 253–71
  Rational, 4, 19, 20, 25, 211, 264
  Regressive, 10, 172, 176

Fine tuning, 12
Fiscal policy, 2
  Measures of, 31–7
  Labour government 1974–79, 39
  Crowding–out and, 48–69
Fix–price market, 193
Flex–price market, 193
Forecast error, 148, 188
Fringe costs, 102
Full employment, 2

Gallup survey, 255, 256, 259
General household survey, 98; *see also* Absenteeism
General index of retail prices, 260
Gross domestic product, 31–44

Herfindahl index of concentration, 195
Historical cost pricing, 231
Human capital, 75

Import penetration, 240
Incomes policy
  Catch–up settlements and, 166
  Conservative government (1973) and, 160
  Costs of, 163

Expectations–augmented
Phillips curve, 161
Inflation and, 139
Public good aspect of, 162
Real wage hypothesis and,
158–60
Supply–side implications,
153–68
Income preferrers, 100
Industrial concentration, 238, 239,
240
Concentration ratio and, 239–41
Determinants of, 241–42
Inflation and, 242–51
Static welfare losses, 242
Inflation
Accelerating, 144
Expectations and, 161
Incomes policy and, 138
Internationally transmitted, 160
Phillips curve and, 181
Subsidies and, 138
Wage push, 143
Inflation tax effect in econometric
models, 56, 66–8
Industrial Reorganisation Corpor-
ation, 251
Input–output relations, 197, 230
Dynamic model of, 246
1971 tables of, 247
Interest parity, 52
Interest rates, 5, 12, 31, 54, 63, 64
IS–LM analysis
Assignment problem and, 7–8
Crowding–out and, 5–7
Effectivess of monetary and
fiscal policy in, 5–7
Floating exchange rates in, 9–10
Lags and, 12
Measures of fiscal policy and,
31–32
Mundell–Fleming paradigm,
51–2
Stochastic *v.* deterministic
framework, 10–12
Wealth effects and, 13–15

Joint hypothesis testing, 255

Koyck transformation, 173

Labour market in Keynesian
model, 73
Labour supply
Absenteeism and, 99–104
Activity rate, 77
Backward–bending curve, 94
Discouraged worker effect and,
87, 89
Household model and, 81–7
Overview of, 75–80
Quantity and quality decisions,
76
Leisure preferrers, 100
Leontief inverse, 247
Leverage, 32
London Business School
econometric model
Crowding-in, 59
Exchange rate determination in,
56
Scandinavian school and, 56

Marginal product of labour, 23
Mergers, 241
GEC–AEI, 252
Leyland, 252
Monetary growth rules,
discretionary policy, 25–26
Monetary policy, 6, 49
Money supply rules and, 12, 13
Monetary targets, 25
Money illusion, 50, 139, 144
Money supply, 8
Monopolies Commission, 252, 253
Multi-geared first-order error-
learning process, 264
Multicollinearity, 270
Mundell–Fleming analysis
Capital mobility (stocks and
flows) and, 53
Constant price assumption, 54
Exchange rate expectations and,
52
In IS–LM framework, 51–2
Wealth adjustment in, 53–4

National Board for Prices and Incomes, 103, 109n
National Institute econometric model, 55
  Crowding–out, 62
  Exchange rate determination, 56
Natural rate, 17, 20, 27, 137
  Unemployment benefit and, 137
  See also Phillips curve
New Earnings Survey, 97
  See also Absenteeism
Non-linearities, 33
Normal cost hypothesis, 213–34

Office of Manpower Economics, 235
Oil price rise, 23, 245
Oligopoly pricing, 194
Overtime, 102

Partial adjustment model, 243
Phillips curve
  Expectations-augmented, 135–51
  Incomes policy and, 16
  Milton Friedman and, 19
  Natural rate augmented, 17
  Open economy expectations-augmented, 141–3
  Optimal trade–off, 16
  Real wage and, 170
  Slope, 16
  Wage inflation and, 181, 186
Policy rules, 12
  Versus discretion, 25–7
Population census, 75
Price determination in the UK, 202
  Expectations-augmented excess demand models, 209–10
  Mark–up models and, 202–9
  See also Phillips curve
Price elasticity of demand, 198
Pricing behaviour
  Influence of industrial market structure, 192–201
Production, technology and, 243
Production function
  Cobb–Douglas, 197
  Linear fixed coefficients, 196

Productivity growth, unemployment and, 140–1
PSBR, 59, 62
Purchasing power parity, 56n

Quantity theory of money, 20

Rational expectations monetarism, 19; *see also* expectations
Rationed equilibrium, 21–5
Real wage
  Exchange rate changes and, 16–17
  Wage theorem, 27n
  Equilibrium, 28n
  See also Money illusion
Real wage resistance hypothesis, 143–51
  Incomes policy and, 155, 158, 159
  Model of, 171–2
  Retention ratio and, 145
  See also Phillips curve
Retail price index, 160
Retention ratio, 145, 175
Risk aversion, 69n

Selective Employment Tax
  Introduction of, 119
  Productivity and, 114
  Reduction and removal of, 121
  UV curve and, 113
SIC–industry categories, 240
Simulations
  With Treasury model, 37–40
  Comparative, 59–64
Slutsky decomposition, for a wage change, 83–6
Social contract, 157, 162, 164, 187
Social Security statistics, 97; *see also* Absenteeism
Social wage, 157
Stabilisation, fiscal policy and, 42
Stagflation, 143
Static equilibrium, 195
Steady state, 48, 137
Sterilisation, 7, 8
Stock adjustment, 53

Strike activity, 106; *see also* Unemployment
Absenteeism
Subsidies, as a means of reducing
inflation, 138
Supply constraints, 15–21
Survey of industrial trends of the
Australian Chamber of Manu-
facturers and Bank of New South
Wales, 258

Temporary employment subsidy,
73
Trades Union Congress, supply
management approach to
economic affairs, 74
Target wage, 171
Tatonnement process, 21
Treasury econometric model
National income forecasting
sector, 37–43
Exchange rate determination
and, 56
Crowding-out and, 63

Unemployment
Adjusted series, 111–29
Benefit–earnings ratio, 114, 115
Classical and Keynesian, 23–4,
82
Model in the non-manufacturing
sector, 115–17
Natural rate and, 72
Percentage in 1950s, '60s and
'70s, 72
Selective employment subsidies,
73
Vacancies and (UV curve),
112–14

Wage inflation, 134–52
Wage service structure, 100
Wage theorem, 28n
Walrasian equilibrium, 23
Welfare function, 99
Wholesale price index, 247
Work sharing, 74